Oracle Hyperion Interactive Reporting 11 Expert Guide

Master advanced Dashboards, JavaScript and Computation features of Oracle Hyperion Interactive Reporting 11 and much more

Edward J. Cody

Emily M. Vose

[PACKT] enterprise
PUBLISHING
professional expertise distilled

BIRMINGHAM - MUMBAI

Oracle Hyperion Interactive Reporting 11 Expert Guide

First published: December 2011

Production Reference: 1011211

Published by Packt Publishing Ltd.
Livery Place
35 Livery Street
Birmingham B3 2PB, UK.

ISBN 978-1-84968-314-2

www.packtpub.com

Cover Image by Anvar Khodzhaev (cbetah@yahoo.com)

Credits

Authors
Edward J. Cody
Emily M. Vose

Reviewers
Jake Vose
Amy K. Gartner
Taoheed Akin Laguda

Acquisition Editor
Rukhsana Khambatta

Development Editor
Rukshana Khambatta

Technical Editors
Joyslita Dsouza
Merwine Machado
Ajay Shanker

Project Coordinator
Jovita Pinto

Proofreader
Aaron Nash

Indexer
Monica Ajmera Mehta

Production Coordinator
Alwin Roy

Cover Work
Alwin Roy

About the Authors

Edward J. Cody is an accomplished data warehouse and business intelligence consultant with over eight years of experience with Oracle Hyperion software. The author of *The Business Analyst's Guide to Oracle Hyperion Interactive Reporting 11*, Mr. Cody's experience with Interactive Reporting began with Brio v6 and has continued through the most recent version. He was a speaker at Oracle OpenWorld 2008, and he has extensive experience with Essbase and Financial Reporting.

Mr. Cody has consulted both private and Government organizations throughout his career. He has a Bachelor of Science in Systems Engineering from the George Washington University, School of Engineering and Applied Science, and he has a Master of Science in Management of Information Technology from the University of Virginia, McIntire School of Commerce. His experience includes managing large data warehouse and business intelligence implementations and providing data warehousing and business intelligence consulting services.

Emily M. Vose is an experienced business process management consultant specializing in Hyperion Interactive Reporting. Hailing from user-oriented graphics design and frontend application development, Ms. Vose brings an unique vision to the reporting process that is rare in the business intelligence world. This perspective led Ms. Vose to construct a framework within Interactive Reporting facilitating rapid report development and enterprise maintenance, even for users with minimal technical expertise.

Ms. Vose has consulted with several organizations, including Hyperion Solutions and Oracle Corporation, and is now the owner of Wagger Designs, LLC, a technology services consulting group, based in the Washington, DC metro area. Ms. Vose has a Bachelor of Science in Cinema and Photography from the Ithaca College Roy H. Park School of Communications and currently resides in Northern Virginia with her husband and two young sons.

Acknowledgments

Edward J. Cody would first like to start by thanking all of you who purchased this book. I hope that you find it a good resource to aid you in your use of the product. Heartfelt thanks to my parents (Ed and Cathy), brother (David), Caitlin, and all of my family and friends for working around my schedule as I wrote this book. I greatly appreciate your patience and understanding.

This book would be neither possible nor successful without the patience and indefatigable work ethic of my co-author, Emily M. Vose. I would also like to thank Jake Vose and Amy Gartner for their valuable input and content contributions. I must thank all of my managers, peers, and employees that have supported me throughout my career, and I must also thank Bob Griesemer, author of two books on Oracle Warehouse Builder, for setting me up with the opportunity to work with Packt Publishing. Bob is a great friend, colleague, and technical expert. His books are great resources for all those interested in learning about data warehousing.

A number of people were key to the production of this book. James Lumsden, Rukshana Khambatta, Zainab Bagasrawala, Merwin Machado, and all of those at Packt Publishing, thank you for your efforts. The team has worked tirelessly with us to produce a quality product and I thank them for their patience and hard work.

Emily M. Vose would like to thank my co-author, Edward Cody, for introducing me to the Packt Publishing family and for his tireless efforts to make this book a reality. I would also like to thank Jake Vose and Amy Gartner for their valuable input and content contributions. Thank you to the managers, customers, peers, and mentors who have supported me throughout my career. Special thanks are owed to both Mark Ostroff for introducing me to Hyperion Interactive Reporting, and to Stanley Quick for providing a supportive development environment rich with creative freedom. Without their encouragement, guidance, and friendship, I would not be where I am today.

Last, but certainly not least, I would like to thank my family for their love and support, without you, I'd be lost.

About the Reviewers

Jake Vose is a web, desktop, server, and mobile application developer of over 12 years, specializing in problem solving and process automation. His wide base of operating system, programming language, and framework knowledge attests his natural curiosity and love of tinkering.

Mr. Vose attended the State University of New York at Oswego and graduated in 1999 with a Bachelor of Arts in Computer Science, specializing in artificial intelligence and is the Chief Technical Officer at Wagger Designs, LLC located in the Washington DC metro area.

Amy K. Gartner is an intelligence analyst, who has worked for several Federal Government agencies in support of a variety of law enforcement related missions. Ms. Gartner has a Bachelor of Science in Justice Studies from James Madison University and is currently working toward a Master of Criminal Justice from Boston University.

Taoheed Akin Laguda is an accredited member of the British Computer Society with over 15 years' Information Technology experience. He is an accomplished and qualified Information and Knowledge Engineer, who understands the range of techniques and principles that improve the management and processing of data, which leads to the realisation of business goals and objectives.

He is an experienced consultant specializing in requirements analysis, design, and development of management information, knowledge management, business intelligence, and operational reporting solutions against data warehouses, ERP systems, and business applications.

www.PacktPub.com

This book is published by Packt Publishing. You might want to visit Packt's website at `www.PacktPub.com` and take advantage of the following features and offers:

Discounts

Have you bought the print copy or Kindle version of this book? If so, you can get a massive 85% off the price of the eBook version, available in PDF, ePub, and MOBI.

Simply go to `http://www.packtpub.com/oracle-hyperion-interactive-reporting-11-expert-guide/book`, add it to your cart, and enter the following discount code:

hir11egeb

Free eBooks

If you sign up to an account on `www.PacktPub.com`, you will have access to nine free eBooks.

Newsletters

Sign up for Packt's newsletters, which will keep you up to date with offers, discounts, books, and downloads.

You can set up your subscription at `www.PacktPub.com/newsletters`.

Code Downloads, Errata and Support

Packt supports all of its books with errata. While we work hard to eradicate errors from our books, some do creep in. Meanwhile, many Packt books have accompanying snippets of code to download.

You can find errata and code downloads at `www.PacktPub.com/support`.

Instant Updates on New Packt Books

Get notified! Find out when new books are published by following `@PacktEnterprise` on Twitter, or the *Packt Enterprise* Facebook page.

PACKTLiB

PacktLib.PacktPub.com

PacktLib offers instant solutions to your IT questions. It is Packt's fully searchable online digital book library, accessible from any device with a web browser.

- Contains every Packt book ever published. That's over 100,000 pages of content.
- Fully searchable. Find an immediate solution to your problem.
- Copy, paste, print, and bookmark content.
- Available on demand via your web browser.

If you have a Packt account, you might want to have a look at the nine free books which you can access now on PacktLib. Head to `PacktLib.PacktPub.com` and log in or register.

Table of Contents

Preface

Oracle Hyperion Interactive Reporting is one of the many products in the Oracle Business Intelligence Enterprise Edition Plus software suite, an industry-leading business intelligence platform. The primary focus of the Interactive Reporting product is to provide strong relational querying and data analysis capabilities, where the software provides significant flexibility for creating custom dashboards, interfaces, and data analysis templates through the use of custom JavaScript programming and built-in software functionality. While Interactive Reporting is extremely flexible, performing advanced operations in the software is complicated and requires basic programming knowledge and an advanced understanding of the software. This *Expert Guide* continues from where *The Business Analyst's Guide to Oracle Hyperion Interactive Reporting 11* left off, and provides the reader with information to successfully leverage the advanced features of the product along with examples and specific techniques applicable to everyday use.

The *Oracle Hyperion Interactive Reporting 11 Expert Guide* provides software users and developers with many examples of techniques used by software experts. The book begins with an introduction to leveraging advanced features of the product along with an introduction to JavaScript. Dashboards are a major focus of this guide, with four chapters focused on building an increasingly complex Dashboard with functions, global objects, and syncing selections across Dashboards. The book places an emphasis on learning methods for data analysis by using advanced programming and built-in functions, and a unique approach to using code to generate batch reports and briefing slides is provided. The Dashboard Studio Optimize Utility and the Dashboard Studio Merge Utility are explained in detail, and the approach to building a central code repository for use across multiple documents in an enterprise is demonstrated.

This book provides the information necessary to evolve Interactive Reporting users into experts, by providing the skills to understand, communicate, and perform advanced level tasks. While this guide displays content and examples from version 11 of the software, the techniques and examples presented are also applicable to previous versions of the software dating back to version 8.

What this book covers

Chapter 1, Advanced Hyperion Interactive Reporting Techniques provides an introduction to the book, a brief review of the main features of Interactive Reporting, and orients the user to the sections of Interactive Reporting where custom scripting and advanced features are utilized.

Chapter 2, Introduction to JavaScript and the Interactive Reporting API provides the background required to understand the developer concepts discussed throughout the rest of the book, including a an in-depth explanation of the Interactive Reporting API and an introduction to the JavaScript programming language.

Chapter 3, Creating a Simple Dashboard presents the procedural steps required to create a simple Dashboard without the use of JavaScript, discusses built-in interactivity, and provides an overview of Live Charts and Gauges.

Chapter 4, Introducing Dashboard Interactivity explores common dashboard interactivity approaches using JavaScript as well as the building blocks for creating a master dashboard layout with navigation, controls, and dynamic objects.

Chapter 5, Building the Dashboard Framework details the steps necessary to create a customized Dashboard Framework within Interactive Reporting by extracting JavaScript to a centralized library of global code objects.

Chapter 6, Advanced Dashboard Techniques provides information on creating and maintaining custom dashboard filters and dashboard controls from a centralized query of filter values, and it provides the steps to keep filter controls synchronized between dashboards.

Chapter 7, Advanced Data Analysis provides an in-depth explanation of the options available in Interactive Reporting for performing data maipulation throughout the document.

Chapter 8, Creating Briefing Slides and Executing Batch Exports educates the user on the methods and features most commonly used for exporting information from Interactive Reporting, including native software export features, leveraging custom programming to perform simple and complex exports, and simple steps for configuring a Report section to produce briefing slide content.

Chapter 9, The Central Code Repository provides information for creating a Central Code Repository to store and programmatically push code into Interactive Reporting documents from a central relational database.

Chapter 10, Optimizing and Merging details the features of the Dashboard Studio and Dashboard Studio Optimize Utility to merge, modify, and fix Interactive Reporting documents.

What you need for this book

This book was written using a standard deployment of Oracle EPM 11.1.1.3. The sections and techniques in this book are primarily version-independent, where almost all of the functionality demonstrated will exist in previous versions of the product. References are made to some of the new features in Interactive Reporting 11, especially in the area of charting and Dashboards as features have progressed throughout the new versions. The Interactive Reporting Sample Database is used throughout the examples in this book.

Who this book is for

The target audience of this book is any Oracle Hyperion Interactive Reporting user looking to improve their skills in the product. The book focuses on the more advanced features of the software, including an introduction to JavaScript, simple to advanced dashboard concepts, advanced analysis, and additional special topics.

Permissions

Security can be set for documents in the Oracle Hyperion Workspace to prevent the user from accessing certain features of the product, including creating custom data models, editing queries, and saving and importing documents. This book is written with full access to all of the features of the product. Contact your system administration resources for more information on your deployment if you cannot access certain features of the product in your environment.

Multidimensional queries

Oracle Hyperion Interactive Reporting provides the capability to query against a multidimensional data source. As most environments leverage Interactive Reporting against relational data sources, the focus of this book is on the relational querying and analysis capabilities of the product. More information on multidimensional queries can be found in the product documentation.

Additional resources

There are many helpful online resources to learn more about Interactive Reporting, including three very common and useful references. The first is the Oracle Business Intelligence 11*g* documentation, which contains the developer references for Interactive Reporting. The second is the "Tips and Tricks Cookbook", by Mark Ostroff, a useful guide containing many Interactive Reporting tips, tricks, and advanced techniques. Both the Oracle documentation and the cookbook can be found on the Oracle website or through a simple web search. Finally, Toolbox.com (http://it.toolbox.com), a website commonly used by developers, contains Hyperion and Brio knowledge groups and provides the ability to search for answers and post questions to a large user community.

Conventions

In this book, you will find a number of styles of text that distinguish between different kinds of information. Here are some examples of these styles, and an explanation of their meaning.

Code words in text are shown as follows: "Within Interactive Reporting, declarations with local scope are defined using the var keyword."

A block of code is set as follows:

```
var vMonth = 1;
var vDay = "06";
var vYear = 1999;
```

New terms and **important words** are shown in bold. Words that you see on the screen, in menus or dialog boxes for example, appear in the text like this: "The **Name** box is for specifying the name of the computed item."

[Warnings or important notes appear in a box like this.]

[Tips and tricks appear like this.]

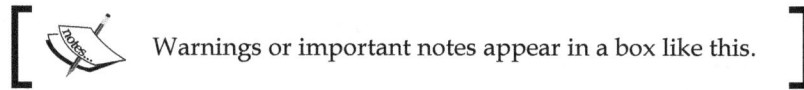

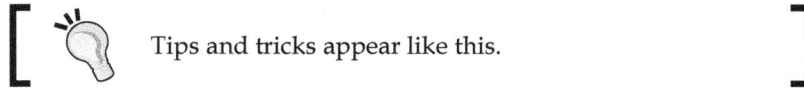

Reader feedback

Feedback from our readers is always welcome. Let us know what you think about this book—what you liked or may have disliked. Reader feedback is important for us to develop titles that you really get the most out of.

To send us general feedback, simply send an e-mail to feedback@packtpub.com, and mention the book title via the subject of your message.

If there is a book that you need and would like to see us publish, please send us a note in the **SUGGEST A TITLE** form on www.packtpub.com or e-mail suggest@packtpub.com.

If there is a topic that you have expertise in and you are interested in either writing or contributing to a book, see our author guide on www.packtpub.com/authors.

Customer support

Now that you are the proud owner of a Packt book, we have a number of things to help you to get the most from your purchase.

Downloading the example code

You can download the example code files for all Packt books you have purchased from your account at http://www.PacktPub.com. If you purchased this book elsewhere, you can visit http://www.PacktPub.com/support and register to have the files e-mailed directly to you.

Errata

Although we have taken every care to ensure the accuracy of our content, mistakes do happen. If you find a mistake in one of our books—maybe a mistake in the text or the code—we would be grateful if you would report this to us. By doing so, you can save other readers from frustration and help us improve subsequent versions of this book. If you find any errata, please report them by visiting http://www.packtpub.com/support, selecting your book, clicking on the **errata submission form** link, and entering the details of your errata. Once your errata are verified, your submission will be accepted and the errata will be uploaded on our website, or added to any list of existing errata, under the Errata section of that title. Any existing errata can be viewed by selecting your title from http://www.packtpub.com/support.

Piracy

Piracy of copyright material on the Internet is an ongoing problem across all media. At Packt, we take the protection of our copyright and licenses very seriously. If you come across any illegal copies of our works, in any form, on the Internet, please provide us with the location address or website name immediately so that we can pursue a remedy.

Please contact us at copyright@packtpub.com with a link to the suspected pirated material.

We appreciate your help in protecting our authors, and our ability to bring you valuable content.

Questions

You can contact us at questions@packtpub.com if you are having a problem with any aspect of the book, and we will do our best to address it.

1
Advanced Hyperion Interactive Reporting Techniques

Welcome to the *Oracle Hyperion Interactive Reporting 11 Expert Guide*! Interactive Reporting is an extremely robust and powerful business intelligence tool providing ad-hoc querying and analysis, dashboards, and reporting capabilities. This Expert Guide picks up where *The Business Analyst's Guide to Oracle Hyperion Interactive Reporting 11* left off, with a focus on providing knowledge of the expert features of the product. While the *Business Analyst's Guide* was an introduction to using the product for the novice to intermediate user, this guide focuses on evolving software users into experts. Interactive Reporting provides many flexible and advanced features that are commonly unknown to the typical business user. One of the most important lesser known features of the software is that it exposes the developer features of the product to the everyday user. These developer features allow the user to leverage scripting in common exercises, to build custom interfaces, and to use code to drive automation. While these features may seem complicated to a user of the product, these features can easily be learned and implemented after reading this book.

This chapter will start with an introduction to the book, highlighting the different groups of content that will be discussed. After the book introduction, the following content is a brief review of some of the main features of Interactive Reporting. The purpose of this review is to baseline terminology that will be used throughout the book and to orient the user to the sections of Interactive Reporting where custom scripting and advanced features are utilized.

This chapter covers the following topics:

- An introduction to the *Expert Guide*
- A review of the EPM Workspace
- A review of Interactive Reporting sections
- Leveraging code throughout the software
- An overview of the Scripting Interface

Introduction to the Oracle Hyperion Interactive Reporting 11 Expert Guide

Interactive Reporting provides users with a significant amount of flexibility in creating dashboards, reports, and analyzing data including the ability to leverage custom programming throughout the document. With this custom programming functionality comes complexity, where users need to understand the best practices in both the software and using JavaScript to create dashboards or custom calculations. This book focuses on providing the reader with an understanding and examples of where custom coding and features of Interactive Reporting can be leveraged to enhance the use of the product in daily activity. These features include introducing JavaScript programming concepts, creating simple to complex dashboards, analyzing content using built-in and JavaScript functions, creating briefing slides and batch exports, building a central code repository for use in the enterprise, and using the developer tools for optimizing and merging two or more Interactive Reporting documents together.

Review of Interactive Reporting concepts

The book begins with a review of the Interactive Reporting sections and highlights the use of Computed Items across each of the sections of the document software. The introduction provides a high-level understanding of the steps needed to perform computations in each section and provides insight into the differences in the sections. The Script Editor is also introduced, and an overview is provided on the features of the editor and the steps to add JavaScript code to dashboard objects and the overall document. This first chapter lays the framework for the book and provides a solid understanding for the content presented across the rest the book.

An Introduction to JavaScript in Interactive Reporting

The book transitions from the overview of the different sections of the product to an introduction to the syntax, methods, and features of JavaScript in Interactive Reporting. JavaScript is an object-oriented scripting language that is commonly used in web development to provide enhanced user interfaces. Within Interactive Reporting, JavaScript is used across all sections of the document, except for the Query section, to perform custom computations and to add interactivity. A solid understanding of JavaScript is needed to become an advanced user of the Interactive Reporting software. The fundamentals described in the second chapter and utilized throughout the rest of the book will provide the user with the confidence needed to build and leverage JavaScript in daily interaction with the software.

Building simple to advanced dashboards

Dashboard sections in Interactive Reporting are used for many purposes, from creating dashboard views of information, to using controls and objects on a dashboard to drive and orchestrate behaviour across multiple sections. This book places a large emphasis on building simple to complex dashboards and provides an understanding for managing code, filters, and interactivity across multiple dashboard sections in a single document. These dashboard chapters provide invaluable information for managing and reusing code inside a document, and the chapters demonstrate best practices for interacting with Interactive Reporting sections and components. Concepts learned in the dashboard chapters can be applied to any business situation where code is needed to perform an operation from processing queries to topics including creating custom programs that produce batch processing, using data from one query to filter another, and exporting to files.

Advanced computations

One of the key aspects of business intelligence is the ability for the user to analyze and manipulate content to answer a set of business questions. Many business users typically prefer to use Microsoft Excel to perform data analysis rather than Interactive Reporting due to their comfort with the software. While Microsoft Excel provides many excellent tools for performing data analysis, Interactive Reporting combines data analysis capabilities with the ability to filter, add computations, leverage data sets, and manipulate data in the millions of records.

Briefing slides and batch exports

Interactive Reporting provides many options for exporting information and formatted reports to different file formats. Users commonly struggle with the best and most appropriate method for creating data or formatted exports, with most users overlooking some of the most effective and efficient exporting methods. In addition to searching for the best export format, many users express interest in exporting information from Interactive Reporting into a Microsoft PowerPoint presentation. While the Hyperion Smart View product can be used to refresh objects in Microsoft documents, another option is available using a few tricks in Interactive Reporting and does not require the use of an additional piece of software.

Another less commonly known feature in Interactive Reporting is the ability to add custom code to generate batch exports of deliverables. Leveraging a few simple programming statements allows the user to save significant time and effort when exporting multiple slices of information from the same document.

The Central Code Repository

One challenge that advanced users encounter with Interactive Reporting's report-centric model is the tracking and maintenance of heavily customized dashboard reports, especially in enterprise-level implementations where the code is used repetitively and transparently across multiple documents. Given the common and straightforward practice of storing similar JavaScript code within each document in an enterprise, it is incredibly difficult and infeasible to individually identify, track, and edit changes across documents.

One simple and invaluable methodology is to store report customization scripts in an accessible database table within the enterprise environment. The chapter on the **Central Code Repository (CCR)** describes building an external code library that allows code to be quickly pushed into some or all documents in an enterprise. This centralized repository provides the capability for agile responses to ongoing business changes and code maintenance without modifying the consuming reporting documents.

Optimizing and Merging

The Oracle Hyperion Interactive Reporting developer tool installation is packaged with two developer tools that are extremely beneficial to users of the software. The products are the Dashboard Studio and the Dashboard Studio Optimize Utility, which allow developers to merge, modify, and fix Interactive Reporting documents in addition to many other operations not included in the Studio developer utility or Interactive Reporting Web Client.

The EPM Workspace

The EPM Workspace, similar to a portal, is where all Oracle Hyperion objects, reports, and files can be accessed and integrated using a shared security model. The Workspace is accessible through the web browser and contains a file system and other document management gadgets, including personal pages, job scheduling, and content subscription.

Interactive Reporting interface and components

Understanding the Interactive Reporting interface is crucial to being proficient in the software. The different sections of the software contain a variety of different options, but the location of where to find and utilize these options is the same across the tool. Knowledge of the interface and how to leverage the features of each section is essential to unlocking the full potential of the product. The terms displayed in the next screenshot will be referenced throughout the book:

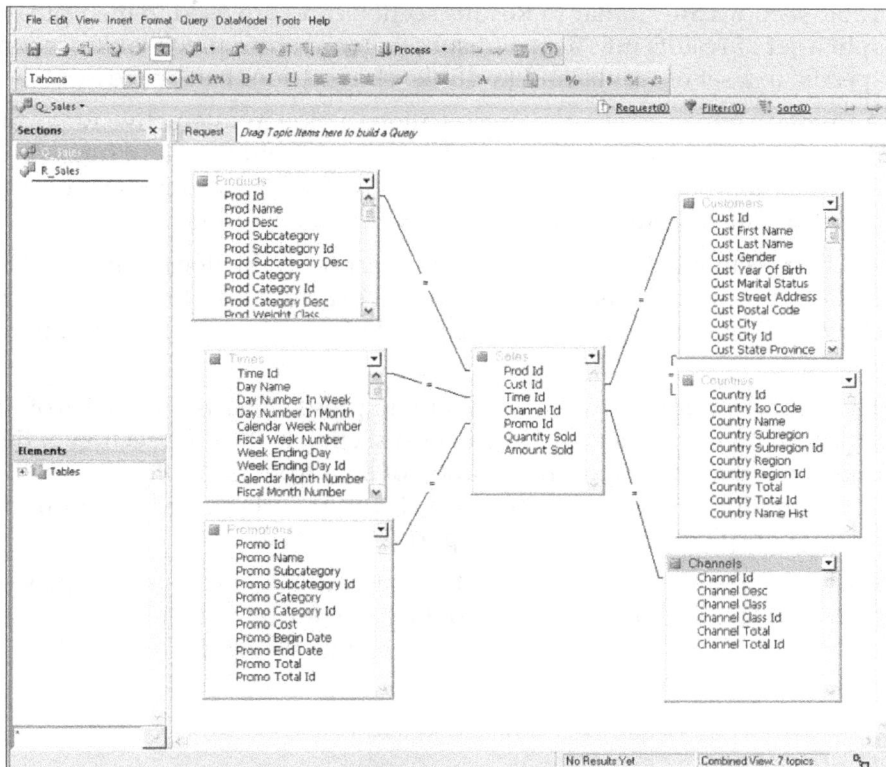

Nearly all features of the Interactive Reporting user interface can be controlled or modified by report authors. Later chapters of the book will describe the methods for controlling the display of the different Web Client Interface menus, toolbars and sections.

Review of Interactive Reporting sections

Before identifying where the advanced features of the product can be leveraged in the document, it is important to review the different sections of the software. The following list provides an overview of each section of the Interactive Reporting software:

- The Data Model and Query sections are used to model database objects and build queries from a data source.

- Each Query section is accompanied by a Results section where data returned from a query is displayed, filtered, and computed. There is only one Results section per Query section, and each Results section displays data in a row by column format.

- Table sections are similar to Results sections and are used to manipulate and split a set of results into different subsets for analysis. Each table section is specific to a set of results and multiple table sections can be created.

- A Pivot section is a common presentation section in Interactive Reporting that aggregates data in a row by column format and the pivot functionality is similar to Microsoft Excel pivots. The Pivot section can use any column of data from the parent Results or Table section.

- A Chart section is another presentation section of the document. The Chart section is commonly used to display data in a graphical format. Different chart formats exist, ranging from bar and pie charts to scatter and bubble charts.

- The Report section provides the ability to present charts and tables of data in a printable report format. The Report section is the only section of the document that allows for the addition of data from multiple queries in the document into a single reporting object, and reports provide an additional method of splitting out data by Report Groups.

- Dashboards are used to create custom interfaces or interactive displays of key metrics. The dashboard section provides the flexibility to leverage custom scripting and interactivity to automate manual features of the product.

Leveraging code

Many methods exist for adding custom code throughout the document. Interactive Reporting provides the flexibility to manipulate data and build custom applications through using a JavaScript programming language throughout all sections of the document except the Query section, where custom fields are defined using database specific SQL.

JavaScript is commonly used in two ways within the document, including - building computations in presentation sections and building logic to force specific behaviours across the document or on a dashboard. When building computations in sections, JavaScript and native functions are used in Computed Items to modify and enhance a set of results. When driving behaviour across the documents or adding interactivity, JavaScript code is used in the Document Scripts or on a Dashboard section. In either approach, Interactive Reporting provides significant flexibility and interactivity to model and solve complex business problems.

Query section Computed Items

Many users require the ability to provide further analysis on data returned from a query. Computed Items can be added to a query to create custom Request line items, which allow the user to modify and enhance the data elements in the data model.

Building Computed Items in the Query section is very different than building Computed Items throughout the rest of the document. The syntax for building Computed Items in the Query section is database specific SQL, while Computed Items throughout the rest of Interactive Reporting are created using JavaScript. The differentiation in syntax is based on the design of the product, where the Query section is the only section that builds a query string that is passed to the database. The rest of the sections in an Interactive Reporting document contain and display data that has already been returned from a data source.

The syntax of the Computed Item in a query is included as a column in the query string that is passed to the database. The following steps are methods to add Computed Items to the Request line:

Right-click method	Query menu method
Right-click inside the Request line	Open the **Query** menu
Select **Add Computed Item**	Select **Add Computed Item**

Upon adding the Computed Item to a query, a window opens as shown in the following screenshot:

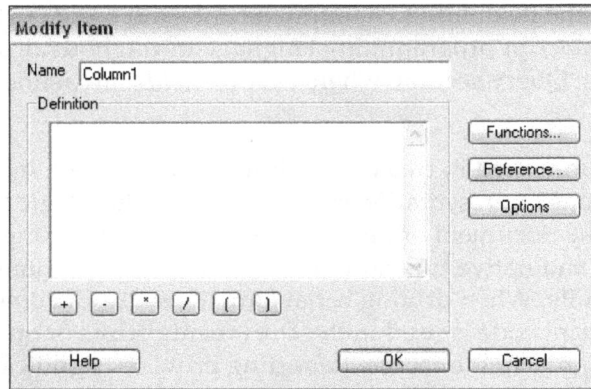

The logic for the blank Computed Item can be typed directly into the Computed Item **Definition** box of the **Properties** window that appears. The **Functions** and **Reference** buttons are included to aid the user in creating the Computed Item definition by providing a selection option for referencing column names and a list of predefined functions. The **Options** button is used to set the **Datatype** of the column, which is important in order to accurately represent the data returned from the query for the column.

> In each Query Element, the Table or Topic name must be added as a qualifier in front of the column name, that is, `Table_Name.Column_Name`. This syntax is similar to qualifying a database table with the table owner, where Interactive Reporting treats the Table or Topic as the owner of the table.

Since the table needs to be qualified (referenced by table name), users commonly add items to the Request line and then edit the item properties by double-clicking on the item to view the **Properties** of the item. By adding an item to the Request line before editing, the item definition is populated in the **Definition** section of the **Properties** window. Upon the completion of editing the Computed Item, the item is added to the Request line with the **Name** specified after pressing **OK**.

> Before completing the custom column definition, it is important to review and adjust the Datatype of the column using the Options of the item. For example, converting a Date field to a string requires the Data type of the column to be set to a string to avoid incorrectly formatted data after processing.

The following are examples of simple Query section Computed Items with Oracle as a data source:

- **Concatenation:** `Products.Prod_Name||' - '||Products.Prod_Desc`
- **String Manipulation:** `SUBSTR(Customers.Cust_Postal_Code,1,5)`
- **Value Replacement:** `NVL(Promotions.Promo_Name, 'No Product Name')`.
- **Date/Time Functions:** `TO_DATE('2009-02-01','YYYY-MM-DD')`

When Computed Items are added to the Request line, the Computed Item element will display at the end of the list of all of the elements in the Request line. Upon processing, the computed column will appear in the data results in the order of the columns in the Request line (if this is the first time the query is processed) or the field will be added at the end of the data results (if the query was previously processed). Computed Items are not differentiated in appearance from any other element in the query, where the Computed Item elements appear similar to the elements mapped from topics or tables. However, any Computed Item or data element containing a function will display with the function notation surrounding the data element name in the Request line. For example, adding a SUM function to a data element in the Query section will display the function name, as shown in the following screenshot:

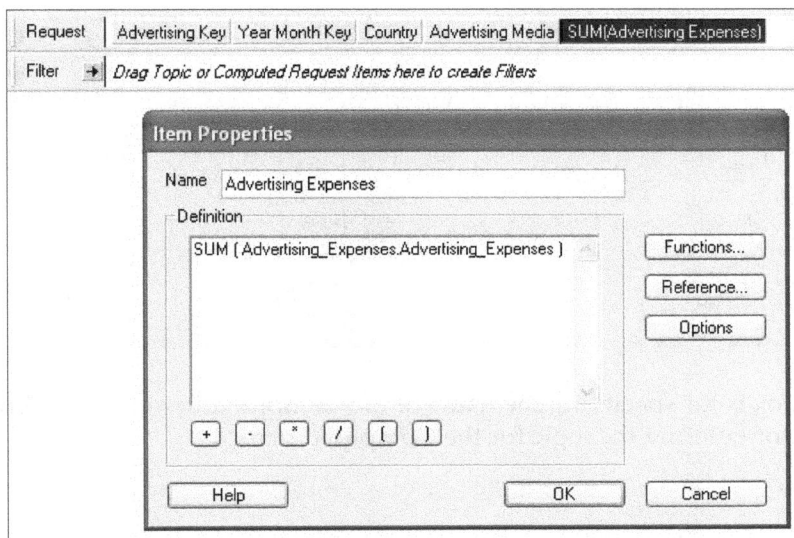

Results section Computed Items

Computed Items are added to the Results section to modify contents and add calculations to data returned from a query. Since the results set is data that has already been processed, the Computed Items in the Results section are based on data stored in the document. While the syntax used in Computed Items in the Query section is the SQL syntax of the database, the syntax used in the Results section to create custom computations is JavaScript. The following steps are methods to add a Computed Item to the Results section:

Right-click method	Results menu method
Right-click inside the Results section	Open the **Results** menu
Select **Add Computed Item**	Select **Add Computed Item**

Once the **Add Computed Item** menu item has been selected, the **Computed Item** window appears, as shown in the following figure:

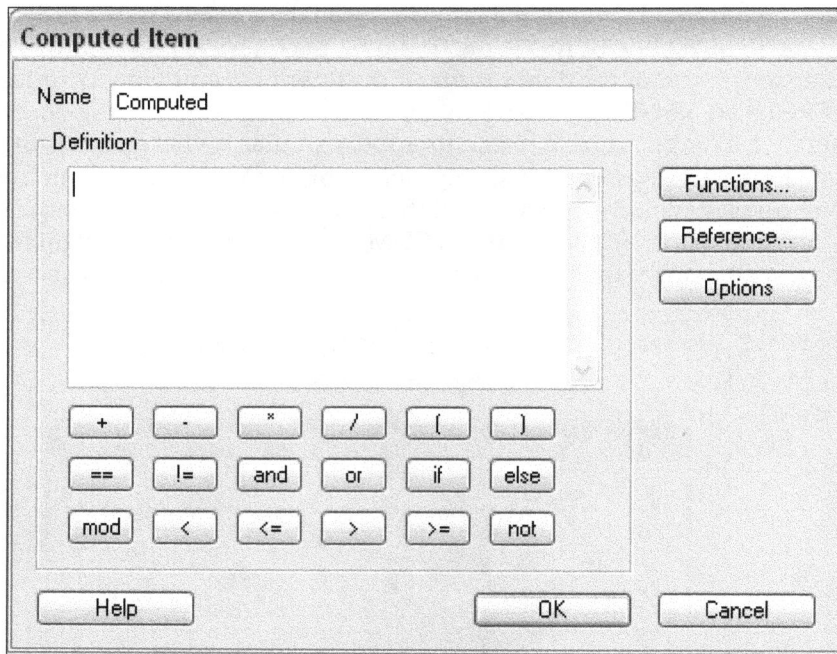

The **Name** box is for specifying the name of the Computed Item. The **Definition** text box is used for entering the logic for the Computed Item.

It is important to note that the column names are case sensitive. It is also important to note that columns with a space in the column name must contain underscores instead of spaces when referenced in Computed Items (that is, Day of Week is referenced as Day_ of_Week in the definition window) and special characters are also replaced with underscores. If adding computations to a column with a special character, it is helpful to use the Reference feature to select the column.

The buttons below the **Definition** text box are the different logic conditions and operators that can be used in the Computed Item definition. These different conditions and operators can be typed into the **Definition** box by the user or the buttons on the screen can be used to populate the definition window with the desired content. The buttons to the right of the text box are similar to the buttons in the Query section, where predefined **Functions** can be used to transform data elements in the section. These predefined functions are specific to Interactive Reporting and provide the ability to manipulate string, date, and text data. The **Reference** button provides the ability to accurately reference data elements in the section without the need to type in the name of the column. The **Options** button is used to set the **Datatype** of the column, which is important in order to accurately represent the column of data after the computation.

Upon the completion of editing the Computed Item, the item is added to the Results section with the **Name** specified after pressing **OK**. The column is added to the end of the Results section and is displayed in the Data Layout window in blue text and in italics. The column can be moved around to the desired location in the Results section, and the column can be easily modified by following one of the two steps:

Right-click method	Results menu method
Highlight the column of data in the Results section	Highlight the column of data in the Results section
Right-click and select **Modify Column**	Open the **Results** menu and select **Modify Column**

The following are a few simple examples of Results section computed items:

- Concatenation: `Products.Prod_Name+" - "+Products.Prod_Desc`
- String Manipulation: `Substr(Customers.Cust_Postal_Code,1,5)`
- Conditional Functions: `Nvl(Promotions.Promo_Name, 'No Product TTarName')`

The examples provided are used to demonstrate simple programming operations that can be performed in the Results section. Future chapters of this book will discuss the different programming functionality and advanced operations that can be added to Computed Items.

Table section Computed Items

Computed Items in a Table section are very similar to Computed Items in the Results section. However, the main difference between the Table section and the Results section is the ability to add multiple Table sections to a set of results. The ability to add multiple Table sections to a set of results allows the user to split Computed Items between the Tables and allows the user to filter on a Computed Item that is created in a parent Results or Table section leveraging the **Prior, Next, Cume** or any other aggregating function.

> Filters cannot be placed on an aggregating function in the section it was created.

The following steps are methods to add a Computed Item to the Table section:

Right-click method	Table menu method
Right-click inside the Table section	Open the **Table** menu
Select **Add Computed Item**	Select **Add Computed Item**

Once the **Add Computed Item** menu item has been selected, the **Computed Item** window appears, as shown in the following figure:

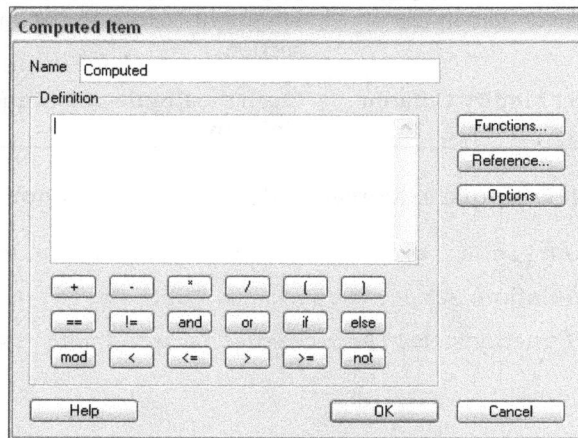

The functionality of the **Computed Item** box is identical to the features provided in the Results Computed Item section and no additional functionality exists that is different from the Results section.

Pivot section Computed Items

Computed Items are common operations performed in the Pivot section, where calculations are easily performed on aggregated sets of data. While items are added to the **Row** and **Column Labels,** the Pivot section only provides the ability to add a Computed Item to the pivot **Facts**. While computations can be completed in the Results section, it is more effective to compute percentages and other division based calculations in the Pivot than the Results or Table sections to accurately calculate totals. A Computed Item is added to a Pivot section by following one of the two steps:

Right-click method	Pivot menu method
Right-click in the main Pivot window.	Open the **Pivot** menu
	Select **Add Computed Item**
Select **Add Computed Item**	

The syntax for a Computed Item is the same as that found in the Results and Table sections and the Computed Item is highlighted in italics in the **Facts** section of the Data Layout. In the next example, a Computed Item has been created to show **Total Sales** over **Quantity Sold**:

Notice the computation of the values in the **Total** lines. Currently the **Total** lines show the sum of the values displayed in the pivot and not the division of the **Total Sales** value by the **Quantity Sold** total value.

Pivot Settings: True Totals and Surface Values

The Pivot section provides the flexibility of calculating the Computed Items and total lines of the document by either the computation of the values shown on the screen or by the values contained in the data results. The settings can be easily configured in the **Pivot Options** menu, where the **Use Surface Values** or **True Computed Item Totals** options checkboxes can be toggled.

When the **True Computed Item Totals** option is selected, the pivot total lines will be calculated by totaling the individual values of the columns that make up the total instead of performing the computation operation on the total column.

When the **Surface Values** option is selected, the pivot calculates the Computed Item from values displayed on the pivot instead of the values in the parent Results or Table section for all columns. The Surface Values setting is necessary when adding one or more Computed Items together in the pivot where the values in the pivot must be used in the calculation.

Editing Pivot Computed Items

Similar to the Results and Table sections, the Computed Item can be modified by one of the following two steps:

Right-click method	Pivot menu method
Highlight the column of data in the Pivot section	Highlight the column of data in the Pivot
	Open the **Pivot** menu and select **Modify**
Right-click and select **Modify**	

Chart section Computed Items

Computed Items can be leveraged in a Chart to display constants or other variations of data elements not contained in the data results. Computed Items are added to a Chart by one of the following two steps:

Right-click method	Chart menu method
Right-click in the main **Chart** window.	Open the **Chart** menu
Select **Add Computed Item**	Select **Add Computed Item**

The syntax for Computed Items in a Chart section is the same as found in the Results and Table sections, where the Computed Item is highlighted in italics in the Facts section of the Data Layout.

> Computed Items cannot be used in the Scatter or Bubble charts.

The chart in the following screenshot is a Bar Line chart, with a Computed Item set to a line and configured to use the scale on the left axis:

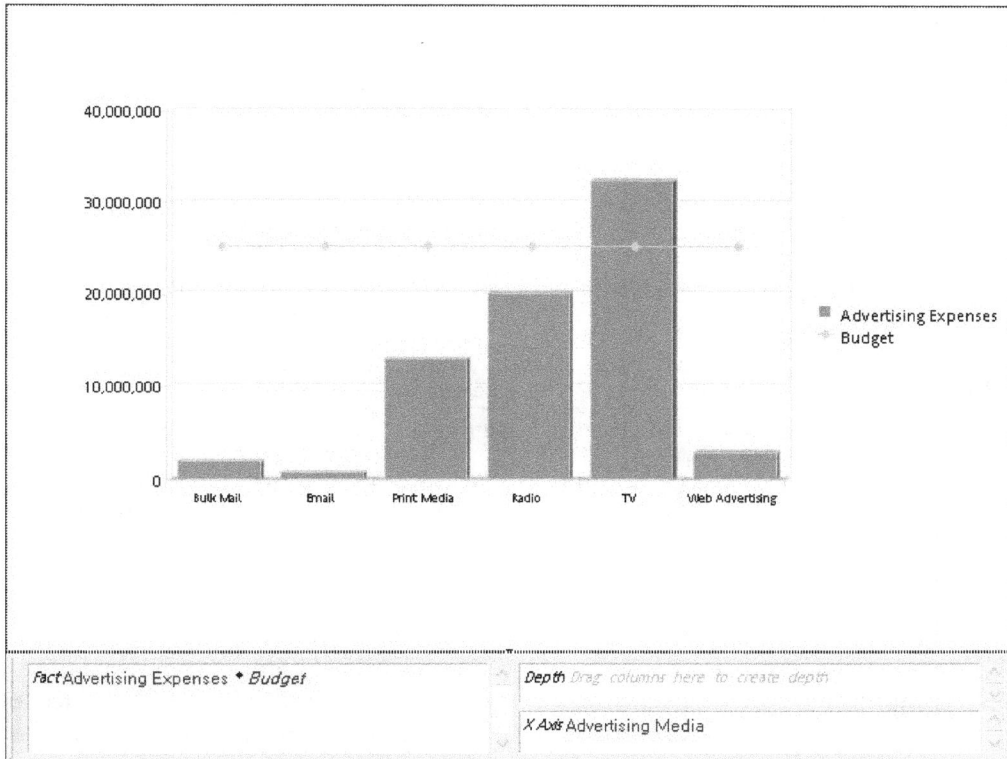

In this example, the Computed Item, **Budget,** is set to a constant value to display a threshold. The following screenshot displays the syntax used to complete the Computed Item. More advanced logic can be used as desired:

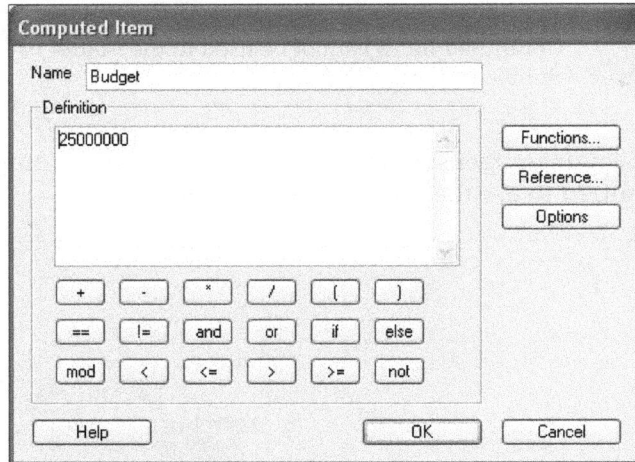

Computed Items in the Chart section are easily modified by one of the two following steps:

Right-click method	Chart menu method
Highlight the data element in the Data Layout window of the Chart.	Highlight the data element in the Data Layout window of the Chart.
Right-click and select **Modify Computed Item**	Open the **Chart** menu and select **Modify Computed Item**

Report section Computed Items

The Report section provides the ability to add two types of computations in a report, where computations can be performed in **Field** expressions as well as in the **Facts** of Report Tables. Computed Items are added to Report Tables through one of the two following methods:

Report menu method	Right-click method
Highlight a column of data inside the table.	Highlight a column of data inside the table.
Open the **Report** menu and select **Add Computed Item**.	Right-click and select **Add Computed Item**.

When a Computed Item is added, the Computed Item window appears as shown in the following screenshot:

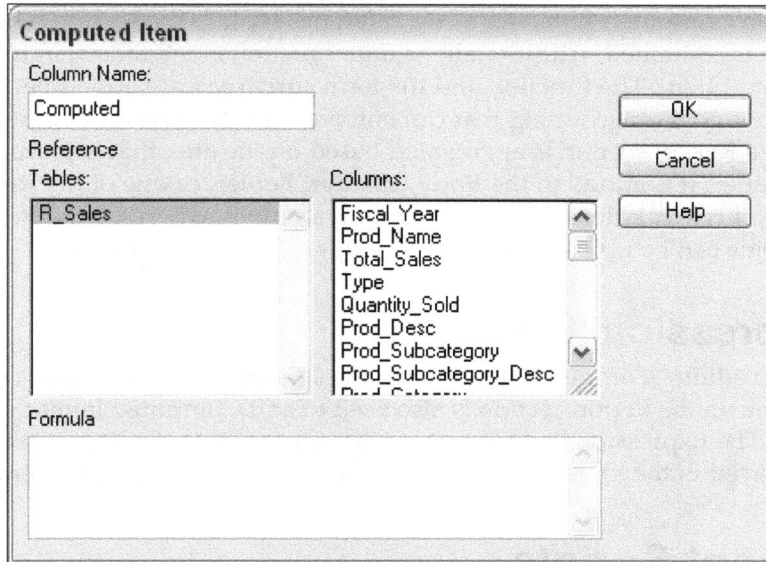

The text box at the top of the window is for adding the desired name for the column. Below the **Column Name** field is the configuration for selecting a field from a table. At the bottom of the window is the **Formula** section for adding the logic to the Computed Item. The following screenshot shows an example of a Computed Item leveraging fields from two Table sections:

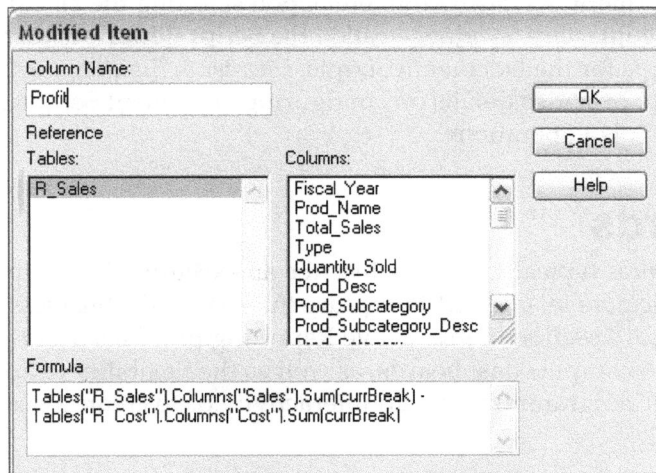

Notice the difference in logic between the Report section Computed Items and the logic for the other Computed Items in the document. Since the Report section Computed Items can reference data from more than one section in the document, Report section Computed Items require a reference back to the section where the data element is contained. Additionally, a data function is referenced at the end of each Computed Item. The function and the term **currBreak** are added because the Report sections contain grouping that can enforce different levels of aggregation. Each item in a Report section is aggregated based on the area that is placed in a report, whether it is added to the **Body**, **Header**, **Footer**, or one of the **Report Groups**. The **currBreak** defines the aggregation to apply, where variations of the **currBreak** logic can be utilized to modify the aggregation performed.

The Expression line

In addition to editing Computed Items using the Computed Item window, the Expression line in the Report section is also used to edit Computed Items as well as **Field** items. The Expression line is a feature that is specific to the Report section and logic is displayed in the Expression line when an item is clicked by the user in a report.

Document Scripts

Each Interactive Reporting document contains the ability to have a predefined set of steps occur when the document opens, before the document closes, before processing, after processing, and upon update of session values. These document level actions are referred to as **Document Scripts** in Interactive Reporting.

Document Scripts are added to the document by clicking on the **File** menu and selecting the **Document Scripts** menu item. Upon selecting the Document Scripts item, the scripting interface window — called the Script Editor — is displayed for adding the logic for the Document Scripts. *Chapter 5, Building the Dashboard Framework* section, provides details on configuring Document Scripts to support dashboards and global operations.

Dashboards

The term *dashboard* is typically used to describe an executive-level report displaying key business indicators in an effort to capture the health of a business at a point in time. The Dashboard section in Interactive Reporting provides users with the ability to create simple to complex dashboards, as well as the flexibility to add controls and custom JavaScript programming to add interactivity or to create a custom interfaces.

The Scripting Interface

The **Script Editor** is the interface where code is written to perform an operation through Document Scripts or the Dashboard section. The Script Editor is opened in one of several ways including: selecting the **Document Scripts** menu item from the **File** menu, selecting the **Scripts** menu item from the **Dashboard** menu, or by *right-clicking* an object on a dashboard and selecting **Scripts**. The following image is an example of the Script Editor open to an item on the Dashboard section:

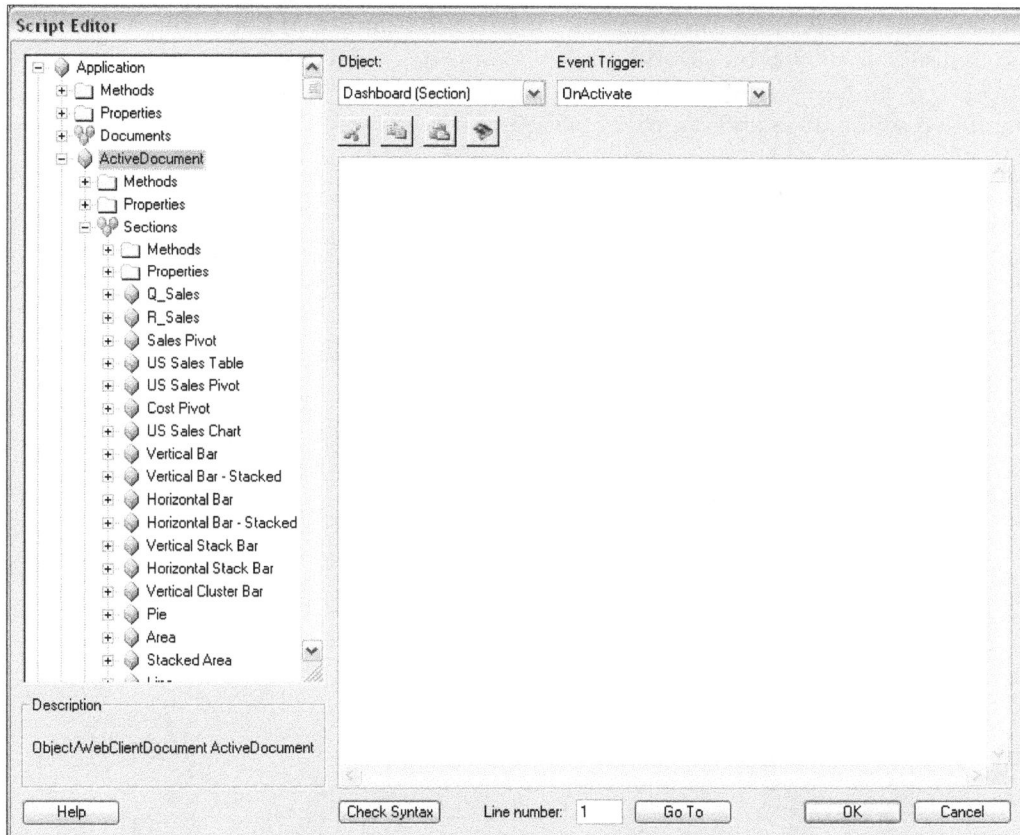

Chapter 2, Introduction to JavaScript and the Interactive Reporting API, provides a detailed introduction to JavaScript and provides a detailed explanation of the Script Editor.

Summary

The goal of this chapter was to provide an introduction to the book and a review of Interactive Reporting terminology, adding Computed Items to sections, and the Scripting Interface. The chapter began with an introduction to the topics that are discussed in future chapters, including JavaScript, Dashboards, Advanced Computations, the Central Code Repository, Batching, and the Dashboard Studio and Optimize Utility. The chapter transitions from an introduction to a review of Interactive Reporting topics and terminology used throughout the book, including the Interactive Reporting Interface and a review of Interactive Reporting sections. The methods to create, build, and modify Computed Items in each section are introduced, and an introduction to Document Scripts is presented. The chapter concluded with a brief overview the Scripting Interface, setting the stage for the following chapter on logical programming in JavaScript.

2
Introduction to JavaScript and the Interactive Reporting API

Building expertise in Interactive Reporting requires a solid working knowledge of the use of the JavaScript programming language, Interactive Reporting built-in functions, and the features of the Interactive Reporting **Application Programming Interface (API)**. The **Application Programming Interface (API)** in Interactive Reporting provides the ability to access objects and events used by the core application. The object properties and event behaviors are orchestrated using JavaScript code to drive a desired application behavior typically in the form of an end-user interface or business application.

The goal of this chapter is to provide users with an introduction to JavaScript and the Application Programming Interface. The chapter will begin with an in-depth look at the Interactive Reporting API and will conclude with an introduction to fundamental concepts of JavaScript.

This chapter covers the following topics:

- Introduction to objects and collections
- The Script Editor
- An introduction to JavaScript

Introduction to objects and collections

The concepts described in this chapter introduce a new set of vocabulary that is referenced through the rest of the book. The Interactive Reporting programming terminology describes the different components of the application, the properties of the components, and the actions that can be performed on each object. The following are the primary definitions used when describing Interactive Reporting components:

- An **object** is defined as either a single entity or a collection of entities. The term object is a fairly generic term used to reference any entity which can be acted upon. These entities range from the Application object to Dashboard Shape objects and control toolbars to Text Labels and beyond.

- **Methods** describe the relevant actions for a given object. The available actions are defined by the object type within the application. For example, the Activate method of a Dashboard section displays the Dashboard section when used and is similar to clicking on the section with the mouse in the Section Catalog.

- **Properties** are the attributes of an object, and may include formatting, data values, or configuration settings. Examples of properties include the text displayed in a Text Label or the operator used in a Query Filter.

- **Collections** are special groupings of objects that are related. A good example of a collection is the Sections collection. This collection contains all of the individual sections that are within a single Interactive Reporting document, regardless of the section type.

- **Constants** are collections of read-only values that represent possible object property states or values. The definition of a constant is determined by Interactive Reporting and cannot be customized by the report author. Interactive Reporting constants always begin with bq.

A real-world example of the concepts presented in this section can be conceptually demonstrated by visualizing an apartment building. The building itself is an object. The building object has properties such as the number of apartments, number of floors within the building, and resident amenities. The individual apartments are also distinct objects with properties, such as the number of rooms in each apartment or the address of the apartment. However, the apartments themselves are also part of the overall building object, making the apartments members, or children, of the building.

Continuing with the apartment example, envision that the building supervisor hires painters to repaint apartments. If the painters are ordered to paint an individual apartment at the object-level, the painter would require the address of the apartment. The resulting request from the supervisor would be to paint apartment 1A. If the painters were needed to paint all apartments within the building, one approach (entailing more work for everyone) might be for the supervisor to give them each apartment address between jobs. Alternatively, the painters could be ordered to paint the collection of apartments and instead be given an order such as to paint all apartments in the building.

The apartment example is a description of how collections work in Interactive Reporting. Orders given to a collection are given to each member until all collection members have received and completed the task. The order in which the members are evaluated is automatically determined by Interactive Reporting when the object is created. The practice of accessing an object by its collection is an incredibly powerful technique that will be demonstrated throughout the code examples in this book.

The Script Editor

The **Script Editor** is the primary interface used to add JavaScript code within different sections of the document. All the customizations in Interactive Reporting are event-driven, meaning that code is executed by either a user-created event such as the clicking of a mouse button, or a system-created event such as the opening of a document. These events invoke JavaScript contained within the object's corresponding Event Trigger.

The Interactive Reporting API categorizes events into three main types. Two of these types, **Dashboard-level Events** and **Dashboard Object-level Events,** are tied to Dashboard sections and are customized using the **Dashboard Script Editor**. A Dashboard-level Event occurs when a dashboard is shown, or activated, to the user and when it is deactivated as the user navigates away from it. This event type is typically used to set and reset default properties of objects users can interact with such as a default radio button selection. Dashboard Object-level events are events that are trigged at the dashboard shape level and are related to actions typically attributed to user interactivity such as a button click. The Dashboard Script Editor is opened by selecting the **Scripts** menu item from the **Dashboard** menu (enabled only on Dashboard sections in **Edit** mode) or through the use of the *F8* hot key.

The third type of event, **Document-level Events,** customize events related either to opening or closing a document or directly before or after a query is processed. An example of using a Document-level Event is enabling or disabling the visibility of a toolbar when a document is opened. The Document-level Events use the **Document Script Editor,** which is accessed by selecting **Document Scripts** from the **File** menu.

The functionality and usage of both Script Editors is the same with the exception that the Document Script Editor allows developers to specify different functionality for different types of client software (that is, the Desktop Studio, Interactive Reporting Web Client, or the HTML client). This feature is commonly used in environments where multiple clients are used to access an Interactive Reporting document. The following image is an example of the Document Script Editor:

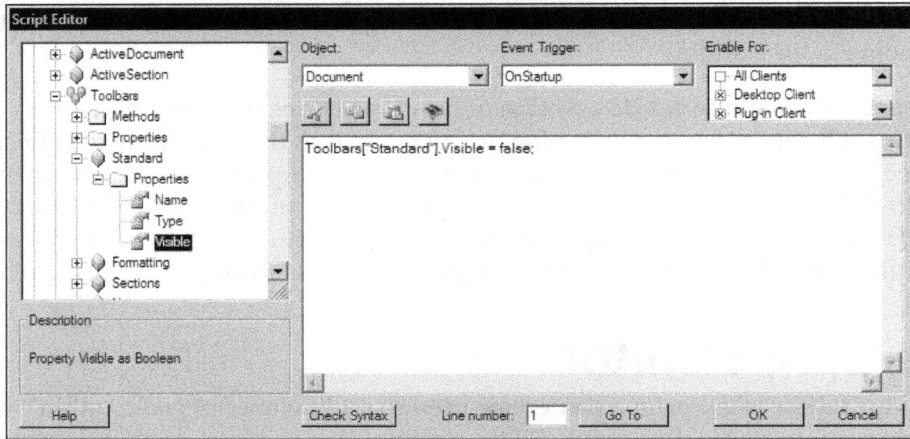

The most important components of the **Script Editor** are the **Object Model** and **Description**, located on the left side of the interface, the **Object** and **Event Trigger** drop-down boxes, located at the top of the interface, and the code pane, located under the **Object** and **Event Trigger** boxes.

The **Object Model** is a visual representation of the contents of the Interactive Reporting API. As shown in the following image, the **Script Editor** displays icons denoting each of the Object Model component types:

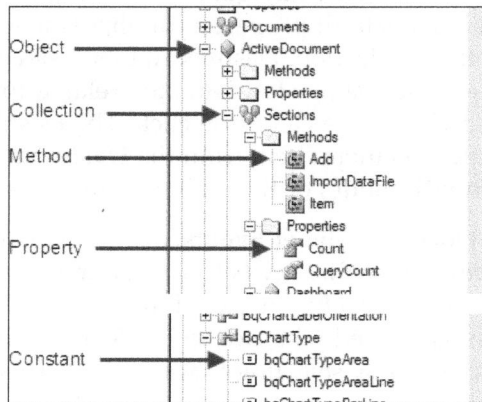

When a selection is made in the Object Model, the section directly under the Object Model displays a description of that object. This description is an invaluable tool when learning to script in Interactive Reporting as it gives an insight of how the API expects the selection to be used. Additional help specific to the item selected in the Object Model can be accessed using the **Help** button below the description box.

The **Object** drop-down list provides the list of available objects that can drive behavior through JavaScript code. The **Event Trigger** drop-down list provides the different events that can be enacted for each object. It is possible for an object to have code on multiple event triggers to perform operations for different events.

The largest area of the **Script Editor** is a text box where customized code is entered, called the **code pane**. Double-clicking on any item from the Object Model will add an appropriate code snippet to the code pane referencing the desired item. Additionally, code can also be manually entered or copied and pasted from other sources.

When the **OK** button is pressed, the code is checked for syntax errors. If no errors are found, the **Script Editor** is then closed and the code is saved.

It is recommendable to occasionally use the **OK** button to validate and save code when scripting large blocks so that progress is not lost should the **Script Editor** exit unexpectedly.

Introduction to JavaScript

JavaScript is a very popular scripting language and is commonly used in websites to provide enhanced user interfaces. This section of the chapter is an introduction to the fundamental concepts of the JavaScript language. The concepts introduced will provide the programming building blocks demonstrated in the code examples throughout this book. In addition to the content described in this chapter, there are many other resources available on the Internet to continue learning JavaScript or to obtain additional code examples.

Variables

Variables are temporary containers used to store information to be recalled at a later point. Once created, the value in the variable can be accessed, or read, across the document and can be manipulated or changed as desired. The following sections of this chapter introduce the many kinds of variables that are demonstrated in the upcoming dashboard and advanced analysis chapters.

Variables are custom names with values assigned to them using the = sign. While most custom names can be used, some names are already defined components of the JavaScript language itself and therefore cannot be used to denote a custom variable. Attempts to use a predefined component, called a Reserved Word, will result in a JavaScript error. Additionally, as JavaScript is a case-sensitive language, all references to variable names must exactly match the combination of upper and lowercase letters.

The visibility, or accessibility, of a variable to different objects across the document is referred to as the variable's **scope**. Scope can be either global, meaning the variable can be accessed from anywhere else in the document, or local, meaning the variable has no presence outside of the object in which the declaration is made. In most cases, local scope would refer to a variable being available only within a particular event or on a particular document section.

Within Interactive Reporting, declarations with local scope are defined using the var keyword. Declarations without the var keyword are automatically considered to have global scope.

Variable data types

Variables contain a reference to the type of data that is stored in each variable. The references are referred to as the data type of the variable, where the common data types are boolean, string, number, and null. In many programming languages, the data type of the variables must be specified at the time the variable is defined. However, in JavaScript, the data type of a variable is associated directly with the stored value instead of to the variable itself. This concept, called **dynamic typing**, allows a single variable to have data with one type associated to it and then later be re-used and have data with a different type assigned. This is useful when converting the data type of a variable throughout the programming process, including from number to string or vice versa.

Boolean variables

Boolean variables contain either a true or false value. This variable type can act as a yes or no flag to signify the state of an object property. For example, the Visible property of a Shape is boolean and can be either true of false. The statement Shape.Visible=false would mean the shape is not visible and Shape.Visible=true would mean the shape is visible.

String variables

Sequences of characters, comprised of any combination of alpha-numeric characters, special characters, and spaces, are stored as **string** variables. When declaring a string, quotes are used to tell the software where the **string** begins and ends. There is no syntax requirement for the use of one type of quotes. Either double or single quotes can be used as long as the start and end quotes are the same type. For example: `myString = "Country"` and `myString = 'Country'` would both declare the variable named `myString` to be equal to the value `Country`.

Strings can be added end-to-end with other strings through a process called **concatenation**. When a string is concatenated with a non-string value such as a number, the result is also stored as a string.

The following example concatenates month, day, and year variables into a single string:

```
var vMonth = 1;
var vDay = "06";
var vYear = 1999;
var stringDate = vMonth +"/"+ vDay +"/" + vYear;
```

> **Downloading the example code**
>
> You can download the example code files for all Packt books you have purchased from your account at `http://www.PacktPub.com`. If you purchased this book elsewhere, you can visit `http://www.PacktPub.com/support` and register to have the files e-mailed directly to you.

When evaluated, the preceding code defines the variable `stringDate` as equal to `1/06/1999`.

Number variables

Data that is strictly numeric is stored as a **number** data type. Variables with the number data type can be evaluated directly with other numbers using an arithmetic operators such as + for addition or * for multiplication. The value resulting from arithmetic operations is a number. In JavaScript the ++ and -- operators are used to increment and decrement a numeric variable, referring to +1 and -1 respectively. For example, `x++` is short hand to mean `x = x+1`.

Null variables

Null variables are variables that are without a value or empty. Conceptually, null is the lack of any value and is not the same thing as a blank string variable or the number zero.

Arrays

An **Array** is an object used to store multiple related values within a single variable. Since all of the values are in the same variable and are identified with a numeric identifier called an index, loop statements (described later in the chapter) are used to iterate through the array to quickly access the stored values.

The following code is an example of the initialization of a global array:

```
gMonthArray = [];
    gMonthArray[0]= "Jan";
    gMonthArray[1]= "Feb";
    gMonthArray[2]= "Mar";
```

While conceptually similiar, it is important to note that an Array index - the starting value stored within the brackets - starts at 0 where as Interactive Reporting objects collections, such as the list of items in a drop-down box or the list of rows in a Results section, start with an index values of 1.

Associative Arrays

Sometimes referred to as a map or dictionary, **associative arrays** are a type of array indexed by a string, instead of a number. Associated arrays are most useful when the relationship between two strings is strongly defined and they are commonly used to create custom look-up references.

The following example declares an associative array with local scope:

```
var vMonthArray = [];
    vMonthArray["Jan"] = "January";
    vMonthArray["Feb"] = "February";
    vMonthArray["Mar"] = "March";
```

Functions

Functions are reusable sets of code that are configured to perform a targeted set of operations. A function must be declared before it can be invoked by an object, and a function is only executed when a separate set of code referred to as a function call is made.

The basic syntax for a function is:

```
function functionName()
{
   //code to be executed;
}
```

Functions can have additional input values to be supplied when the function is called to execute. The input values, called **parameters**, are special variables that are passed into the function allowing the function to be dynamic. Functions accepting parameters have values within the parentheses after the function name. The basic syntax for a function accepting parameters is:

```
function functionName(param1, param2, ...)
{
    //code to be executed;
}
```

A function defaults to a local scope but assigning the function to a global variable makes the function's scope global. A function with global scope can be accessed by any object in the same document. The following example demonstrates the syntax to declare a function with a global scope:

```
function functionName(param1, param2)
{

    //code to be executed;
}


//make the function globally accessible
gfFunctionName = functionName;
```

The syntax for accessing functions is to first call the function by name and then to supply any expected parameters within parentheses immediately following the name. Functions that are bound to a global variable are called by the using the global variable name instead of the function name. The following is an example of the syntax for accessing a function both locally and globally:

```
//Accessing a Local Function
functionName(paramVal1, paramVal2);

//Accessing a Global Function
gfFunctionName(paramVal1, paramVal2);
```

Functions can also return a value back to the user to be used further in the document. For example, if a function was created to perform a mathematical calculation, the user would want the function to produce the output of the calculation. The following demonstrates the function notation and the function call for returning a value:

```
function functionName(param1, param2)
{
    //code to be executed;
    //set output value to var1;
```

```
    //return statement;
    return vOutput1;


}


//make the function globally accessible
gfFunctionName = functionName;


//Call the Function and Receive Returned Value
var2 = gfFunctionName(paramVal1, paramVal2);
```

Decision logic

By default, any custom code is executed line by line from the top down unless otherwise directed. Using basic logic, objects and variables can be assessed allowing a decision to be made between one or more execution paths. Depending on the type of logical statement, code can be executed once, executed more than once, or skipped entirely.

Comparison operators

Comparison operators are a type of operator used to create simple comparisons of the relationship of two entities, such as variables or numbers, where the outcome of that comparison always results in a true or false value. The true or false outcome, which conceptually can be interpreted as a yes or no, is arguably the most important aspect of any decision statement as it ultimately determines the execution path of the code.

Logically, the description of each individual comparison operator is similar to that of its mathematical counterpart, as seen in the following chart:

Comparison Operator	Description
==	Equal (comparison)
!=	Not equal
>=	Greater than or equal to
>	Greater than
<=	Less than or equal to
<	Less than

It is also important to note that the == sign for the equal comparison operator is not the same as the = command. The = is used to define variable values whereas the == is used to compare whether two values are the same. Using a = in a conditional statement to compare values will produce an undesired result.

Conditional statements

Conditional statements, also called **choices**, are the statements and syntax used to build the comparison. There are two main components to a conditional statement, the assessment logic and the code block. The assessment logic is typically the first line the statement and provides the comparison, and the code block is the code to be executed based on the true or false assessment. Opening and closing braces { } are always used to denote a code block in a conditional statement.

The `if()`, `else if()`, and `else` conditional statements are the three statements used to assess if the outcome of a comparative statement is true or false. When an `if()` statement is deemed false, additional statements can be assessed using `else if()`. When it is necessary to define an action for all remaining cases, `else` is used to act for all cases where the result of the `if()` or `else if()` comparison is false. The `if()` statement can stand alone, but `else if()` and `else` statements must be preceded by at least one `if()` statement.

The following code demonstrates the syntax of the `if()`, `else if()` and `else` conditional statements:

```
//Assess one conditional statement
if(conditional statement)
{
    //Current Statement is true
}

//Assess additional conditional statements
else if(conditional statement)
{
    //Prior Statement is false
    //Current Statement is true
}

//Assess all other cases
else
{
    //All Prior Statements are false
}
```

Another type of conditional statement is the `Switch()` statement. Similar to `if()`, `else if()`, and `else` statements, switch statements evaluate the truth of an argument. Switch statements are typically used to evaluate a single object against known cases.

The following code demonstrates the syntax of the switch statement:

```
switch(object)
{
   case 1:
      //code block;
      break;
   case 2:
      //code block;
      break;
   default:
      //code block;
}
```

The **break** statement is used to exit the current statement. It is used throughout switch statements and can be used in loops and conditional statements to exit from the given statement.

Logical operators

Logical operators are used to control the order in which code is executed. The && logical operator denotes AND, the || logical operator denotes OR, and the ! denotes NOT. When two statements are separated by the && operator, both statements must render true to satisfy the condition. When two statements are separated by the || operator, only one of the two statements must be satisfied. When the ! operator is used, it is used to test whether a condition is not true.

Since the &&, ||, and ! operators can be used together, parentheses () are commonly used to segment items in a conditional statement. The following example demonstrates the use of the AND and OR statements used with parentheses:

```
//Using AND, OR and Parentheses
if(A == B || (A==C && B==D) )
{
    //Statement is true
}
```

In the preceding code, the statement that is true is A is equal to B OR A is equal to C AND B is equal to D. From a logical execution, the system would first attempt to validate if A is equal to B. If it were, the statement would be deemed true and the code within the {} would be executed. If A is not equal to B, the system would then check to see if A is equal to C. If A is equal to C, it would then check if B is equal to D. If A is not equal to C or B is not equal to D, the statement is false and code within the {} would be skipped.

Conditional logic is commonly used throughout Interactive Reporting in building dashboards and Computed Items. The following chapters on dashboards and advanced analysis will demonstrate examples of using conditional logic in daily use with Interactive Reporting.

Loops

A **loop** is a programming concept created to run a set of code multiple times. In a simple example, a loop can be used to display a count of 1 to 1000 with only a few lines of code as compared to writing a line of code for each number which would result in one thousand lines of code. Each loop has a condition that is tested to determine if the loop should be executed or exited. Each time the conditional statement is deemed true, the block of code begins again until the statement is proven to be false.

> It is important to note that if a loop statement is unable to be proven false, the loop will repeat infinitely. This error, called an **infinite loop**, cannot be stopped without exiting the program.

The most commonly used loop statement is the `for()` loop. The for() loop is used to execute a block of code a specific number of times and allows developers to specify the start, finish, and increment variables in the creation of the `for` statement.

The following example shows the simple syntax for the `for` loop:

```
for (var v=start; v<=end; v=v+increment)
{
    // until v>end, statement is true
    // code block;
}
```

The shorthand math operators to increment, ++, and decrement, --, can be used to replace the incrementing or decrementing value. With the assumption that the increment is 1, in the preceding example, v = v + increment can be changed to v++ without changing the outcome of the code.

The following example shows an example of a `for` loop:

```
for (var i=0; i<=gArray.length; i++)
{
    // until i is greater than the number of objects in a custom
            array, the statement is true
    // code block;
}
```

The `while()` loop is used to repeatedly execute a code block for as long as the conditional statement remains true. If the logical statement is false when the conditional statement is first reviewed, the code never executes.

```
while (v<=end)
{
   // while v<=end, statement is true
   // code block;
}
```

The `do.while()` loop is a variant of the while loop that executes the code block once and then repeats the code block for as long as the `while()` condition is true. This is very useful when the code should be executed once even if the logical statement is false.

The following example demonstrates the standard syntax for the `do.while()` loop:

```
do
{
   // code to be executed;
}
while (v<=end);
```

There are two commands used to exit the current loop or to exit all remaining loops throughout the loop process. These statements are typically used to save time when searching for specific values or outcomes. The first statement, the `continue` statement, is used to stop the current loop and will continue to run the next loop (if existing). The second statement, the `break` statement, is used to force the current loop to end and will not run any remaining loops. Loops are very common operations in dashboard programming and many loop examples are demonstrated in the following dashboard chapters.

Regular expressions

While not demonstrated in-depth in this guide, an introduction to JavaScript would be incomplete without introducing the concept of **regular expressions**. At the most basic levels, regular expressions are used to deconstruct individual characters within string variables to perform pattern recognition and matching logic. Within Interactive Reporting, the most common role of regular expressions is to assist with data validation of entries made by users on a dashboard. As regular expression is a very advanced programming topic that sometimes eludes even seasoned developers, there are several well-written tutorials and guides that focus solely on regular expressions that are readily available on the Internet.

Summary

The goal of this chapter was to introduce the user to the scripting concepts necessary to perform dashboard development and advanced computations. The chapter began with an overview of the terminology used within the software, including objects, methods, and properties. The chapter continued with an introduction to the Scripting Interface and Interactive Reporting Object Model, providing knowledge on the interface for adding customized code to a Dashboard section or the document as well as the hierarchy/tree structure of objects that can be manipulated through using code. The chapter concluded with a review of the different types of JavaScript components that are utilized throughout the later chapters of the book, providing an overview of the different sets of components that are available and commonly used when building dashboards or performing advanced analysis. The next chapter of the book begins the dashboard development set of chapters in the book, starting with the steps used to build a simple dashboard.

Creating a Simple Dashboard

3

Dashboards are used to quickly and easily monitor the overall health of a business area by providing executive-level insight into key business metrics. In Interactive Reporting, dashboards are created by combining supporting presentation sections of the software with interactivity usually through custom JavaScript programming. The complexity of the dashboard development process can vary widely depending on the number of interfaces and amount of custom interactivity desired.

This goal of this chapter is to present the procedural steps required to create a simple dashboard without the use of JavaScript. The following three chapters will evolve this simple dashboard example and will present methods to appropriately add interactivity across multiple dashboard objects.

This chapter covers the following topics:

- Dashboard planning and preparation
- The BMV USA Executive Dashboard example
- Creating data driven dashboard objects
- Creating a simple dashboard
- Gauges
- Live Charts

Dashboard planning and preparation

The most challenging aspect of developing a dashboard is creating one that is targeted enough to deliver meaningful information to its users while providing quick navigation and clear methods to support further analysis. The most successful dashboards display high-level information, typically in the form of charts and gauges, with clear supporting metrics to either invoke or support business decisions.

Even though the goal of creating a dashboard is to provide a view of the overall health of a business, it is important to avoid the trap of a one-size-fits-all dashboard. While Interactive Reporting provides the ability to store massive amounts of content inside a single document with interactivity and drill-down operations, the maintenance and processing speed will become a burden over time and document usage will decrease.

A more appropriate approach is to create a series of dashboards that provide both a high-level executive view of the organization and a view of individual business areas that provide a more granular view into a subset of the organization. When creating these dashboards, always ensure that the purpose of the dashboard is clearly defined and that the business stakeholder using the dashboard is the driver for the content displayed. Having involved stakeholders through the process will provide governance, encourage dashboard usage, and will drive consistency throughout other metrics created for the organization or organizational subset.

The BMV USA Executive Dashboard Example

The suite of dashboard chapters introduces a number of dashboard specific concepts for a successful dashboard implementation in Interactive Reporting. A single example is used across these chapters to demonstrate different dashboard objects, contents, and interactivity. The example, named the **BMV USA Executive Dashboard**, displays sales and cost data across pivots, charts, tables, and other sections of the document. The data for the example is supplied by the sample database that accompanies the Interactive Reporting installation.

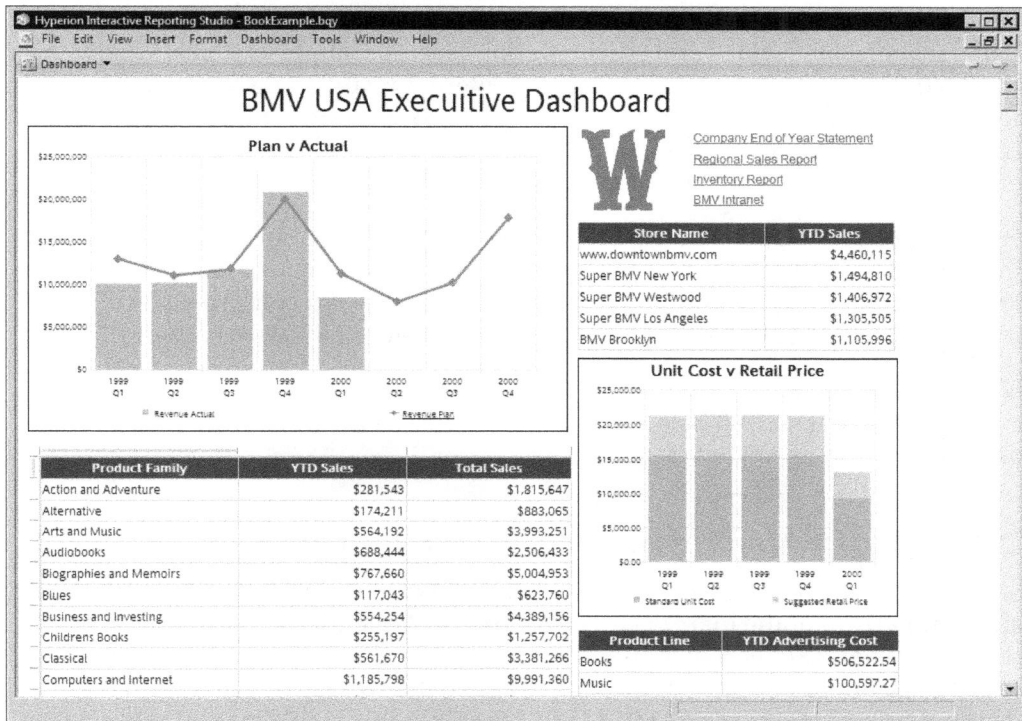

Creating data-driven dashboard objects

The Dashboard and Report sections in Interactive Reporting are unique since these two sections are not tied to a single Query section. Additionally, the Dashboard and Report sections allow content to be combined and presented side-by-side from any section in the document. The combination of content from other sections is the basis for dashboard development using Interactive Reporting.

When a section is presented on a Dashboard section, it becomes an embedded object on the dashboard, creating a presentation window from the dashboard to the existing document section. This connection allows the data presentation, including colors and formatting, to be shown on the dashboard section for analysis. Any effects on the supporting document section, including formatting changes or data refreshes, are reflected on the dashboard.

Interactive Reporting 11 has introduced the Gauges and Live Chart features to dashboard sections. Unlike embedded section objects, Gauges and Live Charts are populated from Results and Table section content directly on the Dashboard section and do not exist elsewhere in the document. The formatting for these objects is performed directly on the dashboard. Gauges and Live Charts are also dynamically refreshed when the supporting Results or Table section content is refreshed.

Although not the focus of this chapter, it is important to note that other dashboard controls and graphics, such as text labels and list boxes, can be data driven using JavaScript programming to control the object's values and properties. The customization of dashboards using code will be explored in later chapters.

The following content of the chapter will provide a step-by-step guide to creating the data driven dashboard objects required to support the BMV USA Executive Dashboard example.

Creating a Vertical Stack Bar chart

This section discusses the methods for creating a Stack Bar chart to demonstrate a quick comparison of the margin between **Cost Per Unit** and **Suggested Retail Price**. Stacked bar charts are best suited for monitoring the relationship between two facts and are most effective when the margin between the two facts remains relatively consistent across data points. In the BMV USA Executive Dashboard example, the **Cost of Units** sold to the **Suggested Retail Price** of the same units are compared.

Creating the Chart Query

The Query for the example Vertical Stack Bar chart is created by inserting a new Query section connected to the Interactive Reporting sample database. Once added, rename the **Query** section to **q Cost v Price** and the **Results** section to **r Cost v Price**. Add the **Periods Months** and **Costs And Prices Fact** tables to the main window of the **Query** section. Once completed and the table joins configured, add **Standard Unit Cost**, **Suggested Retail Price**, **Year**, and **Quarter** to the **Request** line as shown in the following screenshot:

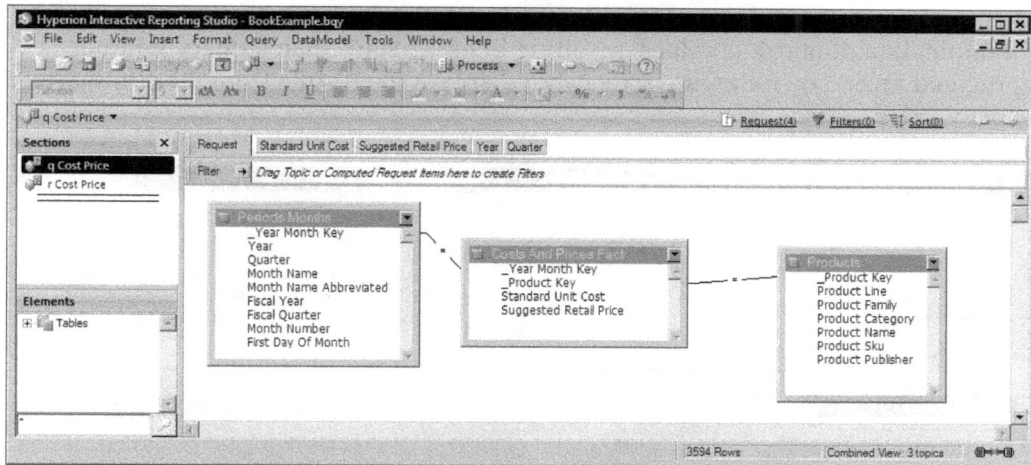

Aggregated data facts

If the data values stored in the data source are more detailed than required for the dashboard, include aggregating functions within the **Query** section, unless there is a business requirement for data drill capabilities. The inclusion of aggregate data functions on facts will result in a faster query and improved dashboard performance due to a smaller data set. The following image shows the addition of the Sum function to the **Standard Unit Cost** element:

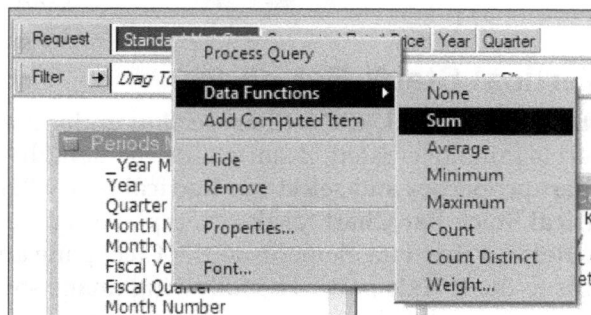

Request line items with data functions applied will display the function name on the object label in the query to denote the function, but the function does not impact the column title in the **Results** section. The following figure shows the addition of the Sum function to the **Standard Unit Cost** and the **Suggested Retail Price** elements:

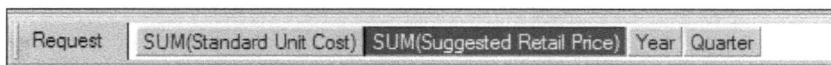

When a query with aggregated facts is processed, the data values are summed by unique data dimension values, resulting in fewer rows than a query without aggregated facts. The following screenshot displays the results from the summarized **q Cost v Price** query:

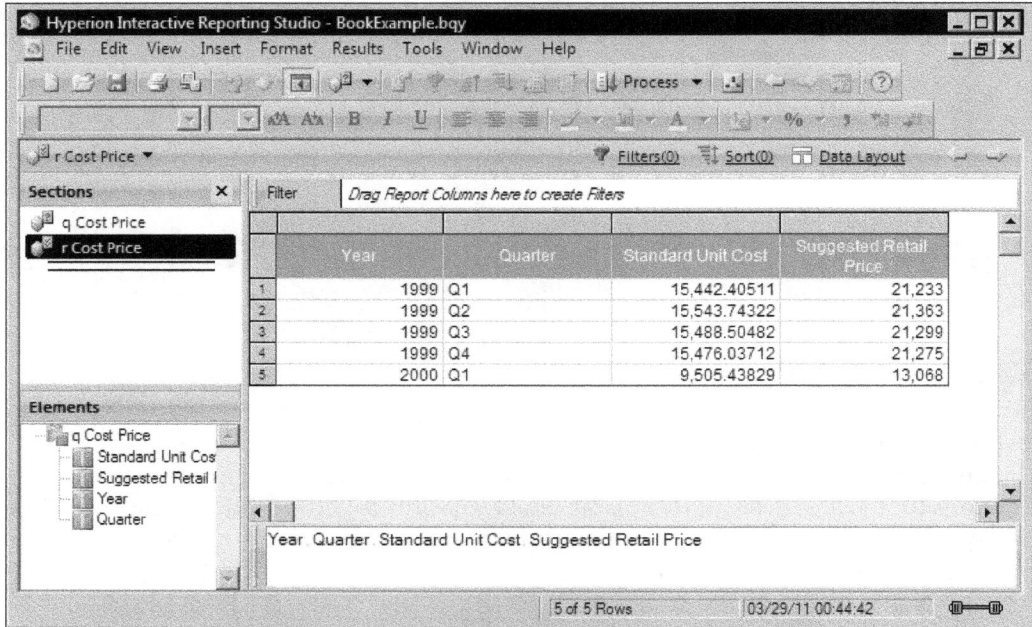

Creating the Vertical Stack Bar chart

Once the **Query** section is processed, add a **Chart** section under the **q Cost v Price** query. When the chart is initially created, it starts with the default Vertical Bar chart. Modify the **Chart** properties and select the **Vertical Stack Bar Chart** format. To populate the **Vertical Stack Bar Chart** for the example, drag the **Standard Unit Cost** and **Suggested Retail Price** data elements to the **Facts** pane and the **Year** and **Quarter** data elements to the **X-Axis** pane. The following image shows the Vertical Stack Bar chart with items populated:

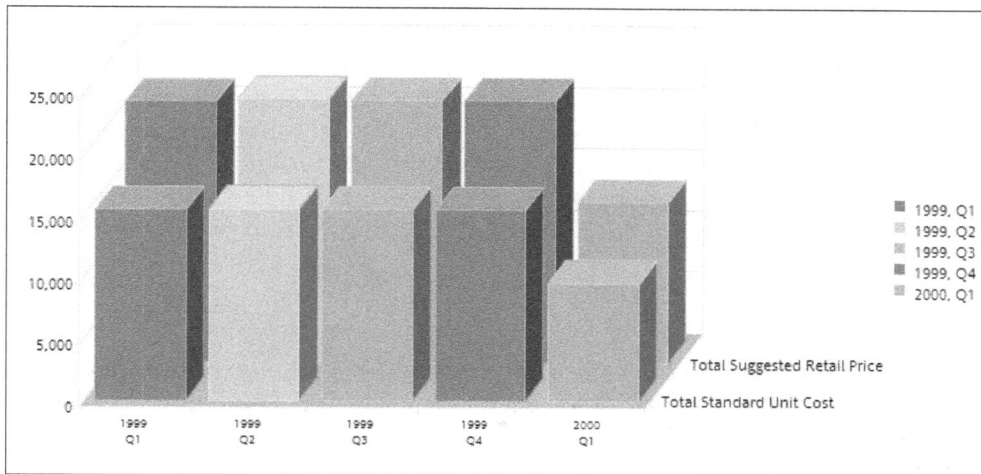

Setting the legend

The legends for bar charts are set on the x-axis by default. As the focus of this Vertical Stacked Bar chart is the Fact information, the legend property must be changed from the x-axis to the y-axis. Use the **Legend** icon on the section toolbar to change the legend on property to **Legend on Y** as shown in the following figure:

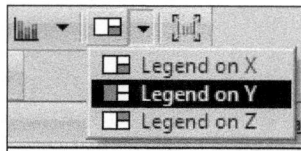

With the legend now applied to the chart facts, the relationship between the two fact items is displayed clearly in the following screenshot:

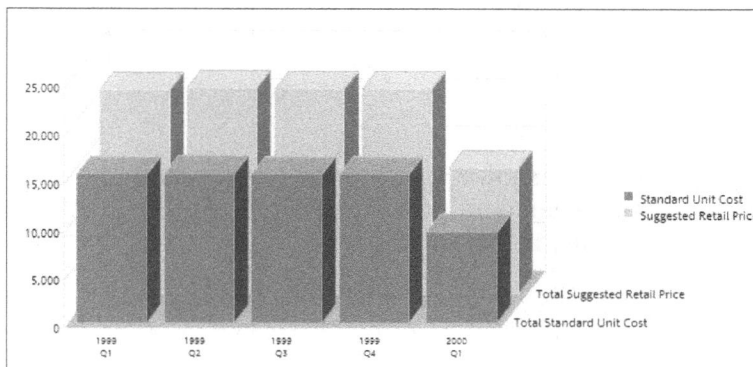

Customizing a Vertical Stack Chart

While the default chart format nicely presents accurate data for analysis, the default format is not well-suited for a dashboard, where objects must be smaller to accommodate multiple objects on a screen. Modifications to chart formatting play a large role in creating readable dashboard sections, where significant time is used to modify formatting to align objects in viewable formats. This section discusses setting the visual properties of the Vertical Stacked Bar chart to prepare it for use in a Dashboard section.

Visually stack the bars

The first approach that should be used is to flatten the chart to give the illusion that the values are physically stacked upon each other, where the flattening will better display the difference between the two values. The chart is flattened by unselecting the **3-D Objects** option in the **Chart Properties** dialog.

Maximizing chart display space

It is challenging to quickly digest data presented by a chart on a Dashboard section when the chart's display area is cluttered with extraneous label and value axis information. While modifications to hide, display, or modify label and value axis settings in the **Chart Properties** can help clear the area for the chart, the simplest way to maximize space is to move the legend location from the default right side location to the bottom of the chart.

To move the legend, select the legend object and drag it to below the X-axis. Resize the legend as desired using the corner anchor points. With the legend out of the way, select the chart and resize it to maximize it in the frame.

Detail-oriented formatting

Dashboard objects should be understood without a supporting explanation. Attention to detail with minor formatting options is important to avoid confusion. Add data masks to facts, title the chart, and label each axis to make fact value types clear.

Color considerations

In situations where data points touch, it is especially important that the chart colors contrast enough so that the values of the chart can be easily distinguished from one another if the chart is printed in black and white.

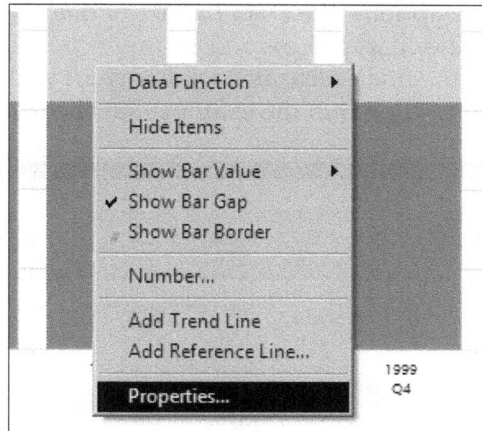

To manually change the color of a data group, click and highlight the data group in the chart or right-click on **Legend** and choose **Properties** (as shown in the previous screenshot) to open the data group **Properties** dialog box. With the **Patterns** tab selected, click on **Foreground** and choose a different color from the color picker or by entering a custom RGB value:

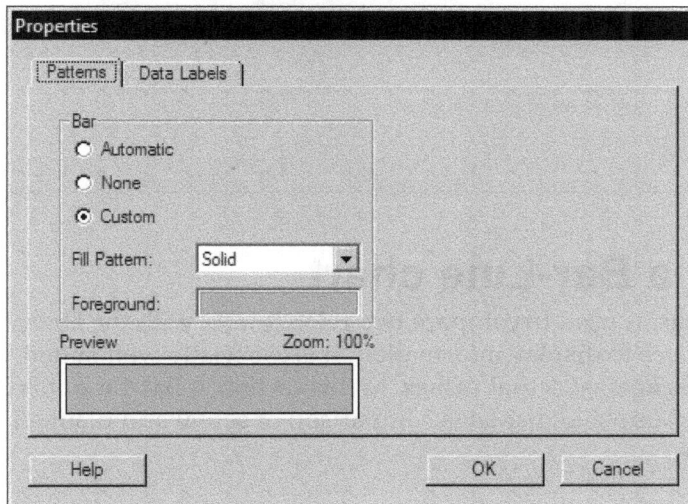

In addition to the Patterns options, the **Data Label** options provide the ability to activate data labels on the chart groups and to apply custom formatting. The following figure displays the final Vertical Stack Bar chart with all of the desired formatting changes for importing into the example dashboard:

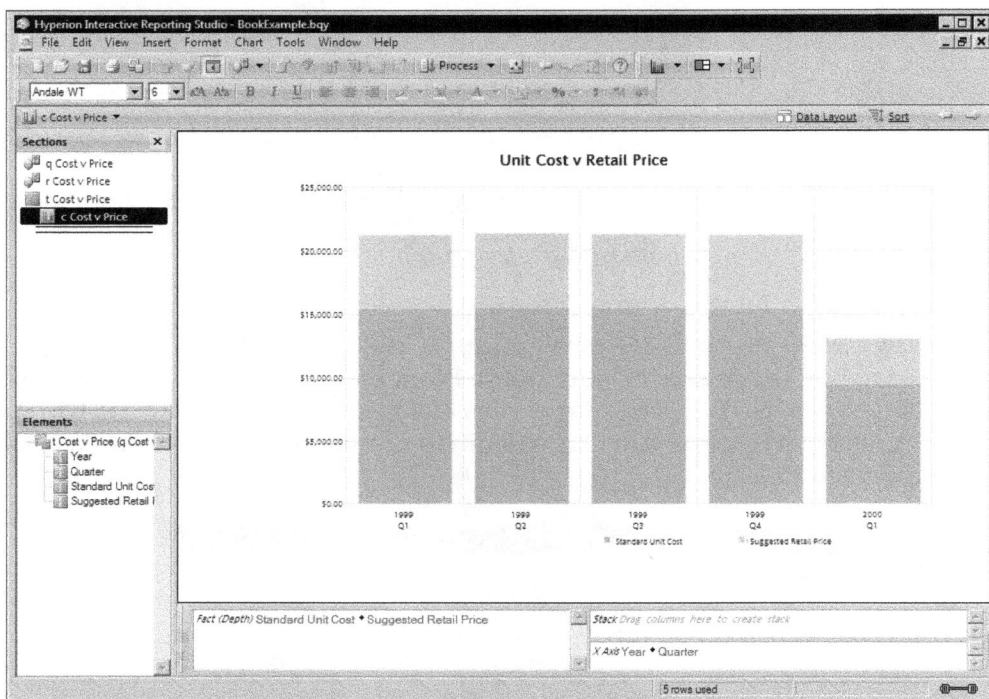

Creating a Bar-Line chart

The Bar-Line chart is used to compare two related facts with the ability of using two different axis scales to display information. It is especially well-suited to compare forecasted values against actual values. In this section, a Bar-Line chart is created for the dashboard example to display a comparison of actual and planned revenue for the country USA.

Creating the chart query

The query for the example Bar-Line chart is created by inserting a new **Query** section connected to the Interactive Reporting sample database. In the example, the **Query** section is renamed to **q Plan v Act** and the **Results** section to **r Plan v Act**. The **Periods Months, Plan Vs Actual Fact, Stores**, and **Regions** tables are added to the main query window. The four tables are joined together using the data key relationships as shown in the following figure:

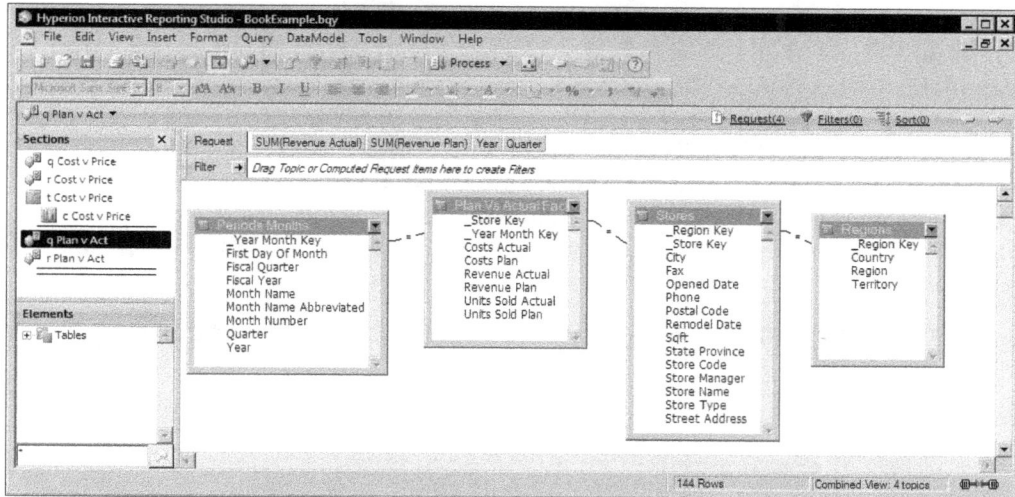

Once the tables are joined, the **Revenue Actual**, **Revenue Plan**, **Year**, and **Quarter** data elements are added to the **Request** line and the **Revenue Actual** and **Revenue Plan** data elements are configured to use the SUM data function.

Limiting the Query data

In the example dashboard, the intent of the Bar-Line chart is to display the comparison of actual and planned revenue for the USA and not the entire data set contained in the database. Place a filter on the **Country** field from the **Regions** table by adding a **Filter** to the query:

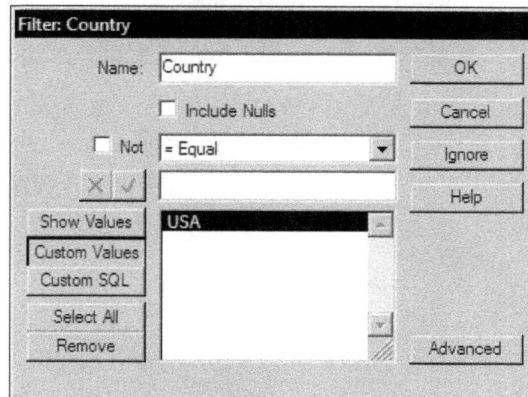

In the preceding screenshot, the **USA** is transferred into the **Custom Values** setting. The **Show Values** filter selection option queries the database to determine a list of all available values before allowing selections to be made. **Custom Values** are not connected to the data source and can be viewed and selected at any time. When creating Filters for dashboards or preparing other filters, use the **Transfer** button to move selections made from the **Show Values** list to the **Custom Values** list. The **Transfer** mechanism will ensure the exact data format is retained and the filter can be selected without needing to query the database each time the filter is opened for the list of values. The following image shows the query configured with the filter:

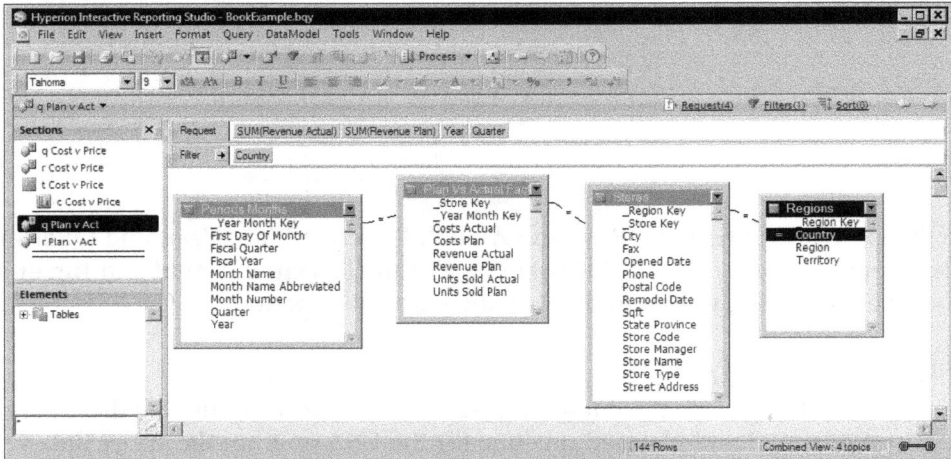

The following screenshot displays the processed data returned from the query, where the data will be used to create the Bar-Line chart:

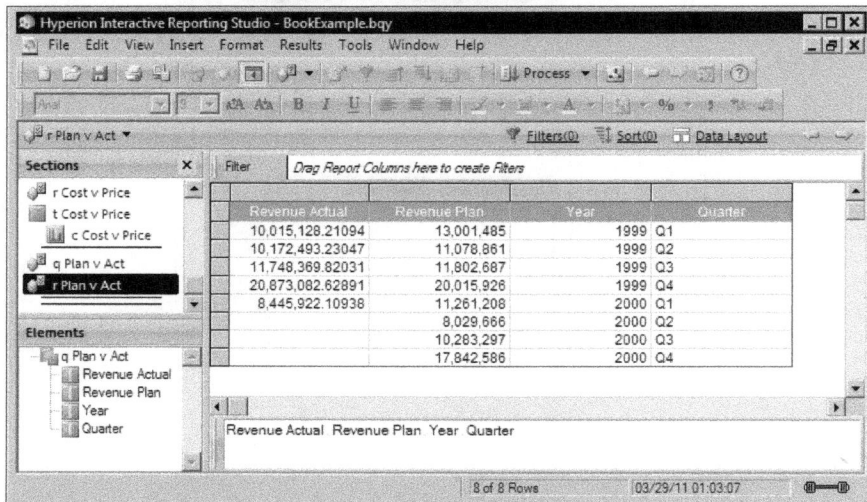

Create the Bar-Line chart

A Bar-Line chart displays two facts simultaneously, where one fact is shown as a traditional Bar chart and the other fact is displayed as a Line chart. The process for creating a Bar-Line chart is similar to for creating a Vertical Stack Bar chart. Once the Chart section is inserted underneath the **r Plan v Act** results, the chart format is changed to the **Bar-Line** format, the **Year** and **Quarter** data elements are set to the **x-axis,** and the **Revenue Actual** and **Revenue Plan** data elements are set to the **Facts**. The following screenshot shows the Bar-Line chart configured with data elements:

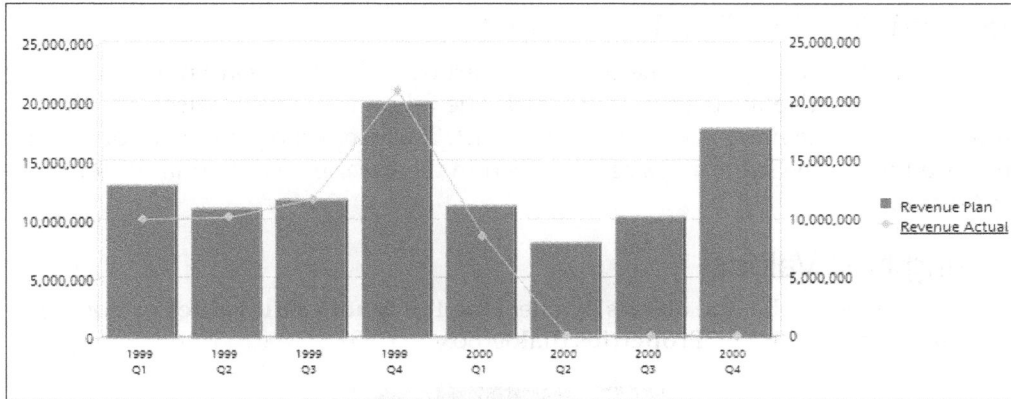

Switching bar and line facts

The Bar-Line chart configures the first fact value to display as a bar and the second fact value to display as a line. In order to switch the bar and line facts on the chart, *right-click* on a bar fact element in the **Data Layout** window and select **Display As Line** as shown in the following screenshot:

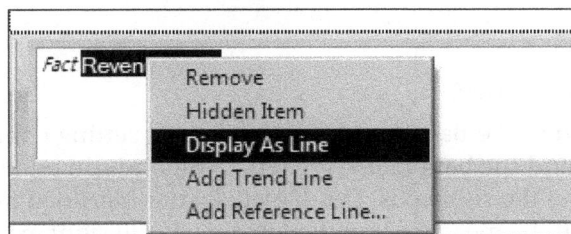

Similarly, a line can be switched to a bar by right-clicking on a line fact element and then selecting **Display As Bar** as shown in the following screenshot:

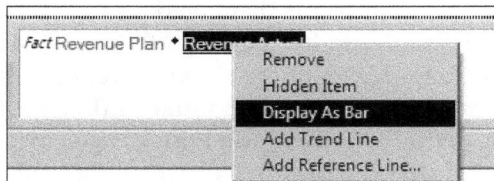

Customizing the Bar-Line Chart

Similar to the Stack Bar chart, the Bar-Line chart default settings are not particularly well-suited to be displayed on a dashboard. The following content discusses the configuration of the line properties on the chart. The properties of the bar object are configured using the same steps as described in the *Creating the Vertical Stack Bar Chart* section.

Ignoring Null Values

Hide null values on the line objects by checking the **Ignore null values** option on the **Data Labels** tab of the line **Properties** dialog box:

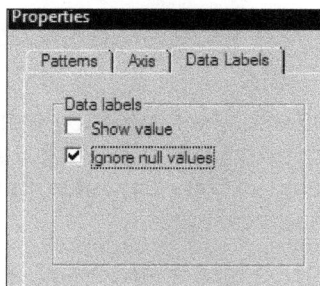

Turning off right values

When facts are added to the Bar-Line chart, the default setting configures the lines to use the right axis and the bars to use the left. Any underlined facts in the Data Layout pane are using the right axis. Double-click an underlined fact to force the Lines and Bars to both be measured on the left axis. If the right axis is needed for chart formatting, but is not needed for display on the dashboard, the right axis labels can be turned off by unselecting the **Show values at right** option to further maximize the display space.

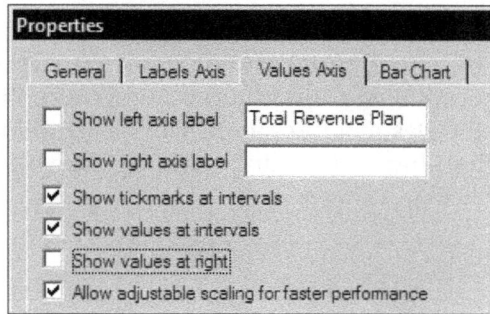

Line properties

Lines have additional options to modify the properties of both the line and the data marker. Adjusting these settings makes the line more visible on the dashboard:

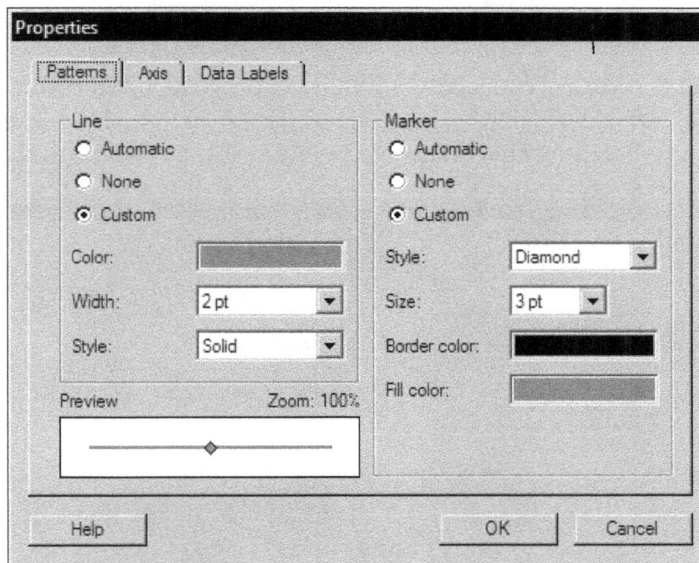

Customizing the grid

The default Bar-Line chart is configured to show only the **Y-Axis** grid lines, which creates horizontal lines. Adding vertical grid lines will make the chart easier to read when it is presented on the Dashboard section. Vertical grid lines are configured by right-clicking with the chart highlighted and selecting **Show X Axis Grid Lines** to toggle the display of vertical grid lines:

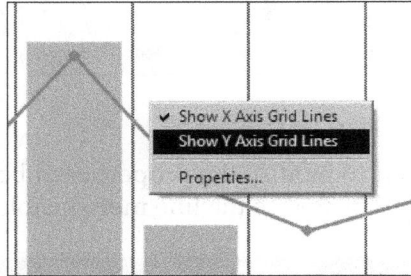

Grid lines on the **X-Axis** are especially good at keeping the relationship between the axis and the line data clear when no bar data entries exist. The following screenshot shows the example Bar-Line chart ready to be imported on the example dashboard:

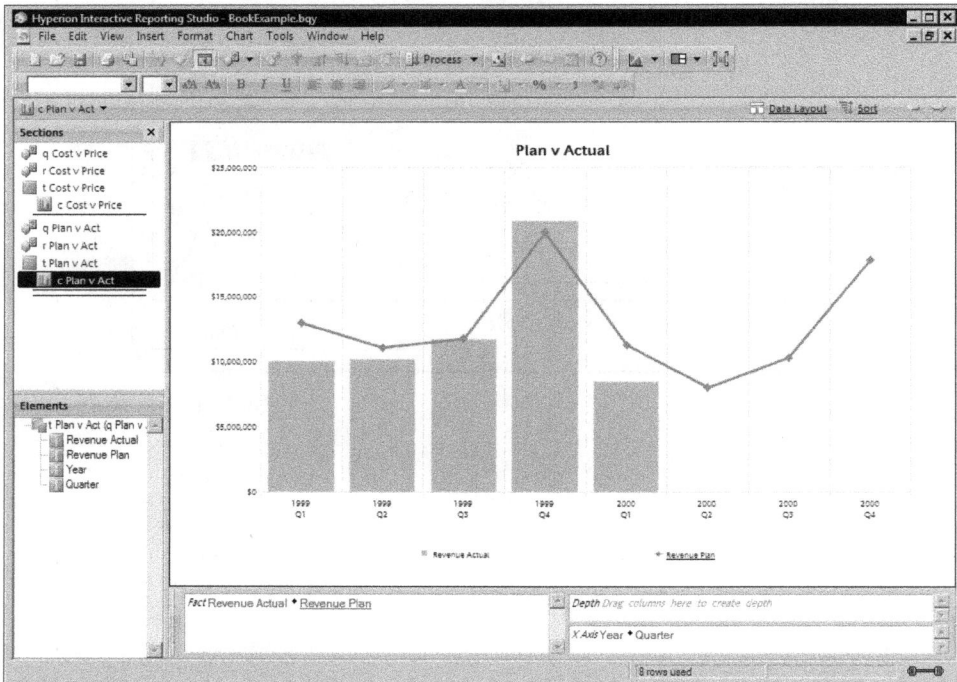

Displaying pivots

Pivot sections can be configured on the dashboard in an active and inactive state. When inactive, **Pivot** sections are great for displaying static data and provide the ability to have actions occur when clicked. When active, **Pivot** sections provide interactivity allowing for powerful dashboard slice-and-dice functionality directly in the dashboard.

This section will discuss the creation of three Pivot sections for the dashboard from two Query sections, where both inactive and active pivots are demonstrated. Additionally, this section will discuss how to limit **Drill Anywhere** paths using Table sections and the methods for creating ranking pivots without using JavaScript.

Creating a simple pivot

Pivot sections are great for displaying data on a dashboard. This section will discuss the steps to create a simple Advertising pivot showing year-to-date (YTD) advertising costs across Product Lines for the sample dashboard:

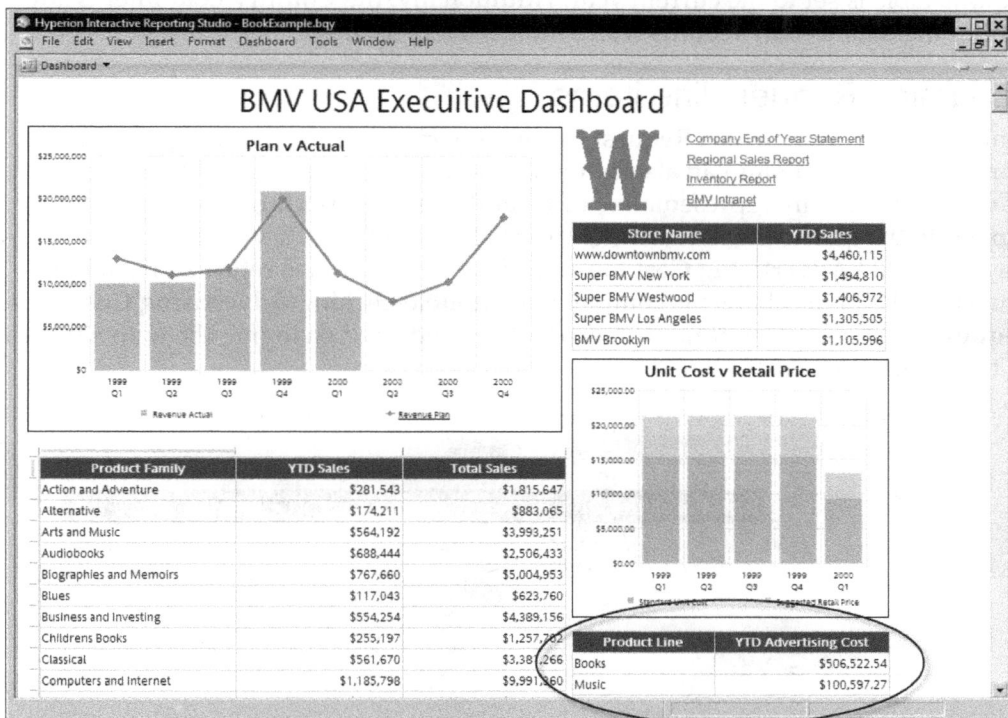

Creating the parent query

The first step in creating the Advertising pivot is to create a simple query to produce the data set for the pivot. The example query to support the Advertising pivot uses the **Periods Months, Advertising Fact**, and **Product** tables with joins on the table keys. The example query uses the **Advertising Cost** and **Product Line** elements in the **Request** line with the Sum function applied to the **Advertising Cost** element.

Limiting by YTD and country

Best practice data warehouses contain a table typically referred to as a date dimension that stores dates with related information, such as fiscal year, quarter, calendar month, and other formats and custom values. With a date dimension, complex date and time manipulation is avoided and system usability is increased. In the sample database, the **Periods Months** table serves as a date dimension.

In the dashboard example, the Advertising query must be filtered to view only the current year data. Since a date dimension table exists, logic for filtering for the current year does not need to be developed. Instead, the **Year** field from the **Periods Months** table is set to the current year. Additionally, the **Country** field filter is added to filter the data to only records related to USA advertising.

Renaming Request line items

Similar to the way in which Request line items can have calculations applied to them, Request line items can also be renamed. It is always a good idea to make sure that column titles are representative of what the fact is reporting. As date filters are applied to the query, the Advertising Cost field would be better represented with the name **YTD Advertising Cost** to better describe the values returned from the database. The name change is completed by double-clicking **Advertising Cost** in the **Request** line to open the **Item Properties** dialog box and changing the item name to **YTD Advertising Cost**:

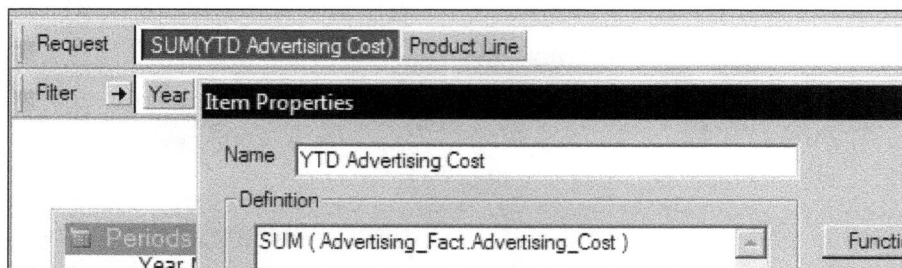

The following screenshot displays the Advertising query ready for processing:

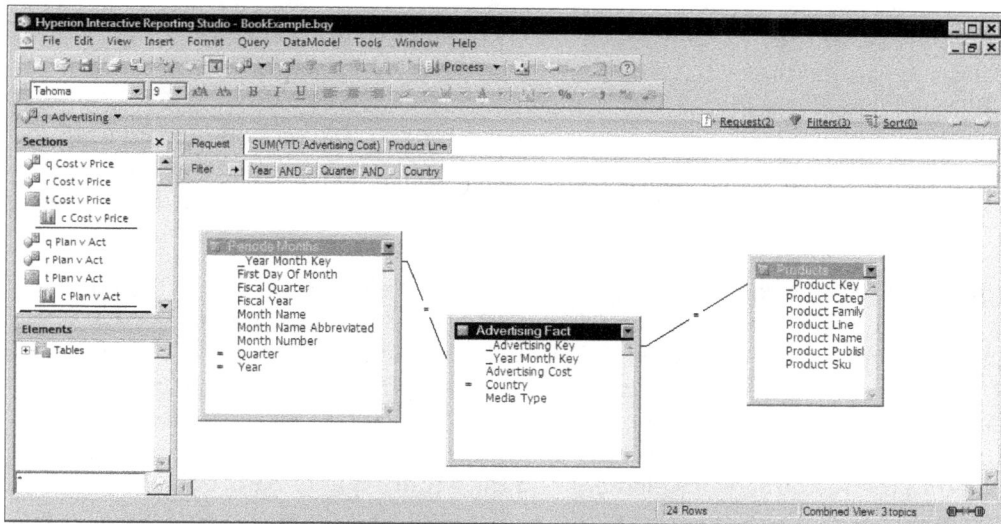

After processing, the fact column title displays the updated name of the data element renamed in the **Request** line. The following screenshot displays the **Advertising** query after query processing is complete:

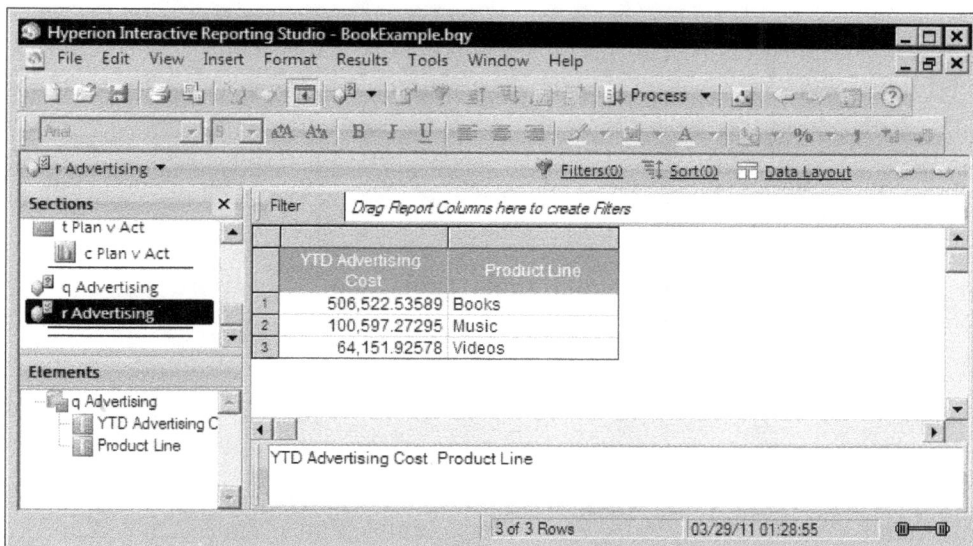

Following the completion of the query, the **Product Line** and **YTD Advertising Cost** are easily placed in a Pivot section to create the Advertising Cost Pivot section for the dashboard. The following content will highlight additional methods to use with Pivot sections, including pivot formatting.

Ranking and Pivot Drill path configuration

While previous examples have demonstrated separate Query sections for each dashboard object, it is productive to produce dashboard objects from a single query when the objects utilize a similar set of results. Since Table sections can be used to segment content and enhance the data set through Computed Items, the reduction of multiple Query sections allows for the same functionality with reduced data storage and processing time.

To demonstrate this concept, the **q Sales** and the **r Sales** sections are utilized to produce the **Product Family** and **Store Sales** reports. The **q Sales** query is constructed from the **Periods Days**, **Products**, **Sales Fact**, **Stores**, and **Regions** tables. The query contains the **Store Name**, **Product Line**, **Product Family**, **Amount Sales**, **Year**, **Quarter**, and **Month Name Abbreviated** with a data filter on **Country** to display only stores located in the USA. Within the Request line, the Sum function is applied to the **Amount Sales** element and the **Month Name Abbreviated** element is renamed to display **Month**. The following screenshot displays the **q Sales** query configured for processing:

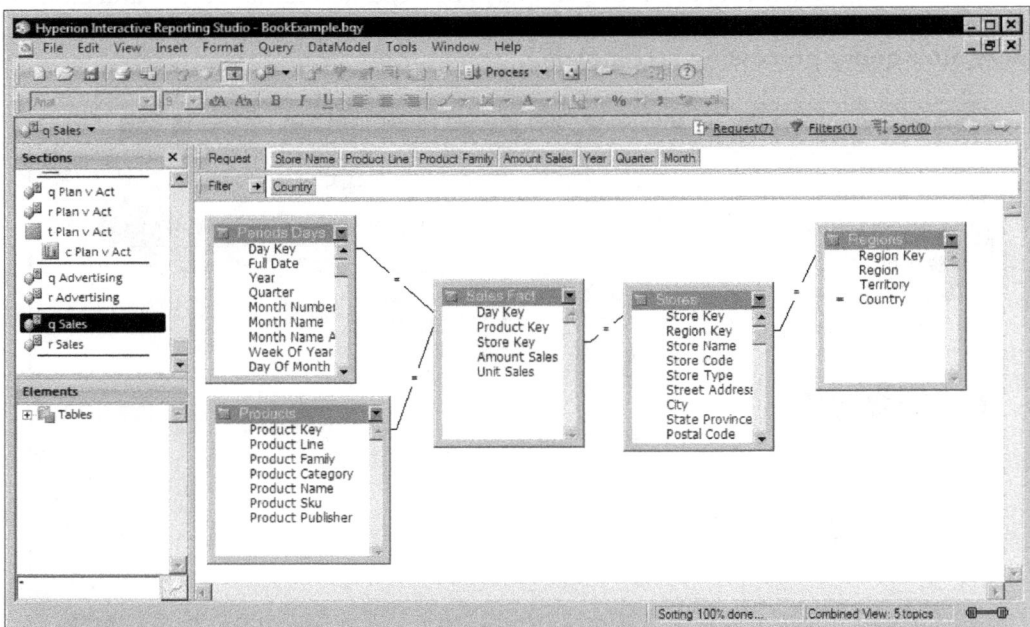

When this query is processed, the **Amount Sales** by **Product Family** is returned as shown in the following screenshot:

From the data results, a table and pivot are created to support both the Top 5 Stores view-only Pivot section and the Sales by Product active Pivot section on the BMV USA Executive Dashboard.

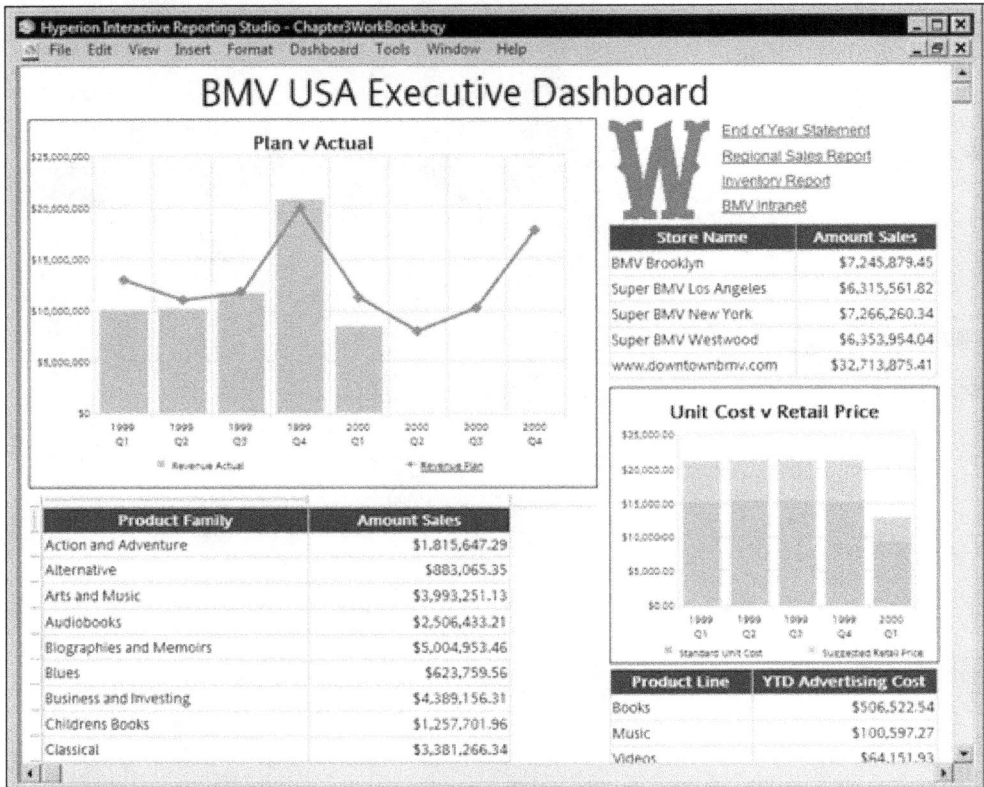

Displaying ranked dimensions

Ranking is a powerful way to identify the most positive or negative contributions. In the case of the BMV USA Executive Dashboard, a table is created that displays the top 5 stores with the highest sales revenues.

With the **Computed Item** dialog box open, select **Functions** and navigate to the Sum function in the **Numeric Functions** category. Set the Sum function parameters to aggregate **Total Sales** broken by **Store Name**:

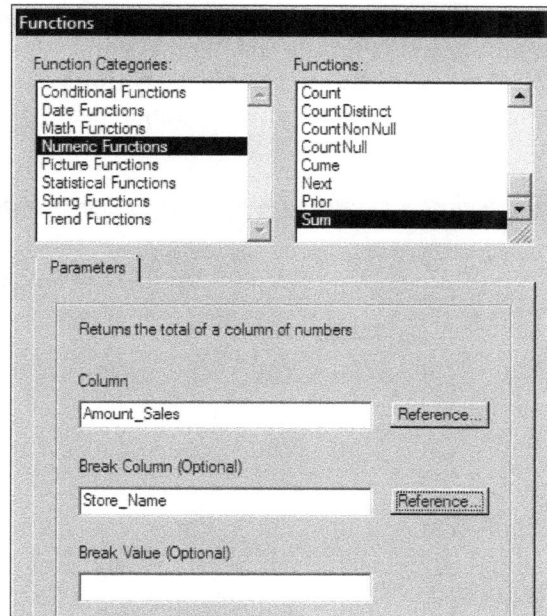

Pressing **OK** closes the **Functions** dialog box, which will display the code in the computed item as shown in the following screenshot:

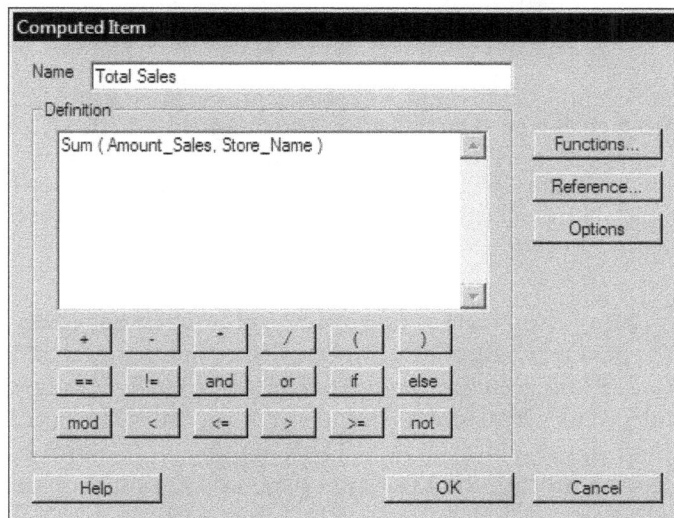

The code populated by the **Functions** window can be further modified or enhanced as desired on this screen. Pressing **OK** to accept any code changes will create an additional column within the Results section to apply this calculation.

Upon completion of the Sum function, a Rank function must be added to the **Total Sales** column. The Rank function will rank the highest value at number 1. Insert a new Computed Item called **Sales Rank**. Use the **Functions** dialog box to select the Rank function under the **Statistical** functions category and rank the **Total Sales** broken by **Store Name**.

When there is a need for a filter on an aggregated or ranked Computed Item, the filter must be performed in a child table. The order of operations for the execution of Computed Items within Interactive Reporting does not allow for the filtering of any comparative calculations, such as rank, sum, next, or prior within the same table section.

The first step in creating this object is to determine the Total Sales for each store. A Computed Item must be created to summarize the total for each store. With the addition of the **Sales Rank** column, the dataset is prepared to be filtered to determine the top 5 performing stores by **Total Sales**. As filtering on the rank column must take place in a dependent section, insert a new **Table** section. Add **Store Name** and **Total Sales** to the **Table** section from the **Elements** pane and a filter on **Sales Rank** to include only rows where the **Sales Rank** value is less than or equal to **5**.

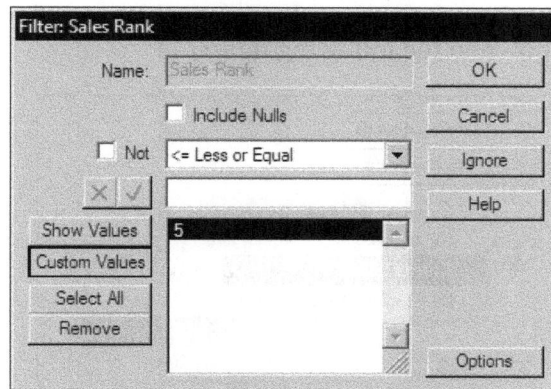

Then, insert a Pivot section and add the **Store Name** to the **Row Labels** and the **Amount Sales** to the **Facts,** as shown in the following screenshot:

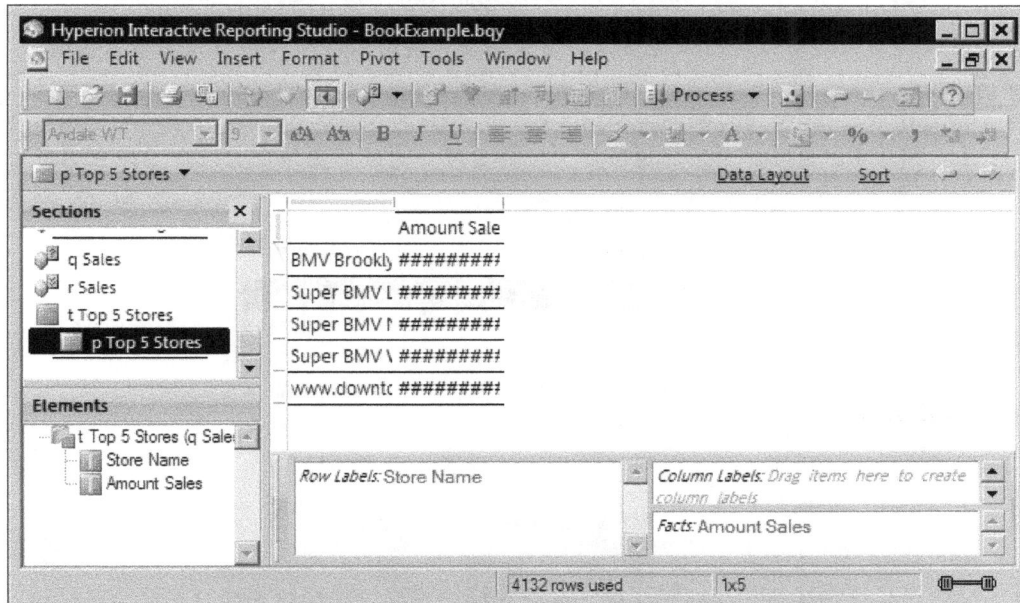

Add **Data Labels** to the Row dimensions by choosing **Row** in the **Corner Labels** right-click menu, as shown in the following figure:

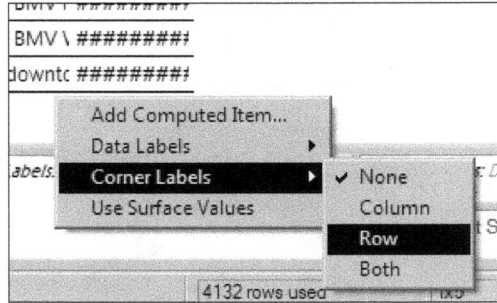

The Row Labels provide a row title for the columns within the pivot. Set the formatting of the pivot to change colors, fonts, numeric formatting, and any miscellaneous visual properties. The following screenshot displays the modified font and color of the Row Labels:

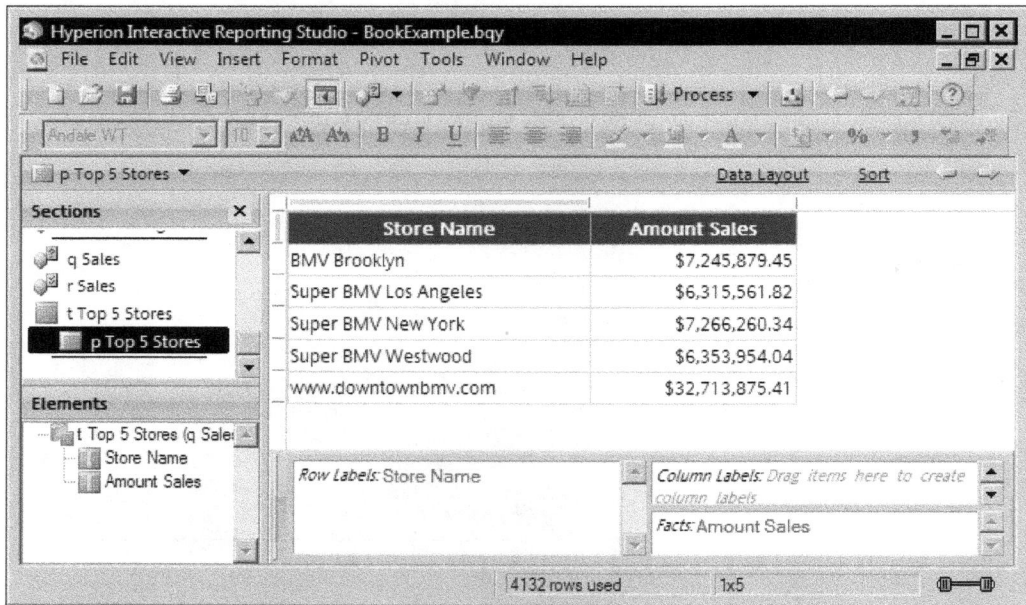

Limiting Drill Anywhere paths

Drill Anywhere, or drill path, options can be limited by using only the desired drillable data elements in the parent table of the section. Configuring a **Table** section with a reduced number of columns allows for hiding data columns used by other objects when the user of the report is utilizing the **Drill Anywhere** capability on a chart or pivot.

To create a pivot with limited **Drill Anywhere** options, insert a new **Table** section. Add only the columns needed to support the pivot and the desired **Drill Anywhere** options and disregard any other data elements from this **Table** section. The following **Table** section, **t Store Sales**, displays a subset of the **r Sales** columns:

Once the new **Table** section is created, populated, and highlighted, add a new Pivot section so it indents under the **t Store Sales** Table section. Add and format dimensions and facts to be displayed to the user by default as shown in the following screenshot. *Right-click* on a dimension and choose Drill Anywhere to see the lateral drill paths available to the user on the dashboard as shown:

Product Family	Amount Sales
Action and Adventure	$1,915,147.29
Alternative	65.35
Arts and Music	51.13
Audiobooks	33.21
Biographies an	53.46
Blues	$623,759.56
Business and I	$4,389,156.31
Childrens Boo	$1,257,701.96
Classical	$3,381,266.34
Computers an	$9,991,359.65
Country	$1,549,145.99
Dance and DJ	$943,094.13

Drill Anywhere ▶ Store Name / Product Line / Year / Quarter / Month

Add Computed Item...
Focus on Items
Hide Items

Font...
Style ▶
Justify ▶

Data Labels ▶
Corner Labels ▶
Use Surface Values

Setting the default pivot formatting

When end users drill through active pivots, items added to the pivot will follow the default pivot options set within the document when the document was created. To reduce the manual pivot formatting, the default pivot formatting should be consistent with the display properties of the pivot, as items added to the pivot will follow the default pivot options unless the options are overridden in the pivot.

To set the program's default formatting style, navigate to the Default Formats in the **Options** submenu located in the **Tools** menu:

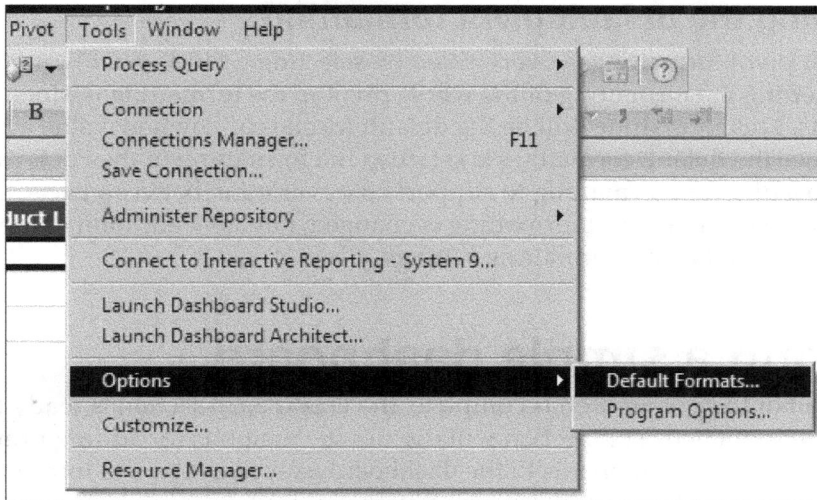

Set the default values for **Data Values** and **Labels** on the Pivots table of the **Options** dialog box as shown in the following screenshot:

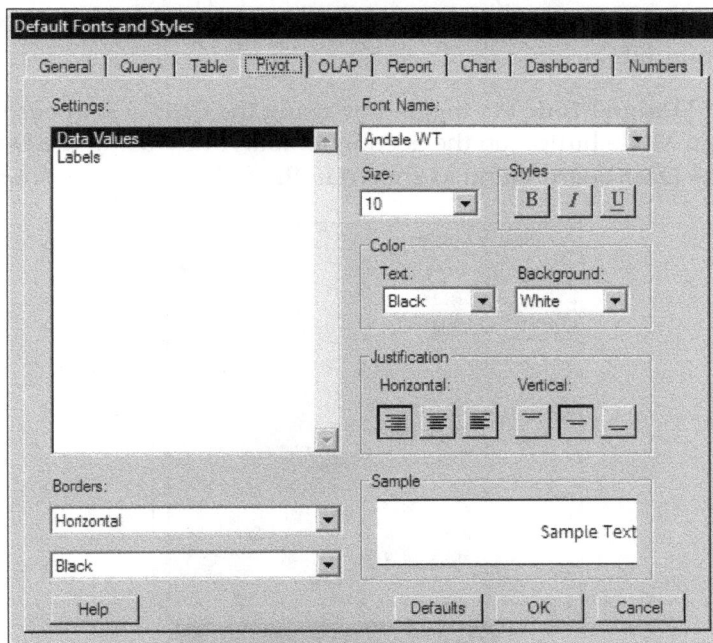

Overriding the default pivot formatting

The default pivot formatting is overwritten by selecting *Ctrl+A* on a Pivot section and then setting the formatting of the whole pivot to the formatting desired for the Row Labels. This formatting will be the default format for any new value added to a pivot. Once the default formatting is set, then the formatting of the Facts can be changed to a different formatting to support color variation between Facts and Row Labels. Even though the Fact formatting is changed, any new addition to the Row Labels will retain the new formatting settings.

Creating a simple dashboard

Now that all of the preparation is complete, the **Dashboard** section is ready to be created and populated. This section will discuss the methods for adding previously created data-driven components to the dashboard as well as steps to introduce adding graphics, controls, and basic user interactivity.

Dashboard sections have a **Run Mode** and a **Design Mode**. When a new **Dashboard** section is inserted into Interactive Reporting, the section starts in **Design Mode**. When the dashboard is in **Design Mode**, dashboard objects can be added and edited. When the dashboard is set to **Run Mode**, the dashboard is fully operational for use by the user community.

Run Mode and **Design Mode** are toggled by using the *Ctrl+D* keyboard method, by using the Design Mode button on the Section toolbar, or by using the **Design Mode** toggle under the **Dashboard** menu as shown in the following screenshot:

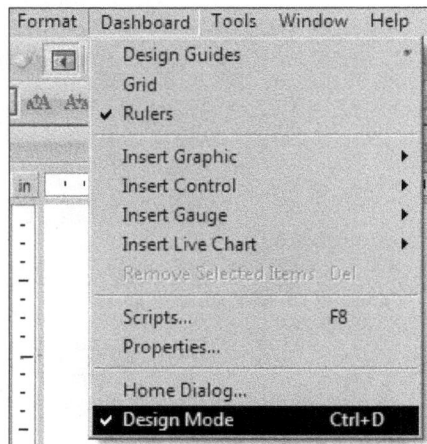

> The rulers are displayed only in **Design Mode**.

Adding dashboard objects

Objects are added to the dashboard using the **Elements** window displayed in the bottom left of the next screenshot. The **Elements** window has a tree structure displaying content across the sections in the document as well as configurable objects native to the dashboard such as Controls, Live Charts, and Gauges. To add objects to the dashboard, navigate to the desired object in the Elements pane and drag-and-drop the element to position it on the dashboard. Once the object is added, it can be resized as needed. The following screenshot displays the sample dashboard with all of the embedded sections added, resized, and positioned:

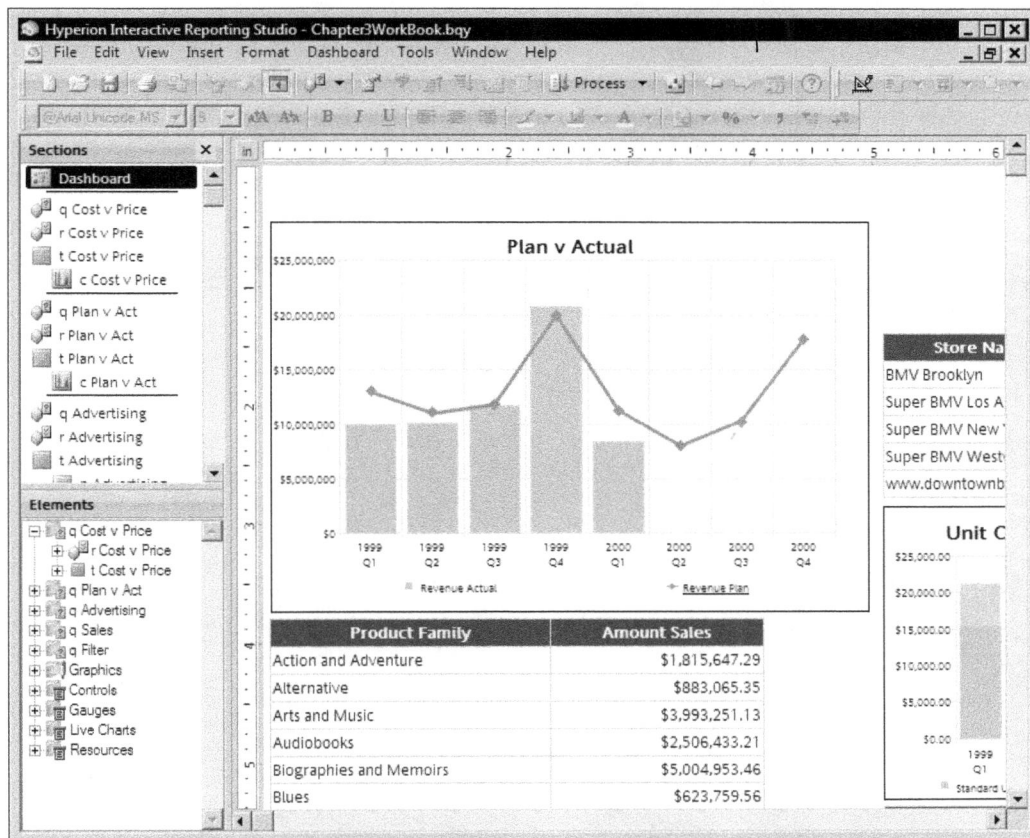

Adding graphics and controls

In addition to adding sections of the document to the dashboard, objects such as images, labels, and buttons can be added to enhance the dashboard display and to add user interactivity. This section touches on the addition of graphics to a **Dashboard** section and the following chapters will discuss the use of controls with custom programming.

Graphics are added to the dashboard by dragging an object from the **Elements** pane to the dashboard while in **Design Mode**. The most common graphic is the Text Label object, which is used to provide titles and text descriptions. Lines and shapes are also used to define borders and separate content. The effective use of graphics will significantly enhance the dashboard display and visual appeal.

Adding custom images

Custom pictures, such as company logos, can be easily added to a Dashboard section using the Picture graphic. Drag the Picture graphic to the dashboard and, when prompted, choose the graphic from the file navigator. Use the **Picture** tab in the **Properties** menu of the Picture object to modify display properties of the picture.

Adding Hyperlinks

The Hyperlink dashboard control object creates hyperlinks from a dashboard to either repository objects or external web pages. Hyperlinks are added to the dashboard by dragging the Hyperlink object from the **Control** group in the **Elements** pane to the dashboard. The Hyperlink name can be edited similar to a Text Label on the dashboard, but the link properties must be configured by selecting the **Properties** of the Hyperlink object. A URL can be supplied and the Display Method can be configured to allow the link to open in either a new window or the current widow. Future chapters will discuss advanced techniques regarding the methods for using the Hyperlink control to create dashboard menus linking dashboards in different Interactive Reporting documents.

The following screenshot shows the full configuration of the dashboard with an image, title, and hyperlinks to outside documents:

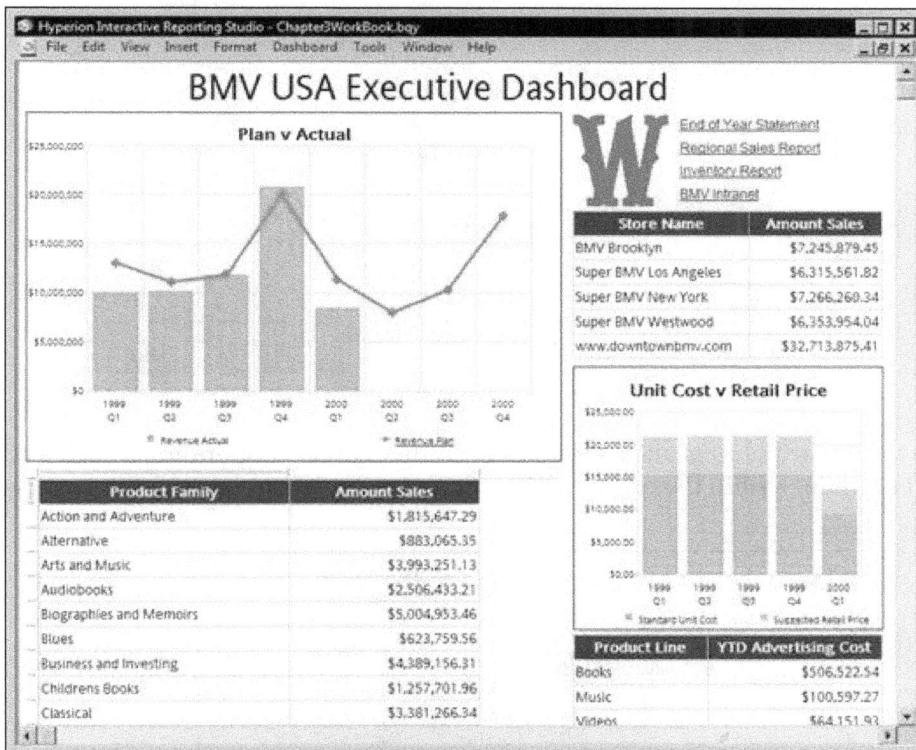

Basic interactivity

Interactive Reporting provides dashboard interactivity for Chart and Pivot sections without the need to use JavaScript customization. Chart and Pivot sections placed on a dashboard by default have no interactivity. However, charts and pivots can be made interactive by setting the **embedded section** property to either **Active** or **Hyperlink**. The sections can be modified by selecting the desired object on the dashboard and use the right-click menu to select the **Properties** of the object. Notice the configuration change of the **embedded section** setting from **View-only** to **Active**:

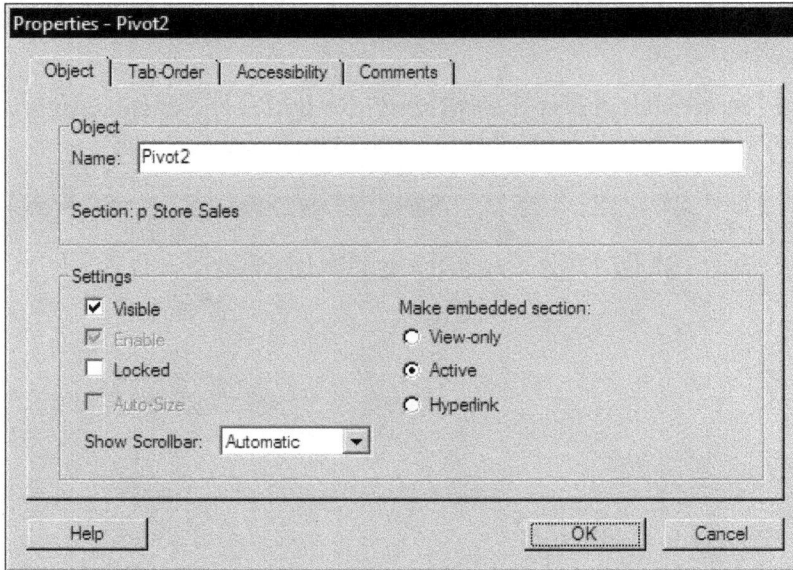

Active dashboard objects allow users to perform analytical operations, such as drill, focus, and hide, within the embedded section object without leaving the dashboard:

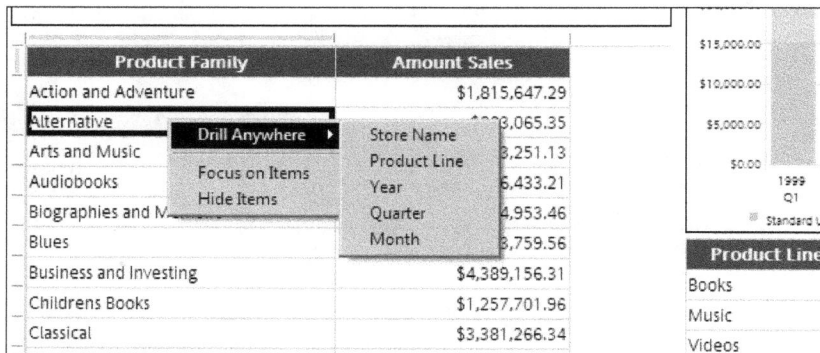

The **Hyperlink** option invokes code in the `onClick` method of the object when a user clicks on the object in **Run Mode**. The default code behind each object takes the user from the **Dashboard** section to the section that was clicked, where the user can perform analysis directly on the specific section. Future chapters will discuss modifying the default hyperlink behavior to navigate to other dashboard sections for further analysis.

Gauges

In addition to the items discussed on the sample dashboard, **Gauges** are a more recent addition to Interactive Reporting and are used to display a quick view of a key business indicator. The gauges in Interactive Reporting are limited to a **Bullet**, **Speedometer**, **Thermometer**, and **Traffic Light**. Each gauge has a **Configuration** tab in the gauge properties, allowing for the custom configuration of the thresholds of each object when the dashboard is in **Design Mode**.

Configuring gauges

When a gauge is added to a dashboard, the gauge must be populated with data elements produced from a query, and the properties of the gauge can be configured to produce the desired view of interest. The following image is a sample of each of the four gauges on a dashboard:

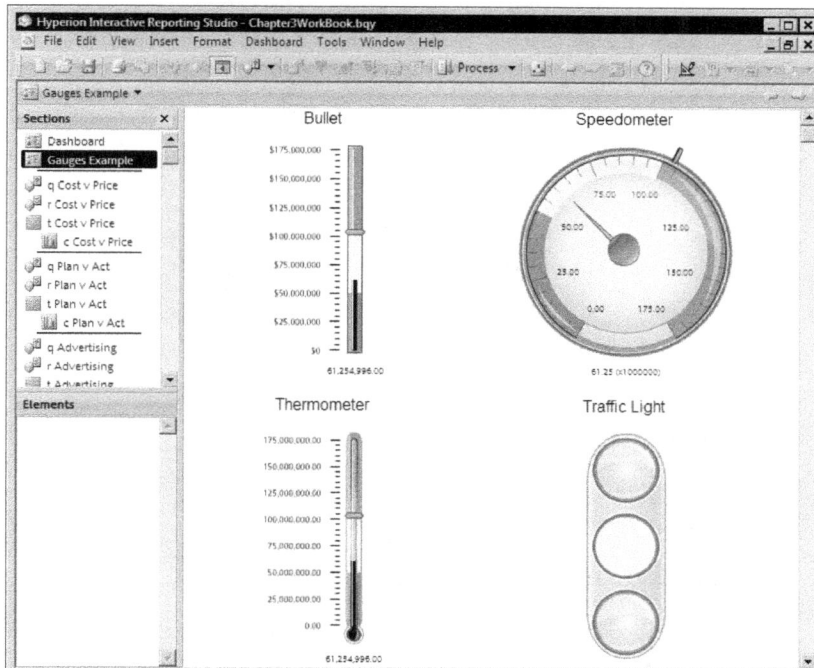

Each gauge contains a **Fact** element and all of the gauges besides the **Traffic Light** contain a **Target Fact** element. When a gauge is clicked and highlighted on the **Dashboard** during design, a Data Layout window appears at the bottom of the main screen with areas to add data elements from Results or a Table section. Dragging-and-dropping the desired elements from the **Elements** window into the Data Layout area will configure and populate the object with data. After adding the elements to the section, toggling the **Dashboard** to **Run Mode** will display the populated object.

When viewing the gauges (other than the **Traffic Light**), notice the gauges show the Fact in either the black line or speedometer needle and the Target Fact is displayed with the blue object. The Stoplight does not contain similar features, but is configured to display a color status based on a range of values. All of the gauges are dynamic and are updated based on the data contained in the referenced query.

Gauge properties and color ranges

Notice the color ranges specified on the gauge objects. Each of these ranges is configured in the **Properties** menu of each gauge. The **Properties** menu of the gauge is accessed by highlighting the gauge on the **Dashboard**, right-clicking, and selecting the **Properties** menu item or by highlighting the gauge and then selecting the **Properties** menu item from the **Dashboard** menu. The following image is an example of the **Bullet** gauge **Properties** menu open to the **Bullet** tab:

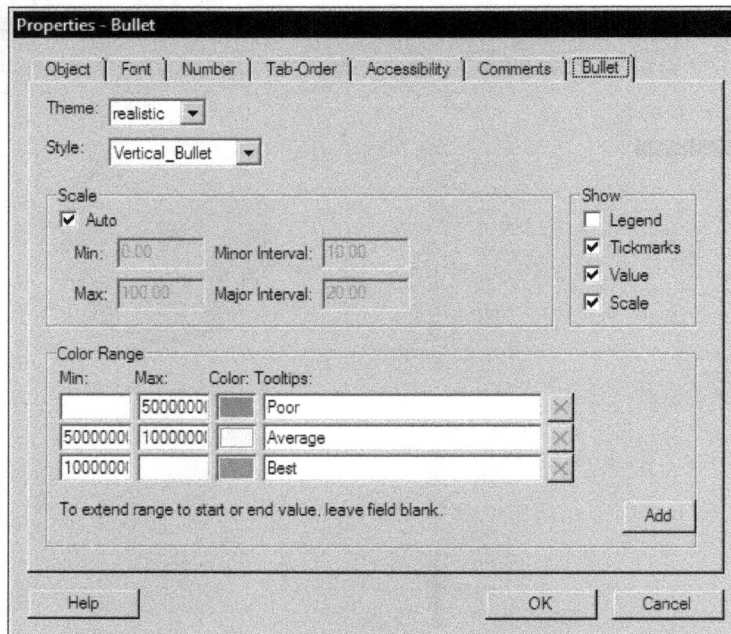

Each gauge object contains a gauge-specific properties tab, where the tab provides the same general settings as the previous screenshot where the **Theme**, **Style**, and **Color Range** settings exist for each gauge type. In the example screenshot of the **Gauge Properties**, the default configuration is used and **Color Range** has been configured based on the data in the Sales sample to show the different color ranges on the gauge. When configuring a **Color Range**, **Min** and **Max** values as well as the desired color are required. However, the min of the first range and the max of the final range can be left blank to specify no bound on the lower and upper ranges of the gauge. In addition to the range and color, the **Tooltip** setting is used to add a text label to the gauge. The tooltips are displayed when the mouse cursor is highlighted over the **Color Range** in the gauge. Pressing the **Add** button allows for additional ranges. The other tabs in the **Properties** menu are specific to setting the generic object, number, and font formatting for the gauge.

Live Charts

Live Charts are also a more recent addition to Interactive Reporting and are similar to a Chart section but can only be used in a **Dashboard** section. There are six types of charts including **Bar**, **Block**, **Funnel**, **Line**, **Pie**, and **Radar**. The Live Charts are limited in functionality compared to the **Chart** section, but Live Charts are more graphically appealing and scale better than the **Chart** section when used on a dashboard.

Configuring Live Charts

Configuring the Live Chart objects is similar to configuring Gauges. When a Live Chart is added to a dashboard, the Live Chart must be populated with data produced from a query. Additionally, the Properties of the **Live Chart** can be modified to produce the desired Chart display of interest. The following two screenshots are examples of the six types of Live Charts available for use in the document.

The next screenshot shows the **Block, Pie, Funnel**, and **Radar** Live Charts:

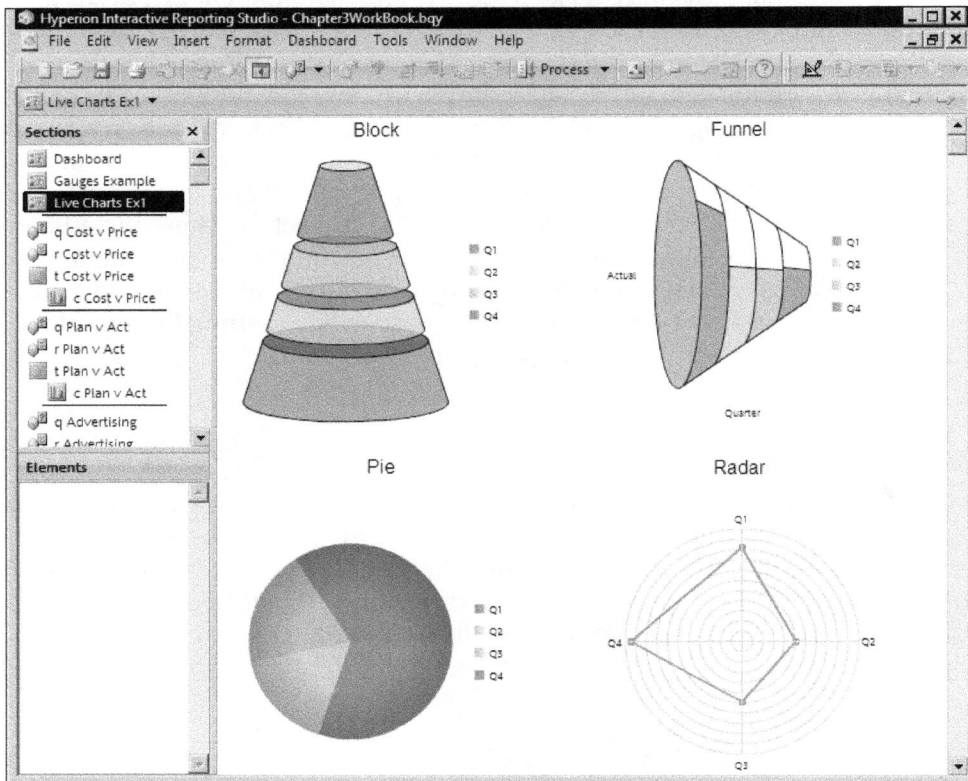

The following screenshot displays an example of a **Bar** and a **Line** Live Chart:

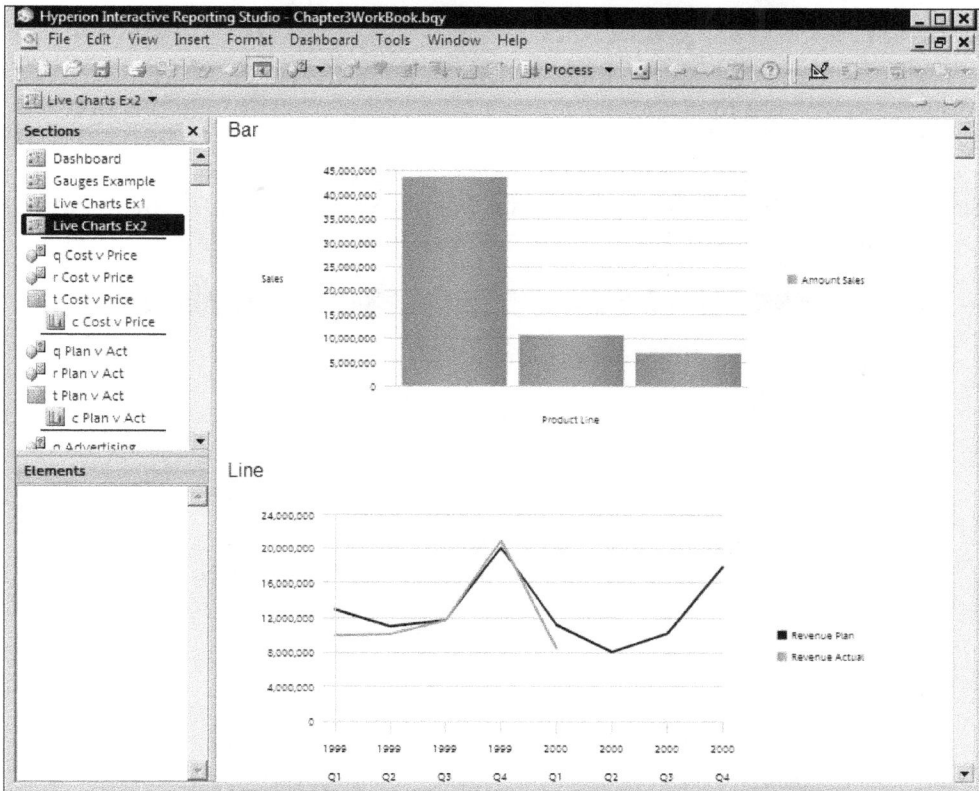

When the dashboard is under design, clicking and highlighting the Live Chart will bring up the Data Layout window. Each Live Chart contains a Fact area and chart specific non-fact areas for adding data elements. Dragging-and-dropping the desired elements from the **Elements** window into the Data Layout area will configure and populate the object with data. After adding the elements to the section, making the dashboard active will display the Chart populated with data. The Live Charts are dynamic with the data contained in the related Results or Table section. Any changes to the data will update the display of the Live Chart on the Dashboard.

Live Chart properties

Similar to Charts and Gauges, Live Charts contain a chart-specific tab in the **Properties** window for modifying the Live Chart display. The **Properties** menu of the Live Chart is accessed by highlighting the Live Chart on the dashboard and right-clicking and selecting the **Properties** menu item, or by highlighting the Live Chart and then selecting the **Properties** menu item from the **Dashboard** menu. The following image is an example of the Bar Live Chart Properties menu open to the **Bar** tab:

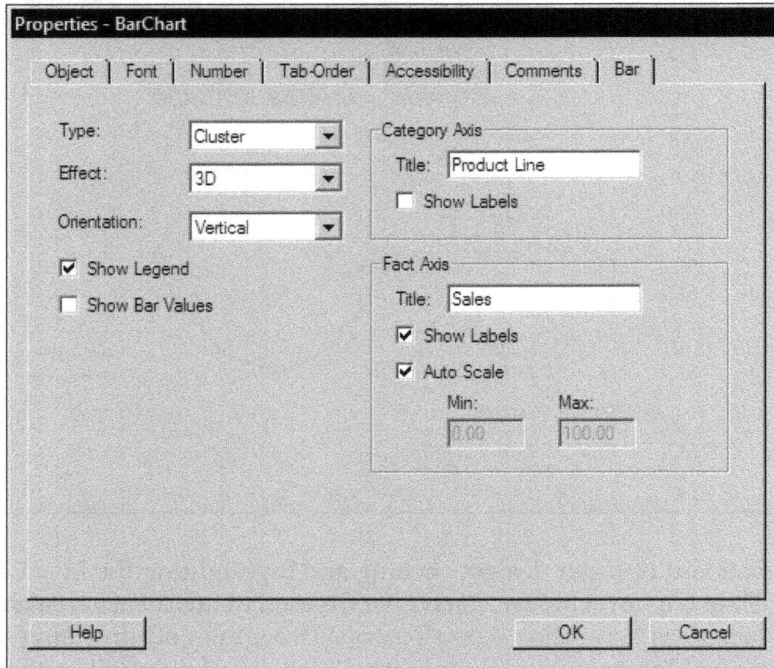

The chart-specific properties tab provides all of the features that can be modified for the Live Chart. This menu provides the ability to modify the chart display **features**, **axis scales**, **legend**, and **labels** for each of the chart objects. The other tabs are used for setting the formatting of the chart and the **Object** tab contains a text box for the chart **Title**.

Summary

The goal of this chapter was to present the steps to create content for a simple dashboard and the steps to display the content on a **Dashboard** section. The chapter begins with a discussion on dashboard planning and the steps used to produce effective dashboards. The chapter continues with an introduction to the BMV USA Dashboard example and then progresses to creating sample pivot and chart content for the example dashboard. An overview of custom drill paths and methods for creating a Top 5 pivot are discussed, and the methods for creating and formatting Stacked Bar and Bar-Line charts for dashboards were presented. Then the methods for configuring and displaying content on a **Dashboard** section was discussed with an introduction to images, graphics, and hyperlinks, and adding interactivity on the dashboard without custom programming through active pivot and chart features. Finally, Live Charts and Gauges were discussed to provide an introduction to newer dashboard specific objects to provide additional dashboard flexibility. The next three chapters will explain methods for adding interactivity to the sample dashboard.

4

Introducing Dashboard Interactivity

The next steps in building an advanced dashboard is expanding from the introductory dashboard knowledge presented in the previous chapter to creating custom interactive components, modifying presentations sections, and applying filtering. This chapter will build upon the dashboard example in *Chapter 3, Creating a Simple Dashboard*, to create a customized dashboard with interactive components, including examples of several commonly-used Hyperion Interactive Reporting dashboard components and approaches.

This chapter will present approaches using JavaScript as well as key controllers and graphics tools, including the role the tools play in providing intuitive and useful dashboard capabilities to end users. The goal of this chapter is to provide the building blocks for creating a master dashboard layout with start-up scripts, navigation, controls, and dynamic objects.

At the end of this chapter, the reader will have a better understanding of the following concepts:

- Dashboard Section Objects
- Creating a Master Dashboard
- Implementing Custom Dashboard Navigation
- Toggling Object Visibility using Radio Buttons
- Modifying Pivot and Chart facts using a Drop-Down Control

Dashboard Section Objects

Dashboard Graphics and Controls are objects authors use to customize Dashboard sections beyond embedding presentation sections such as Charts and Pivots onto the Dashboard. The Graphics and Controls objects can be combined allowing report authors the option to provide custom tailored Dashboards that are consistent with the visual presentation for the end user. This section introduces the different types of Dashboard Graphics and Controls available to report writers for creating interactive Dashboards that are functional and visually appealing.

Graphics

Dashboard Graphics are commonly used to enhance the look and feel of a Dashboard section. When customized with JavaScript, Graphics can also be used to provide button-click interactivity.

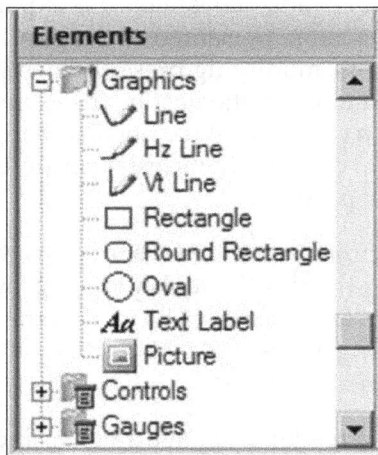

Several shapes are made available to report authors to customize the visual properties of a Dashboard section. These shapes, **Rectangle**, **Rounded Rectangle**, **Line**, **Hz Line**, **Vt Line**, and **Oval** can be layered and customized to provide visual characteristics that are consistent with an established image or branding.

Text Label Graphics can be dynamic data labels, such as a date to indicate when the data was last refreshed, or static labels such as section headings. Text Labels are also very well-suited for making custom buttons, since the Command Button Dashboard Control has very few customization options.

Picture Graphics display images. It is best to resize, crop, or perform modifications to the image outside of Interactive Reporting, as the properties of the Picture Graphic do not provide many options for modification.

Each time a Picture is placed on a Dashboard section, the image is saved as a resource. **Resources** are custom dashboard objects, usually images, imported by report authors. Images placed on the dashboard using the Picture Graphic are automatically saved as resources even if the Picture is a duplicate. Use the **Resource Manager** accessible from the **Tools** menu to remove unused or duplicate resources.

Controls

Controls are dashboard objects that provide interactivity to the end user. The most effective dashboards use controls that are intuitive for the end user to understand and are consistently applied across documents within the same application. In fact, a key consideration when planning for user interactivity is ensuring that Controls remain as consistent as possible across dashboards and applications, as this will expedite user adoption of the dashboards. From a development perspective, the combinations of functionality and overall look of dashboard Controls are practically limitless with significant flexibility and customization allowed.

The following screenshot displays the Control objects available to customize a Dashboard section:

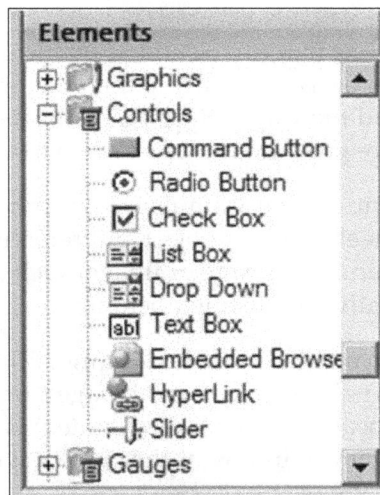

The **Command Button** dashboard Control is an object that can be clicked by the user. While other objects can also behave like Command Buttons, this is the only object with an on-press visual event to give the user a clear indication that the object has been clicked.

Radio Button dashboard Controls are used when the user is presented with a group of options, only one of which may be selected. Radio Buttons are used in situations where the options are well defined and a selection is required. The **Group Name** property is the name of the group that a Radio Button belongs to. Users can select only one option per radio group.

The **Check Box** dashboard Control object allows users to make more than one selection from a defined list. This object is well suited for sections where the responses are limited and where the user is allowed to make multiple selections. A good example of using a Check Box would be to allow users to select the quarters a chart covers, as the number of options represented are static.

List Box dashboard Control objects present users with the option to select one or more values from a predefined list. The values available to the user, commonly called the **List of Values (LOV)**, can be either static, meaning they never change, or dynamic, meaning they change automatically.

The **Drop Down** dashboard Control allows the user to select only one item from a list of available values. Like List Box controls, Drop Down Controls can also contain either static or dynamic LOVs.

Text Box Controls are text areas that can be edited by the user. Since the values entered into the Text Box can be accessed using the Title property of the Text Box, JavaScript can be used to read the value supplied by the user. Searches requiring the user to supply a date filter are good examples of when to use this Control.

The **Embedded Browser** Control is very similar to an embedded section except the content is rendered in a web browser object and referenced by an URL. The reference URL can be an external webpage or image, such as a company portal, help document, or another Interactive Reporting document.

Hyperlink Controls, introduced in *Chapter 3, Creating a Simple Dashboard*, create traditional web links to external documents, web pages, or other Interactive Reporting documents. The location of the linked content is defined by the report author and can be set to in a new window or the current window.

The **Slider** Controls are used to control the indicator for one or more associated Gauge within the same Dashboard. This Control can be tied only to existing Gauges.

Creating a Master Dashboard

A **Master Dashboard** is a Dashboard section that acts as a template for the visual properies and placement of objects repeated across one or more Dashboard sections to easily enforce visual consistancy. During the development process, the Master Dashboard is replicated each time a new dashboard is added and is either hidden or removed when the document is prepared for production. While use of the Master Dashboard is not compulsory when creating an Interactive Reporting document with more than one Dashboard section, it can greatly decrease the hours spent during the development phase as it eliminates the need to recreate the dashboard elements for each Dashboard section.

In addition to the visual properties and placement of the objects, any repetitive shape-specific code can also be included in the Master Dashboard template. Any code included in this manner is duplicated across the Dashboard sections that use those shapes.

This section discusses the specific concepts required to create the Master Dashboard shown in the following screenshot:

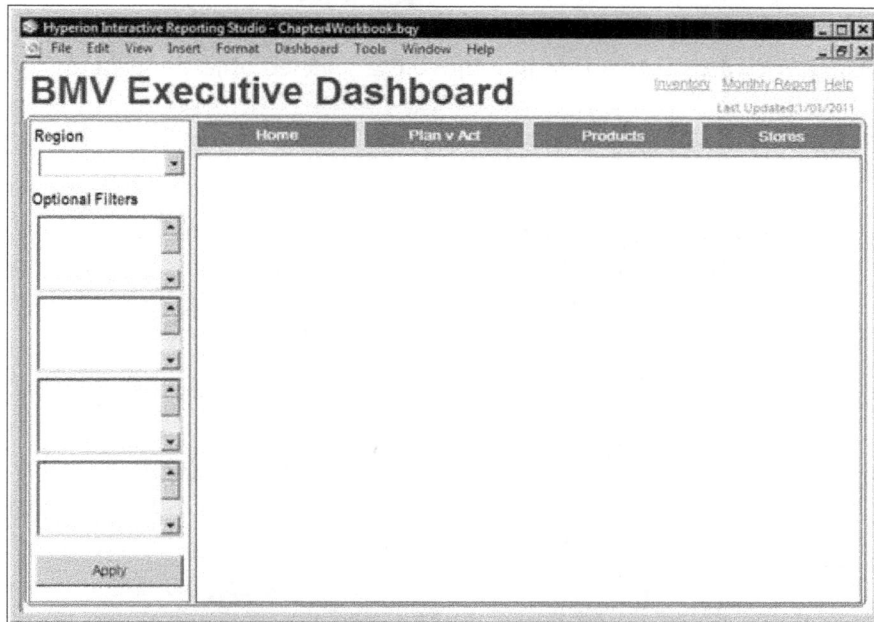

This Master Dashboard will be used to create a new **BMV Executive Dashboard** from the example from *Chapter 3, Creating a Simple Dashboard*.

Placing Objects

The sample Master Dashboard for the BMV Executive Dashboard uses Graphics and Controls to define a customized visual style. This example uses Rectangle, Rounded Rectangle, and Text Label Graphics as well as the Drop Down, List Box, Command Button, and Hyperlink Controls.

When created, each dashboard object is automatically assigned to a **layer**. The first item created is assigned to the first layer, also referred to as the background, and the last object created in the top layer, also referred to as the foreground. The layer feature allows report authors to modify the default layer an object is assigned to, allowing objects to be stacked on top of each other to control the visibility of all or part of an object.

The options available to report authors for moving object layers within a Dashboard section are:

- **Bring To Front**: The selected object will be assigned to the front-most layer and all other objects will appear behind it.
- **Send To Back**: The selected object will be assigned to the bottom layer and all other objects will appear in front of it.
- **Bring Forward**: The option will move the selected object one step closer to the front.
- **Send Backward**: This option will move the selected object one step backward.

To change the layer of an object, first select the object to be moved. Using either the **Layers** submenu in the **Format** menu or by using the **Layers Tool** icon located within the **Section** toolbar, select an option to move the object. The following screenshot shows a close-up view of the Layers Tool icon in the Section toolbar:

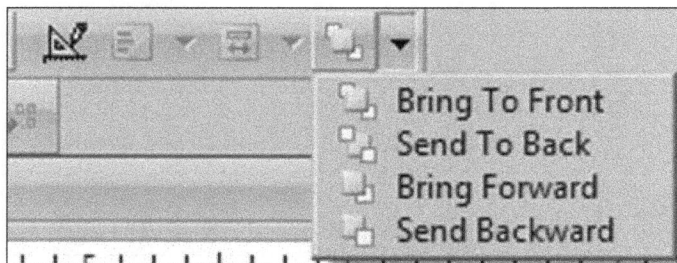

The **Align** feature is another useful formatting tool which allows report authors to align two or more objects with each other. Report authors can choose to align selected object both horizontally or vertically.

The options available for aligning two or more selected objects are:

- **Left**: This option will align all objects to the left-most point within the selected objects.

- **Right**: This option will align all objects to the right-most point within the selected objects.

- **Center**: This option will align all objects to the average center point within the selected objects.

- **Top**: This option will align all objects to the top-most point within the selected objects.

- **Bottom**: This option will align all objects to the bottom-most point within the selected objects.

- **Middle**: This option will align all objects to the average vertical midpoint within the selected objects.

To align two or more objects, hold the *Ctrl* key and click on each object to be aligned. With the objects selected, access the **Align** submenu in the **Format** menu or the **Align Tool** icon in the **Section** toolbar and choose the desired alignment option. The following screenshot shows a close-up view of the Align Tool icon in the Section toolbar:

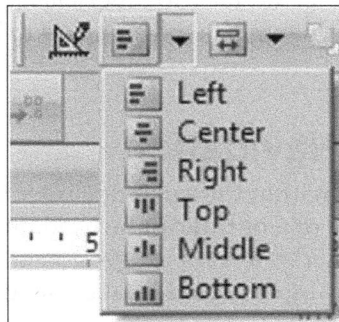

The **Make Same Size** feature makes two or more objects of the same height and/ or width as the first object selected. Report authors can use this feature to make multiple Dashboard objects exactly the same height or width automatically.

The Make Same Size options are:

- **Width**: This option will make all selections the same width as the first object selected in the group.

- **Height**: This option will make all selections the same height as the first object selected in the group.

- **Both**: This option will make all selections the same width and height as the first object selected in the group.

To use the Make Same Size feature, hold the *Ctrl* key and click each object to select all of the objects to be resized. With the objects selected, access the Make Same Size submenu in the Format menu or the Make Same Size tool in the Section toolbar, as shown in the following screenshot:

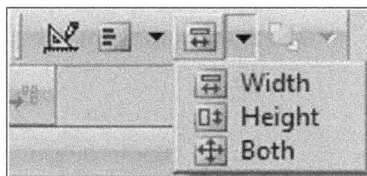

Implementing Custom Dashboard Navigation

Dashboard navigation can be implemented to provide end users with links to both internal and external document sections and to other websites. This provides report authors the ability to create customized navigation structures beyond the options supplied by default. In the sample Master Dashboard, there are two navigation menus. One menu navigates the end user to other Dashboard sections within the same document, and the other navigates the end user to links that are external to the document.

Scripting Internal Navigation

To navigate between sections within the same document, the OnClick() Event Trigger of almost any Graphic or Control can be used. However, Graphic objects, especially the **Text Label**, provides a wide range of visual customization options. The BMV Executive Dashboard example uses text labels to allow the end user to navigate between Dashboard sections.

For example, the code required to display, or activate, the **Home** section is as follows:

```
ActiveDocument.Sections["Home"].Activate()
```

Notice in the code, the Home section is referenced by name. If the name of the Home section were to change, this code would also have to be adjusted since the section name is directly referenced. While the Home section could be referenced instead by its index in the Section collection, this would still require maintenance on all supporting dashboards if the Dashboard designated as Home were to change.

A better solution is to synchronize the names of the Dashboard sections with the text displayed on the navigation link. For example, the Text Label representing the link to the Home Dashboard section would also display the text **Home** through the Text Label's Title property. This synchronization allows report authors to leverage a concept called **Reflection** to access the properties of the text labels without addressing the object by name or collection index. Consider the following code statements:

```
//Statement 1:
ActiveDocument.Sections["Home"].Activate();

//Statement 2:
ActiveDocument.Sections[tlHomeNav.Text].Activate();

//Statement 3:
ActiveDocument.Sections[this.Text].Activate();
```

Assuming that the Text property of the `tlHomeNav` object is equal to `Home`, meaning the Text Label displays Home to the user, and this code is applied to the `OnClick()` Event `Trigger` of the `tlHomeNav` text label, all three statements will activate the Home Dashboard section when `tlHomeNav` is clicked by the user. Statement 1 is the code required to activate the Home Dashboard section as described previously in this section. Statement 2 accesses the `Text` property of `tlHomeNav`, which is `Home`, and then activates the Home Dashboard section. Statement 3 leverages Reflection to access the Text property of `this`, which references the `tlHomeNav` text label when clicked, and then activates the Home section.

While each of these three statements will end with the same results, the third statement can be reused because it does not reference the name of the section or the name of the object directly. For report authors, this means that as long as the text displayed to the user matches the section to be activated, the statement will work without modification.

External Navigation

As introduced in *Chapter 3, Creating a Simple Dashboard,* Hyperlink Controls are used to link to external documents from Interactive Reporting. The Hyperlink Control is the only supported option for linking to external documents when the Interactive Reporting document is presented in Interactive Reporting Studio or the Interactive Reporting Web Client plug-in. However, when an Interactive Reporting document is presented to the end user in HTML mode through the Hyperion Workspace, HTML code can be used in sections. This means the `@HTML` command and the JavaScript `link()` method can be used to create HTML links in addition to using the Hyperlink control.

Since leveraging Hyperlink Controls to link to external URLs and document paths was already discussed in *Chapter 3, Creating a Simple Dashboard*, this section focuses on using Hyperlink Controls to link to other Interactive Reporting documents. The use of the Hyperlink Control in this manner requires that the document be published in, or have access to, an online Hyperion Workspace environment. When selected, the option to link to a repository object steps the report author through the process of creating a link to an object in the Workspace. This approach allows the user to add additional parameters such as the displayed section and whether the document opens in HTML or plug-in mode. Similar activities can be performed by using the Smart Cuts path as the URL to the report, but as these Smart Cuts need to be updated if the main URL of the site changes, this approach may require more maintenance than using the repository object method.

Creating Supporting Dashboard Sections

With the Master Dashboard completed, additional supporting Dashboard sections can be created by simply duplicating the Master Dashboard and then renaming it as desired. This section of the chapter focuses on creating a loading Dashboard, a Home (default), and a supporting details dashboards created from the Master Dashboard.

Loading Dashboard Section

Using a Dashboard section and JavaScript code, report authors can customize a loading screen with a message, either static or dynamic, that can be displayed to the end user. These screens are commonly used when the document is opened and document processing commands are executed, most commonly the processing of Query sections. The message is used to let the user know the application is still running and did not freeze while opening.

To build the loading message in Interactive Reporting, it is necessary to create a new Dashboard section specifically for the loading message. There should not be any interactive elements or any data driven objects on the Loading Dashboard, since this section will be shown to the user before any other code is executed and then replaced with the active Dashboard when all of the preprocessing is complete. The following screenshot shows the Loading Dashboard section created for the **BMV Executive Dashboard** example:

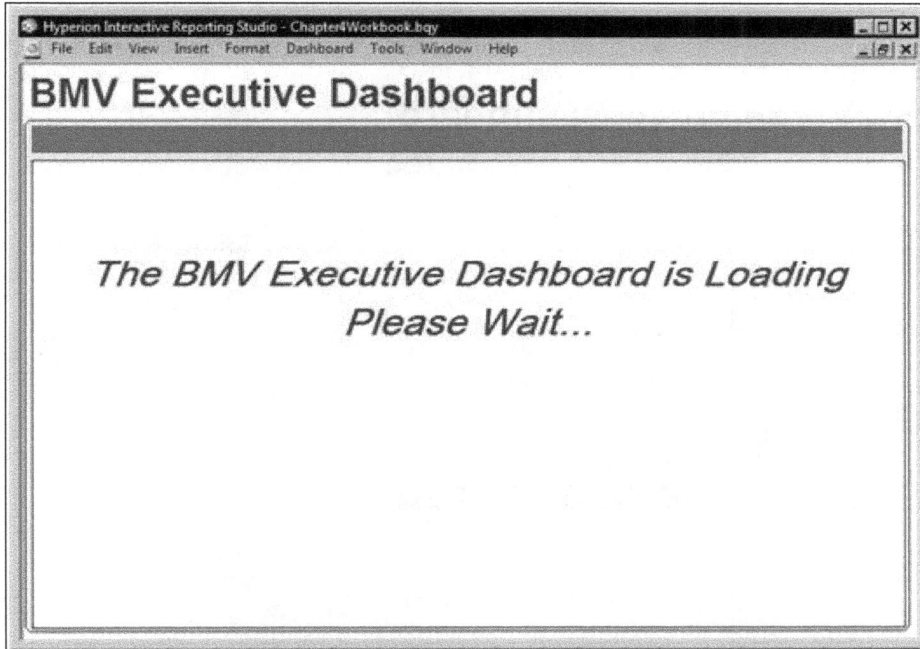

Home Dashboard Section

The Home Dashboard is the main dashboard. In the case of the **BMV Executive Dashboard** example, it presents a top-level view of data presented across all Dashboard sections. Since it will be the section the user sees first, the different data views have been grouped together so the user can quickly assess the data presented in a single screen. The following screenshot shows the expected final product of the BMV Executive Dashboard Home section:

By default, all of the Chart and Pivot embedded sections are **inactive**, meaning the end user cannot click or drill on them. By opening an **embedded section's** properties, and changing from the default **View-only** to **Hyperlink**, the shape can be used a link. This activates the OnClick() event trigger for the embedded section, allowing the report author to customize the user's interaction with the object.

An Embedded Section with the Hyperlink feature enabled will prepopulate the Hyperlink code of the section to activate the respective section by default. In the case of the example dashboard, the embedded section representing the Plan v Act data should link to the **Plan v Act** Dashboard section when the end user clicks on it. The following screenshot shows the system-generated JavaScript for the OnClick() event trigger of the chPlanvAct chart object in the BMV Executive Dashboard once the Hyperlink option is set.

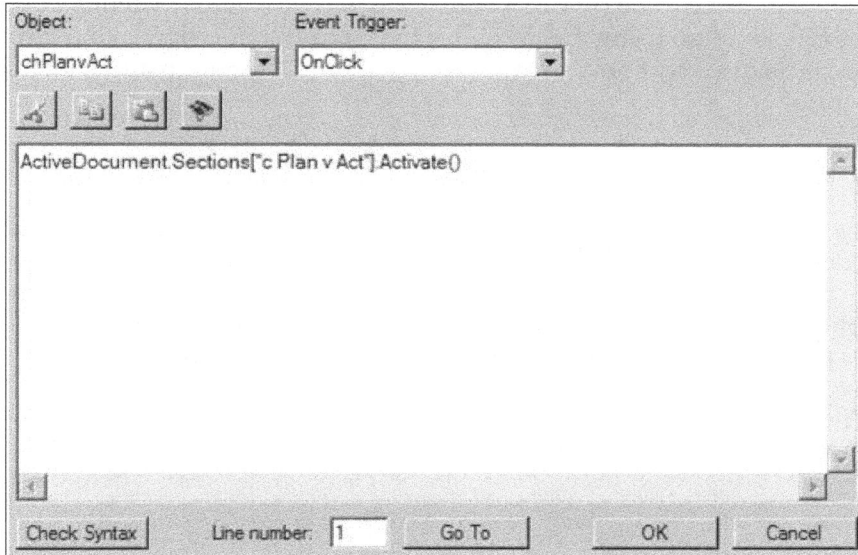

The section to be displayed, or activated, is the section referenced between the [ ] characters. Note that the default section in the code is the **Chart** section that was embedded on the screen. The following code displays how the default script should be modified to display the Plan v Act supporting dashboard instead of the c Plan v Act Chart section:

```
/* Activate the Plan v Act Dashboard section*/
ActiveDocument.Sections["Plan v Act"].Activate()
```

Detail Dashboard Sections

The purpose of a detail Dashboard section is to provide the user with an opportunity to perform a deeper level of analysis than that which is provided on the Home Dashboard. The following screenshot shows the **Plan v Act** detail dashboard of the BMV Executive Dashboard sample, which allows end users to analyze revenue, cost, and units plan versus actual data in either a Chart or Pivot.

This section will discuss the process of allowing users to toggle visibility between a Chart or Pivot section using the Radio Button Controls, and how to dynamically change the facts of a Pivot or Chart section based on a selection made with a Drop Down Control.

Toggling Between Objects

The Plan v Act Dashboard in our example allows a user to choose between seeing a Pivot or Chart view of the data. This is accomplished by using Radio Button Controls to change the Visible property of identically-sized embedded sections that are layered on top of each other. When a Radio Button is selected, the Visible property of one of the embedded section is set to true and the other to false.

When applied to the OnClick() event trigger of the Pivot Radio Button Control, the following code will set the Visible property of the embedded Pivot section to true and the Visible property of the embedded Chart section to false when selected by the user.

```
// Show the pPlanvAct shape by setting visible to true
ActiveDocument.Sections["Plan v Act"].Shapes["pPlanvAct"].
Visible=true;

// Hide the cPlanvAct shape by setting visible to false
ActiveDocument.Sections["Plan v Act"].Shapes["cPlanvAct"].
Visible=false;
```

The first statement sets the Visible property of the pPlanvAct embedded Pivot section to true, making it visible to an end user, and the second statement sets the Visible property of the cPlanvAct embedded Chart section to false, hiding it from the user. Alternatively, report designers can leverage the relationship between the Dashboard section and the Shapes collection to accomplish the same result. The following code shows the revised statements using a direct reference to the Shapes collection:

```
// Show the pPlanvAct shape by setting visible to true
pPlanvAct.Visible=true;

// Hide the cPlanvAct shape by setting visible to false
cPlanvAct.Visible=false;
```

This code works because objects on a Dashboard section belong to a collection of shapes accessible only by that Dashboard. This allows code that remains in the local scope of the Dashboard to access shapes by name.

In order to toggle the Chart and Pivot visibility, the second Radio Button Control must set the Visible properties of the two embedded sections to be the opposite of the Visible properties from the first option. The following code sets the Visible property of pPlanvAct to `false` and cPlanvAct to `true`:

```
// Hide the pPlanvAct shape by setting visible to false
pPlanvAct.Visible=false;

// Show the cPlanvAct shape by setting visible to true
cPlanvAct.Visible=true;
```

With the code in place on both buttons, the end-user is now able to toggle between related data in a Chart or Pivot section.

Modifying Element Facts

Presenting the end user the option to control the Plan v Actual fact displayed using a Drop Down Control can be accomplished using a few different methods. One approach would be to set up a Chart and Pivot for each of the three factual views views, using the logic demonstrated to toggle the visibility of the embedded sections. However, this method would result in both an increased document load time and an increased dashboard load time. Another approach is to use JavaScript to programmatically switch the data in both sections, requiring only one Chart section and one Pivot section. Using this approach, the need for redundant document sections is eliminated, since the same sections will be used for all three data displays.

From a functional standpoint, the facts displayed on the Chart and Pivot section are determined by a Drop Down Control on the Dashboard. This is accomplished in the code by first reading the selected value in the drop-down list, swapping the data on both the Pivot and the Chart, and finally performing any formatting.

To begin, add a Drop Down Control to the dashboard. With the **drop-down** menu selected, *right-click* and choose **Properties**. Click on the **Values** tab to view the list of values displayed for the user to choose.

To add a value, type the text which will be displayed to the user in the **List Value** textbox, and click on the **Add** button to add it to the list of values to be displayed.

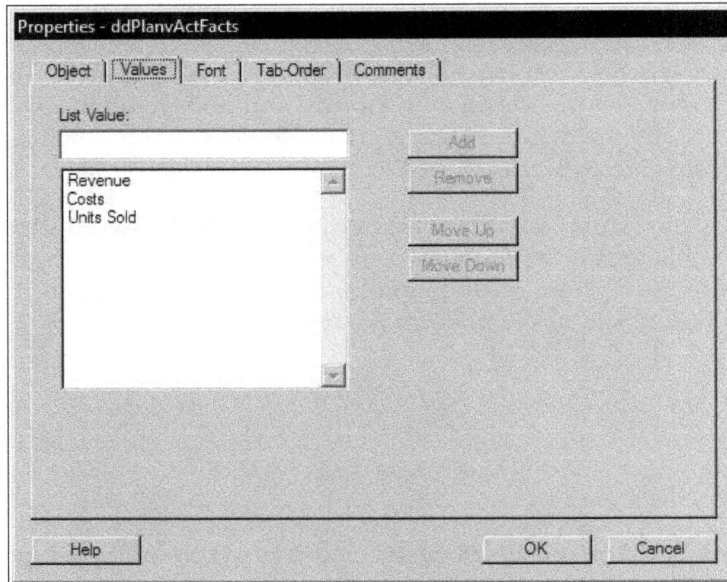

By default, the values are presented in the order entered. Use **Move Up** and **Move Down** to rearrange the List of Values as needed.

Once complete, click on **OK** to close the **Properties** dialog. When the Dashboard is in the run mode, the LOV will be displayed as shown in the following screenshot:

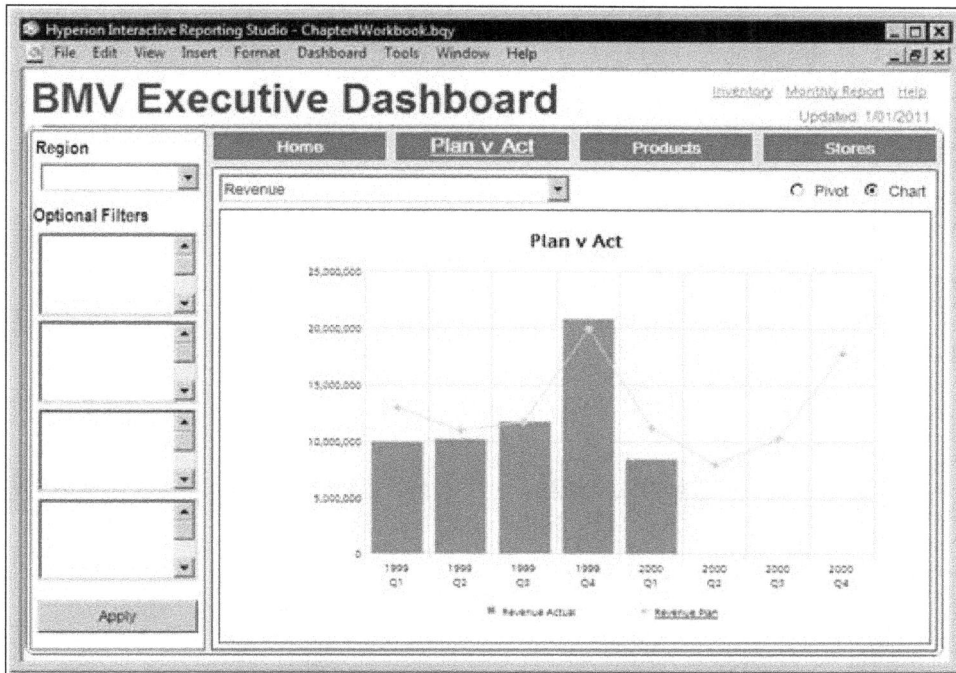

Next, with Design Mode active, select the Drop Down Control. *Right-click* and select **Scripts** to open the **Script Editor**. Since this code needs to be run when the user makes a selection, the code should be contained within the default `Drop Down OnSelection` event trigger.

With the Script Editor open, first identify what selection the user made from the Drop Down List of Values, so we can determine what facts should be shown on the Pivot and Chart.

```
// Declare a local variable to represent the user selection
var ddSelection = ddPlanvActFacts.Item(ddPlanvActFacts.SelectedIndex);
```

The code interprets the user-selected value and stores that string as a local variable.

The next step is to remove any Facts currently on the Chart or Pivot section that is to be changed:

```
// Remove all existing chart facts
ActiveDocument.Sections["c Plan v Act"].Facts.RemoveAll();

// Remove all existing pivot facts
ActiveDocument.Sections["p Plan v Act"].Facts.RemoveAll();
```

The above code uses the `RemovalAll()` method of the Facts collection in both the Pivot and Chart section to remove any Facts currently on the Chart and Pivot sections respectively.

Add the new facts to both the Pivot and the Chart sections:

```
// Add the Actual Fact to the Chart
ActiveDocument.Sections["c Plan v Act"].Facts.Add(ddSelection + "
Actual")

// Add the Actual Fact to the Pivot
ActiveDocument.Sections["p Plan v Act"].Facts.Add(ddSelection + "
Actual")

// Add the Plan Fact to the Chart
ActiveDocument.Sections["c Plan v Act"].Facts.Add(ddSelection + "
Plan")

// Add the Plan Fact to the Pivot
ActiveDocument.Sections["p Plan v Act"].Facts.Add(ddSelection + "
Plan")
```

After all of the code is added to the Drop Down, the script editor will appear as shown in the following screenshot:

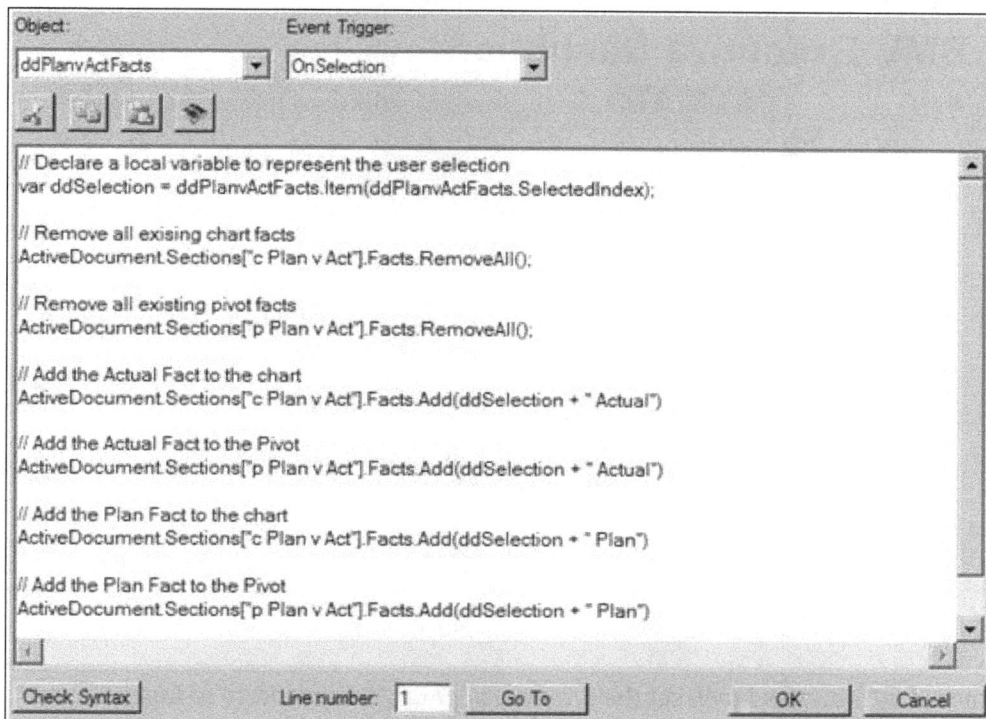

```
Object:                        Event Trigger:
ddPlanvActFacts          ▼    OnSelection              ▼

// Declare a local variable to represent the user selection
var ddSelection = ddPlanvActFacts.Item(ddPlanvActFacts.SelectedIndex);

// Remove all exising chart facts
ActiveDocument.Sections["c Plan v Act"].Facts.RemoveAll();

// Remove all existing pivot facts
ActiveDocument.Sections["p Plan v Act"].Facts.RemoveAll();

// Add the Actual Fact to the chart
ActiveDocument.Sections["c Plan v Act"].Facts.Add(ddSelection + " Actual")

// Add the Actual Fact to the Pivot
ActiveDocument.Sections["p Plan v Act"].Facts.Add(ddSelection + " Actual")

// Add the Plan Fact to the chart
ActiveDocument.Sections["c Plan v Act"].Facts.Add(ddSelection + " Plan")

// Add the Plan Fact to the Pivot
ActiveDocument.Sections["p Plan v Act"].Facts.Add(ddSelection + " Plan")

Check Syntax    Line number: 1    Go To          OK        Cancel
```

Dynamic Section Formatting

While the code necessary to change the embedded section Facts has been added, any custom formatting applied to the display properties of the Chart or Pivot Facts has been reset to the program defaults. Any display properties that had been modified from the section default values will have also reverted back to the default settings.

First, the chart has the right-axis label visible which needs to be hidden:

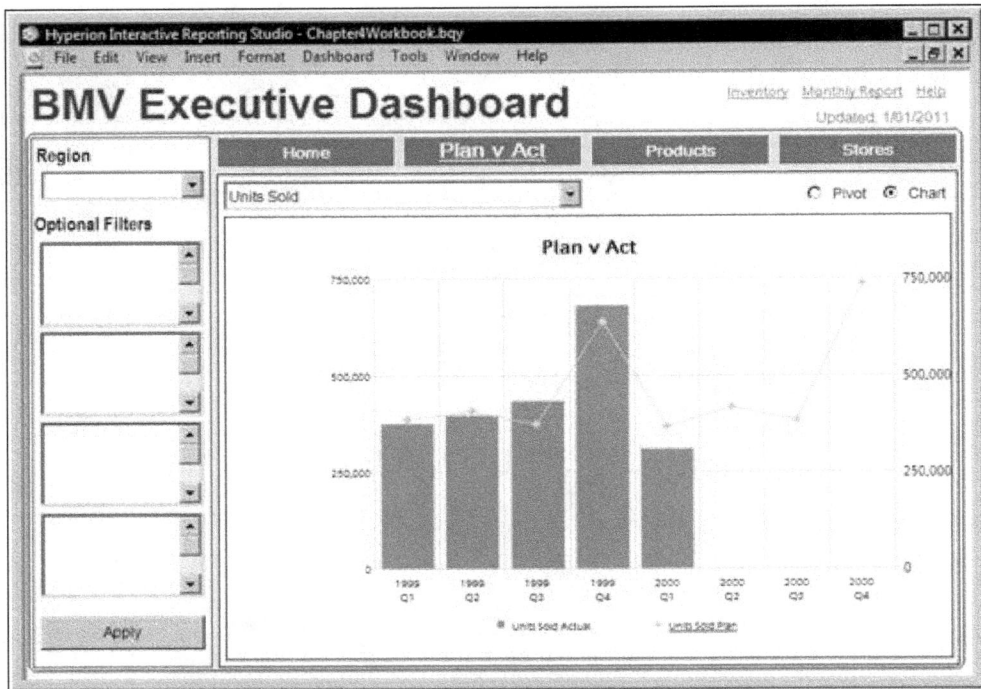

To hide the right-axis label, set the `ShowValuesAtRight` property to false.

```
// Hide right data labels on the chart
ActiveDocument.Sections["c Plan v Act"].ValuesAxis.
ShowValuesAtRight=false;
```

Second, the Pivot section number formatting needs to be set to **Currency** since the displayed Fact represents dollars:

Number formatting needs to be applied to both Facts. Define the `NumberFormat` variable to represent currency rounded to the nearest dollar.

```
// Set currency formatting on the pivot
ActiveDocument.Sections["p Plan v Act"].Facts[ddSelection + " Plan"].
NumberFormat = "$#,##0."

ActiveDocument.Sections["p Plan v Act"].Facts[ddSelection + "
Actual"].NumberFormat = "$#,##0."
```

If there were a business requirement requesting the currency to be reported to the penny, set the `NumberFormat` property to be equal to `S#,##0.00` which would round values to the nearest penny.

When completed, the `OnSelection` event trigger of the Drop Down Control object should appear as shown in the following screenshot:

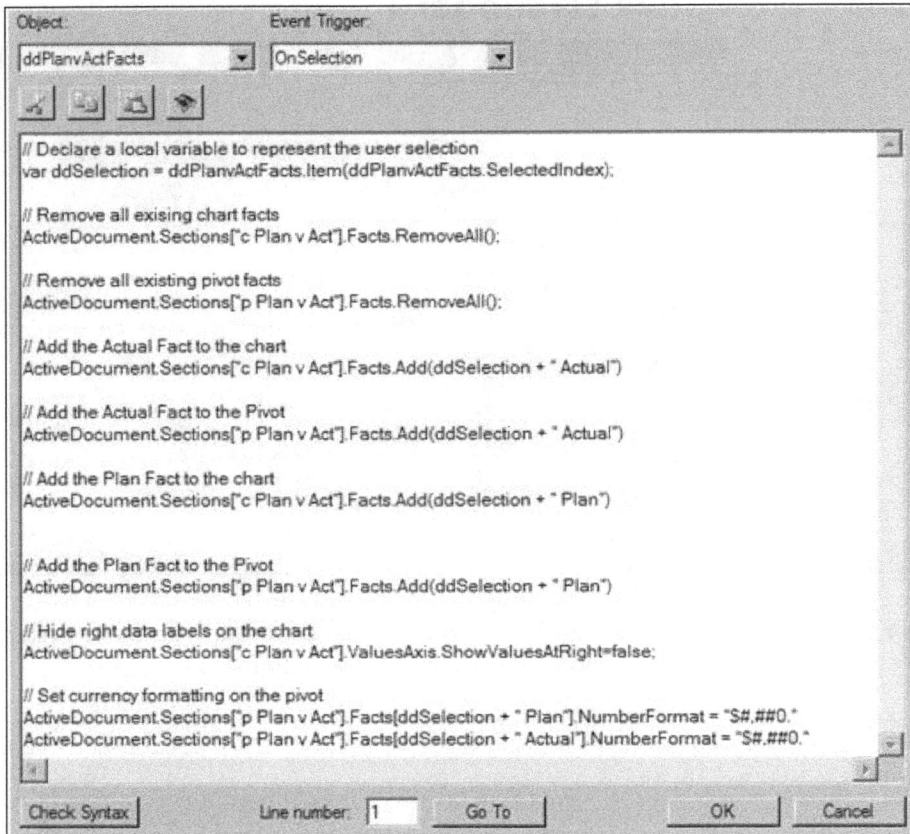

```
Object:                          Event Trigger:
ddPlanvActFacts          ▼       OnSelection          ▼

// Declare a local variable to represent the user selection
var ddSelection = ddPlanvActFacts.Item(ddPlanvActFacts.SelectedIndex);

// Remove all exising chart facts
ActiveDocument.Sections["c Plan v Act"].Facts.RemoveAll();

// Remove all existing pivot facts
ActiveDocument.Sections["p Plan v Act"].Facts.RemoveAll();

// Add the Actual Fact to the chart
ActiveDocument.Sections["c Plan v Act"].Facts.Add(ddSelection + " Actual")

// Add the Actual Fact to the Pivot
ActiveDocument.Sections["p Plan v Act"].Facts.Add(ddSelection + " Actual")

// Add the Plan Fact to the chart
ActiveDocument.Sections["c Plan v Act"].Facts.Add(ddSelection + " Plan")

// Add the Plan Fact to the Pivot
ActiveDocument.Sections["p Plan v Act"].Facts.Add(ddSelection + " Plan")

// Hide right data labels on the chart
ActiveDocument.Sections["c Plan v Act"].ValuesAxis.ShowValuesAtRight=false;

// Set currency formatting on the pivot
ActiveDocument.Sections["p Plan v Act"].Facts[ddSelection + " Plan"].NumberFormat = "$#,##0.";
ActiveDocument.Sections["p Plan v Act"].Facts[ddSelection + " Actual"].NumberFormat = "$#,##0.";
```

```
Check Syntax        Line number: 1        Go To                OK        Cancel
```

Click on the **OK** button to close the Script Editor and save the scripts. Switch the dashboard to run mode and use the Drop Down to begin testing the code. The Drop Down will change the data Facts for both the Chart and Pivot sections, based on the selection made by the user.

Document Start-up Scripts

Document Scripts, also known as Document Start-Up Scripts, describe the `OnStartup()` event trigger of the Document Object. The API at the document level is accessed from the **Document Scripts** selection in the **File** menu.

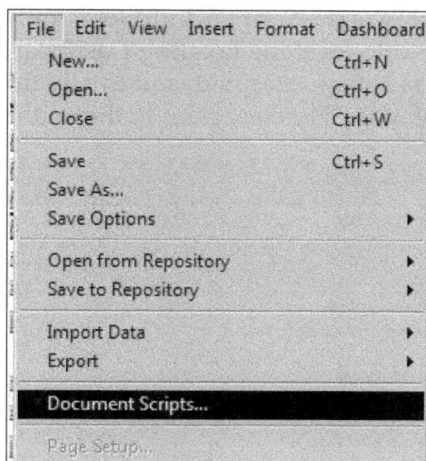

The Document Scripts API, while similar in appearance to the Object API, allows the report writer to create code specifically for each Interactive Reporting application type that is accessing the interface.

Loading Screen Script

In this section, the steps needed to activate the Loading Dashboard section will be displayed using the Document Start-Up Scripts. Activating the Loading Dashboard section upon start-up makes the Dashboard section visible while the remainder of the document is prepared for viewing. To set the Document Start-Up Scripts to make the Loading section appear upon start-up:

```
//Display the Loading Dashboard section
ActiveDocument.Sections["Loading"].Activate();
```

Since the goal is to show the Home Dashboard section to the users as the primary section once all of the preprocessing is complete, the Home section must be activated once the Loading Dashboard section splash screen is no longer needed. Set the Home section to active to display the Home screen after all of the processing is complete.

```
//Display the Home Section after all startup scripts have completed
ActiveDocument.Sections["Home"].Activate();
```

The following screenshot shows the Script Editor open to the Document Scripts `OnStartup` event trigger. Notice that the Loading Dashboard section is activated first, the preprocessing code is then executed, and finally the Home Dashboard section is activated to display the Home section to the end user for use.

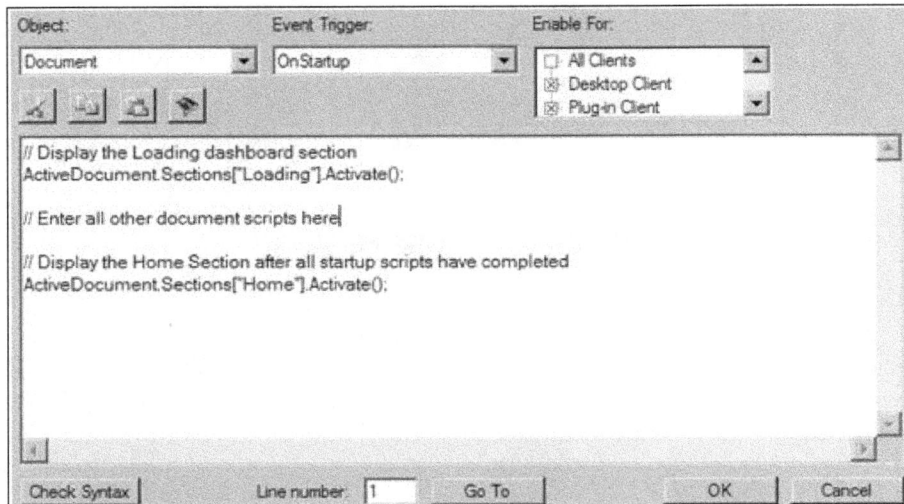

Understanding Toolbars and Menus

When Dashboard sections contain custom navigation, end users typically do not need access to the default application menus and document toolbars. Controlling the visibility of toolbars and menus is also a great way to increase the viewing area for a dashboard. Executive-level Dashboards, which typically do not require advanced ad-hoc data analysis, should always have toolbars and menus carefully controlled to keep the dashboard clear of unnecessary distractions.

Application Toolbars

Toolbars provide quick access to a variety of application, section, and formatting options using icons. In Interactive Reporting, there are five toolbars that are members of the Application Toolbar collection. The toolbars are as follows:

- **Standard**: The Standard toolbar presents icons to represent application level functions such as save, print, query process, insert new section and connections. The Standard Toolbar, when active, is available on all sections.

- **Formatting**: The Formatting toolbar grants quick access to text properties such as font, font size, font alignment, background colors, and number formatting. When active, the Formatting toolbar is available on all sections.

- **Sections**: When the Sections toolbar is active, it allows the user to quickly access section specific formatting functions unique to the active section type. For example, on Dashboard sections, the Section Toolbar displays the layout tools discussed earlier in this chapter.

- **Navigation**: The Navigation toolbar presents icons to allow users to navigate document sections. One of the Navigation toolbar icons is the Dashboard Home button that sets the Dashboard section that has been defined as the main Dashboard section of the document.

- **Paging**: The Paging toolbar is an abbreviated version of the Standard toolbar accessible only when a document is opened in Intelligence iServer using a direct URL. When code references to this toolbar are encountered by other clients, the command is ignored and the script continues without error.

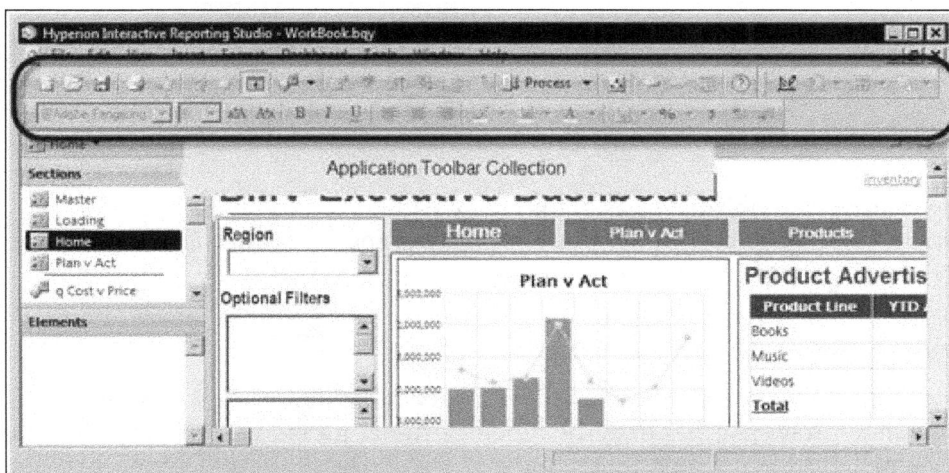

Each of these Toolbar objects contains a Boolean `Visible` property that can be set to `true` (visible) or `false` (invisible) using JavaScript code.

To hide all five toolbars, one approach would be to turn each toolbar off individually by using the following code:

```
// Hide the Standard Toolbar
Toolbars["Standard"].Visible=false;

// Hide the Formatting Toolbar
Toolbars["Formatting"].Visible=false;

// Hide the Sections Toolbar
Toolbars["Sections"].Visible=false;
```

```
// Hide the Navigation Toolbar
Toolbars["Navigation"].Visible=false;

// Hide the Paging Toolbar
Toolbars["Paging"].Visible=false;
```

Alternatively, since all five toolbars reside in the Toolbars collection, a `for` loop can be used to step through the collection and set the `Visible` property to `false` as demonstrated in the following code:

```
/* Hide all Toolbars in the Toolbar collection by using a for loop
statement to increment a value until it becomes equal to the number of
toolbars in the toolbar collection. */

// Use a for loop and cycle for each item in collection
for (var i=1; i<=Toolbars.Count; i++)
{
    // Set the visible property of toolbar[index] to false.
    Toolbars[i].Visible=false;
}
```

The preceding code means for as many times as there are toolbars in the Toolbar collection, referenced using the Count property of the Toolbars collection, set the `Visible` property of each toolbar to false.

Application Menus

Hiding the **Application** Menu Bar makes it very difficult for users to interact with the document in ways other than the report designer intended. Since the Menu Bar is very small, it does not gain much in the terms of usable space. Therefore, hiding the Menu Bar is more about controlling the user's access to sections of the document than a space-saving methodology.

The `ShowMenuBar` property of the Application is a Boolean property that is set to `true` by default. Unlike the members of the toolbar collection, the `ShowMenuBar` property is displayed each time the document is opened. The code required to hide the Menu Bar is shown in the following code snippet:

```
//Set the ShowMenuBar application property to false to hide the
MenuBar
Application.ShowMenuBar=false;
```

Section Catalog

The **Section Catalog** provides users with a hierarchal view of all visible sections in a document. When dashboards have custom navigation, the Section Catalog should be hidden, so the user is not confused or lead astray from using the custom navigation options. Hiding the Section Catalog also adds a significant amount of screen space for the dashboard, which is always at a premium.

The ShowCatalog property of the document is also a Boolean property that is set to true by default. The code required to hide the Section Catalogue is shown in the following code snippet:

```
//Set the Show Catalogue document property to false to hide the
Section Catalogue
ActiveDocument.ShowCatalog=false;
```

Section Title Bar

The **Section Title Bar** provides two specific purposes: the bar contains a navigation drop-down on the left, and the bar provides specific controls for each section on the right. The SectionTitleBar property of the document is a Boolean property that is set equal to true by default each time a document is opened.

With the Script Editor open for Document Scripts, add the following code to hide the Section Title Bar from view.

```
//Set the SectionTitleBar property to false to hide the section Title
Bar
ActiveDocument.ShowSectionTitleBar= false;
```

The state of the SectionTitleBar property is not saved across document sections. Each time the document is opened, the value of the SectionTitleBar document property is set to true and must be hidden using JavaScript code.

Quickly show all menus

Create and hide a button on the Home Dashboard that enables all of the menus and toolbars when clicked. Then set the Visible property of the button to false so it is hidden, forcing the user to have the permissions to go into design mode to unhide the button. This feature allows report writers quick access to the toolbars and menus at any time.

Prompting the User to Save

Interactive Reporting prompts the user to save the document when exiting an unsaved report for all client software versions. When creating or modifying reports in the Interactive Reporting Studio, the prompt to save is a helpful feature to prevent data loss by forgetting to save session changes before exiting. When end users are accessing the document with the Interactive Reporting Web Client plug-in, however, the additional prompt created by this feature maybe undesirable as it allows all users to save the document to their local machine. The easiest way to disable the Prompt To Save feature when the document is accessed using the Web Client plug-in is to set the `PromptToSave` document property to `false` during the Document Start-up event.

The save prompt is disabled by first referencing the `PromptToSave` document property, either by navigating through the Object Model to the `PromptToSave` property of the `ActiveDocument` group, or manually entering `ActiveDocument.` `PromptToSave` to reference the `PromptToSave` property. Once referenced, the property is set to false by typing `=false;`. With the property set to false, the prompt will not be displayed when the end user closes the document.

The following screenshot shows the Code Pane of the Document Script Editor with the start-up scripts displayed:

When the document is opened, the application will first activate the loading screen. It will then set the visible property of each of the toolbars in the toolbar collection to `false`. The Menu Bar, Section Catalog, Section Title Bar, and Prompt to Save dialog will be disabled, and finally the Home Dashboard section will be displayed.

Summary

The goal of the chapter was to demonstrate the steps for evolving the simple dashboard into a master dashboard with start-up scripts, navigation, controls, and dynamic objects. The chapter began with an overview of the building blocks for creating interactive and presentable Dashboard sections, including Graphics and Controls. Dashboard development tools are described in detail with an overview of the alignment, sizing, and layering toolbars. The concept of the master dashboard was introduced and dashboard navigation was presented with the methods for reducing code maintenance through the use of reflection. The chapter presented the concept of start-up scripts and the use of the Loading screen and the Home dashboard, and the chapter provided detail on embedded section linking and visibility toggling. The methods for modifying section content (Facts) through the use of controls and JavaScript was demonstrated and discussed at length, and methods were presented for hiding the menus, the Section Catalogue, and various toolbars. The chapter concluded with details on writing code for the different Interactive Reporting client tools and the methods to preventing the user from saving the document upon exiting the software.

5
Building the Dashboard Framework

Dashboards evolve over time and a standard development best practice is to construct dashboards with the ability for growth and modification without using repetitive code through the document. An effective method to streamline dashboard programming with areas for growth is to create and extract the standard code statements of the document into a customized Dashboard Framework within Interactive Reporting. While there are various approaches to constructing a Dashboard Framework, the strategy detailed within this chapter demonstrates one approach to achieve an optimal configuration. In addition to the information provided for building the Dashboard Framework, this chapter provides information on the options for managing document size, delivery, and document security.

This chapter covers the following concepts:

- Understanding the Dashboard Framework
- Implementing the Dashboard Framework
- Document Save Options
- Working Offline, File Compression, and Document Security

Understanding the Dashboard Framework

The previous chapter introduced the basic scripting concepts required to assign code directly to the Script property of an object. However, as dashboards become more complex, repetitive code across shapes should be extracted to create global functions that can be used by all objects in the document. The process of creating a set of global functions permits report authors to create and maintain a customized framework of JavaScript code in a centralized location within the Interactive Reporting document.

The strategy used in this guide, called the **Dashboard Framework**, is simply an organization of global code contained within reusable global functions invoked by objects across the document.

Chapter 9, The Central Code Repository, goes one step further and demonstrates the process for storing the global functions of a document in a database for use across multiple documents.

Framework Naming Conventions

Interactive Reporting allows any name to be used as long as it conforms to the requirements of the object type and is unique within the object's collection. For example, the Section collection allows names to contain spaces, but the Shape collection does not. The requirement that an object name be unique within a collection can quickly escalate into an organizational challenge.

Naming conventions make code easier to write, understand, debug, and maintain. Naming Conventions also ensures consistent standards when multiple report authors are working in a collaborative environment, writing and maintaining customized reports together. When operating within the Dashboard Framework, using a naming convention is very important.

Section Names

Since all section names within a single document are a part of the same Section collection and must be unique, it is recommended that the section names be prefixed to denote the section type the name is referring to. For example, when a Query section is inserted into a document, the Query section and the Results section are created by default and named Query and Results respectively. Assuming the purpose of the Query section is to return information related to sales figures, it is recommended that the Query section be renamed to `q Sales` and the Results section be renamed to `r Sales`. Should a table be subsequently added, that Table section should be named `t Sales`. Additional sections representing sales data should also be prefixed with a single character representing the section type.

The addition of the prefix to denote the section type is extremely helpful as the document grows to easily identify the objects that relate to each other and quickly determine the type of those section objects.

Variable Names

Variable names should always be descriptive. While it may seem unimportant, having good variable names goes a long way when the code is being tested or maintained by another report author. It is also recommended that variables be prefixed to denote the scope of the variable. Global variables should be prefixed with the letter g and local variables should be prefixed with the letter v. The use of g and v is an immense help when documents move into testing or maintenance as the variable's scope, and therefore the potential impact the variable has on other code, is immediately known to report authors. The variable vLimitName is a good example of a local variable with a descriptive name. The variable gLimitName is an example of how the same variable would look if the variable's scope was global.

In a situation where a variable is representing an array of values, the name should indicate the scope of the variable and that it is an array. For example, gMonthsArray would be indicative of an array with global scope; vMonthsArray would represent an array with local scope.

Function Names

As the declaration process for a global function and a local function differ, it is recommended that only global functions are prefixed to denote that the function is being referenced and that the function is global. Additionally, within the Dashboard Framework, the use of local functions is very limited so the presence of a local function would be immediately noticed. An example of the recommended prefix is the name gfResetDashboardSelections to denote a global function that would execute code to reset dashboard selections.

Dashboard Shape Names

The dashboard Shape naming convention is the most important aspect of the naming convention, as the shape type can be very important when determining how to respond to an end-user action. It is recommended that the shape name be preceded by a two character prefix to denote the type of shape. The following chart displays commonly used dashboard shape types, including the ones used in this guide and their suggested prefixes:

Shape Type	Shape Prefix	Example Shape Name
Command Button	bt	btSubmit
Radio Button	rb	rbYes
Check Box	cb	cbCurrentYear
List Box	lb	lbState
Drop Down	dd	ddRegion
Text Box	tb	tbUserName
Embedded Browser	eb	ebHelpPage
Embedded Pivot	pv	pvSales
Embedded Chart	ch	chSales
Embedded Table	ta	taSales
Embedded Report	rp	rpSales
Hyperlink	lk	lkHomePage
Text Label	tl	tlRefreshDate

Any shapes accessed by JavaScript code that are not included in the chart displayed above should be preceded with a unique two character prefix that clearly indicates the type of shape the variable is representing. Generally speaking, shapes that are not acted upon by code, for example, a static label or a background box do not need to have a customized name as the impact the object would have, if modified, is easily understood by a report author.

The concept of the Master Dashboard discussed in *Chapter 4, Introducing Dashboard Interactivity*, is a key component of template design within the Dashboard Framework. As one of the most powerful aspects of the framework is using loop statements to step through related document sections to perform repetitive operations, the synchronization of names and properties of related dashboard objects is imperative. Any individual Controls shared between Dashboard sections must have the same name in each Dashboard section. If the object names differ, attempts to react to end-user selections using global JavaScript functions will results in an error indicating that the object was not found.

Understanding the JavaScript Workflow

The JavaScript used to define the Dashboard Framework contains three primary components:

- **Global Library Shapes** are the shapes that contain code used to customize the Dashboard Framework. This includes code for declaring any variables or arrays and defining JavaScript Functions.
- **Start-up Events** refers to the scripts, which are run directly by the OnStartup event of the document. Actions processed during the Start-up Events include the definition of any Global Library Shapes and the execution of the Activation Scripts.
- **Activation Scripts** It contains single-use code that prepares the document to be shown to the end user after the Dashboard Framework has been defined. Any document default selections, such as radio button selections, are defined here before the script to display the home dashboard, also in this component, is executed.

Implementing the Dashboard Framework

The use of a single Dashboard section to act as the code library for the document is the basis of building out a framework within Interactive Reporting. The Dashboard Framework refers to this section, which contains the necessary global support code, as the **Globals** section.

Continuing with the BMV Executive Dashboard example, insert a new Dashboard section called Globals into the document. Once the Globals Dashboard section is created and named, shapes which will contain code used by the Dashboard Framework are added, and scripts are written on their onClick() event triggers. Although any Graphic or Control with an onClick() event trigger could be used to contain global scripts, the Text Label Graphic is a convenient option as it provides the flexibility for customizing the text and visual properties of the object, such as the title, name, color, and border.

Global Library Shapes

Within the Dashboard Framework, **Global Library Shapes** are the individual objects that contain the JavaScript code responsible for defining the behaviors of the framework. Each shape in the library contains JavaScript that can define variables, functions, or execute code. While the organization and structure of code across the shapes within the library are defined by the report author, there are a few rules that must be followed for the Dashboard Framework to recognize a shape as a member of the Global Library.

Global Library Shapes must be named in the order they are to be executed starting from the number 1. Additionally, the number must be prefixed with the letters gs to denote their inclusion. For example, the first Global Library Shape must be named gs1 and the second, gs2. This naming convention allows the Dashboard Framework to use a loop statement to call the onClick() method of all shapes starting with the prefix on the Dashboard section without requiring the report author to define the number of shapes present.

Global Variables

It is recommended that the first shape in the Global Library be used to contain any global variables in a document. While local and global variables can be defined at any time, a best-practice is to group all of the global variables used across the document into a single object to assist with testing and maintenance.

Continuing with the example, add a Text Label to the Globals dashboard. Set the **Name** property of the newly created shape to gs1, as the code on this shape will be executed first, and add a descriptive title, such as Global Variables, to be displayed as the **Title** property.

Any global variables, including arrays, should be defined in the onClick() event trigger of this shape. When defining the variables in the Global Variables section, it is useful to create one array containing the Dashboard section names, as well as other arrays for other sections that can be accessed instead of repeating the section names in each block of code. These arrays will provide the ability to make identical changes throughout related sections of the document as configured in the array. The following code demonstrates a method for configuring the Dashboard section array in the BMV Executive Dashboard example:

```
// ---Array of Dashboard Sections accessible by users
gDashboardArray = [];
    gDashboardArray[0]="Home";
    gDashboardArray[1]="Plan v Act";
    gDashboardArray[2]="Products";
    gDashboardArray[3]="Stores";
```

By using arrays, sections can easily be added or removed from the collection without breaking any of the code in the document. Examples in the following chapter will demonstrate the use of these arrays and discuss their benefits in further detail.

Framework Start-up Events

The shape containing the Dashboard Framework Start-up Events will be directly called during Document **OnStartup** event and will either directly contain or call any code to be executed during the initialization of the document. While global functions and code may be housed directly within the Document **OnStartup** event itself, it is important to note the possibility of creating an infinite loop upon start-up. An infinite loop in the start-up scripts of the document will crash Interactive Reporting and will prevent the opening or recovery of the document. Use of the StartUp Events shape within the Dashboard Framework prevents this from occurring by allowing the code to be tested before being connected to the Document OnStartup event.

To create the StartUp Events shape, add a Text Label graphic to the Globals dashboard. Name the newly created shape **startUpEvents** and set the **Title** object property to **StartUp Events**. Once this is completed, the shape is ready for code.

The code to be contained within the `onClick()` event trigger of the **startUpEvents** shape will first activate the Loading dashboard, then define the state of any document-level properties such as the visibility of toolbars and menus, then execute a for loop to declare any Global Library Shapes, and finally invoke the Activation Scripts.

As an added benefit, this method allows the code to be executed without having to invoke the document start-up code. Instead, report authors can test any document start-up processes simply by clicking on the **StartUp Events** shape with the Globals dashboard in **Run** mode.

Initializing the Loading Screen and Document Properties

In *Chapter 4, Introducing Dashboard Interactivity*, code used to activate the Loading dashboard, hide the different application toolbars and menus, and disable the **PromptToSave** document property was written directly within the OnStartup event trigger of the document. This code should be moved to the `onClick()` event trigger of the StartUp Events shape on the Globals dashboard. To do so, open the **Document Scripts** editor using the **Document Scripts** item from the **File** menu, highlight the code in the window, and use *Ctrl+X* or **Cut** from the right-click menu to cut all of the code from the **OnStartup** event.

Navigate to the **StartUp Events** shape on the Globals dashboard, right-click, and open the **Script Editor**. Paste the scripts into the OnClick event trigger as shown in the following screenshot:

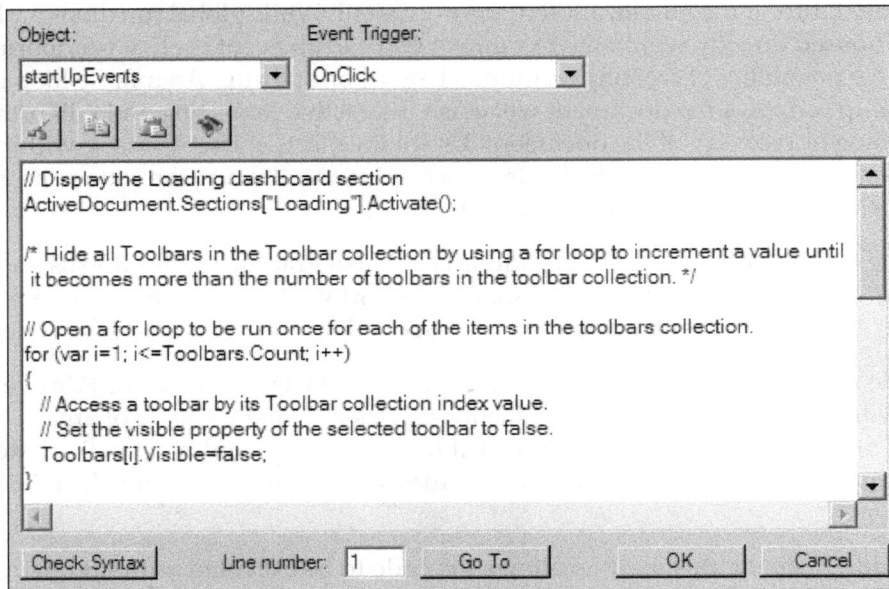

```
Object:                          Event Trigger:
startUpEvents            ▼       OnClick                ▼

// Display the Loading dashboard section
ActiveDocument.Sections["Loading"].Activate();

/* Hide all Toolbars in the Toolbar collection by using a for loop to increment a value until
 it becomes more than the number of toolbars in the toolbar collection. */

// Open a for loop to be run once for each of the items in the toolbars collection.
for (var i=1; i<=Toolbars.Count; i++)
{
    // Access a toolbar by its Toolbar collection index value.
    // Set the visible property of the selected toolbar to false.
    Toolbars[i].Visible=false;
}

Check Syntax     Line number: 1        Go To           OK          Cancel
```

Declaring Global Library Shapes

Since the number of objects will vary depending on the customized requirements of each framework, the Dashboard Framework uses a loop statement to ensure all objects are appropriately defined. The code required to execute the JavaScript code for each of the Global Library Shapes is shown in the following code snippet:

```
// ---- Make sure required globals have been activated
for (var i = 1; i < ActiveSection.Shapes.Count - 1; i++)
{
   var vGs = "gs" + i;
   ActiveDocument.Sections["Globals"].Shapes[vGs].OnClick();
}
```

The value of the incrementing variable, i, is used to control which shape is being accessed. Each time the loop runs, the OnClick() method of the shape represented by the vGs local variable is executed. The variable i then increments by one and, if the conditional statement of the for loop is still true, the next shape is similarly accessed.

Notice the conditions of the for loop statement. The incrementing value, defined as i, starts at one and the loop continues until the value i is less than the number of shapes on the Globals dashboard -1. The less than operator and the -1 are required because there are two other shapes on the Globals Dashboard, StartUp Events and Activation Scripts, besides any Global Library Shapes. This prevents the loop from running too many times while providing report authors the flexibility to add or remove shapes from the Global Library without requiring additional scripting to support the StartUp Event scripts.

Calling Activation Events

The final statement included in the StartUp Event scripts is the code required to execute the code contained within the Activation Scripts shape. The code, as shown below, executes after the Global Library Shapes have been defined:

```
// --- Execute the Activation Events
ActiveDocument.Sections["Globals"].Shapes["ActivationScripts"].
OnClick();
```

Activation Scripts

In the Dashboard Framework, code that is executed solely for the purpose of preparing a document for end-user interaction is part of the Activation Scripts and should be contained within a separate object. The reasoning behind the strategy of separating this code is that functions defined within the framework are used in conjunction with other scripts to set default state of the document. Because attempts to call a function prior to it being defined results in an error that would terminate the start-up sequence, the use of a separate object ensures any functions have already been defined.

Create a shape to represent the Activation Scripts by adding another **Text Label** to the **Globals** dashboard. Set the set the **Name** to **ActivationScripts** and the **Title** property to **Activation Scripts**. This object will contain code specific to any initial user interface objects, such as default filter selections or populating a last updated date on the dashboard header, and end with the following code to activate the **Home** dashboard object:

```
// Activate Home Section
ActiveDocument.Sections["Home"].Activate();
```

Setting the Document Scripts on Start-up

Test the code thoroughly by clicking the **StartUp Events** shape on the Globals dashboard while in **Run** mode. If no errors are encountered and the code executes as expected, the code is ready to be executed when the document opens. To execute the code during the opening of the document, the **OnStartup** event of the **Document Scripts** needs to be modified to call the `onClick()` method of the **StartUp Events** shape on the **Globals** dashboard. Open the **Document Script Editor** using the **Document Scripts** menu item in the **File** menu and add the following code:

```
// Click the Start-Up Events shape
ActiveDocument.Sections["Globals"].Shapes["startUpEvents"].OnClick();
```

When the Interactive Reporting document is opened, the script within the `OnClick()` event trigger is executed and the Dashboard Framework is defined.

Understanding Document Save Options

Interactive Reporting offers various save options to give the report author additional control over the visibility of the code contained in the document as well as options that impact the size and performance of a document. The **Save Query Results With Document, Work Offline in Web Client,** and **Compress Document** options allow report author the ability to control document size and performance. The **Password Protect Document** and **Password Protect Design Mode** options give report author the ability to protect the coding and dashboard interface.

Save Query Results With Document

The **Save Query Results With Document** option provides the option to save the data in a Results or Table section in the Interactive Reporting document. When the option is active for a section, Interactive Reporting saves the data in the document for the section. This setting is active by default and is very beneficial, since the document can be saved with data for the user without requiring the user to reprocess the query. Saving the data in the document increases the file size of the document, which will impact the speed at which the dashboard opens. Deciding to save the results with the document should depend on the purpose and use of the document. The following steps demonstrate the methods for editing the **Save Query Results With Document** settings:

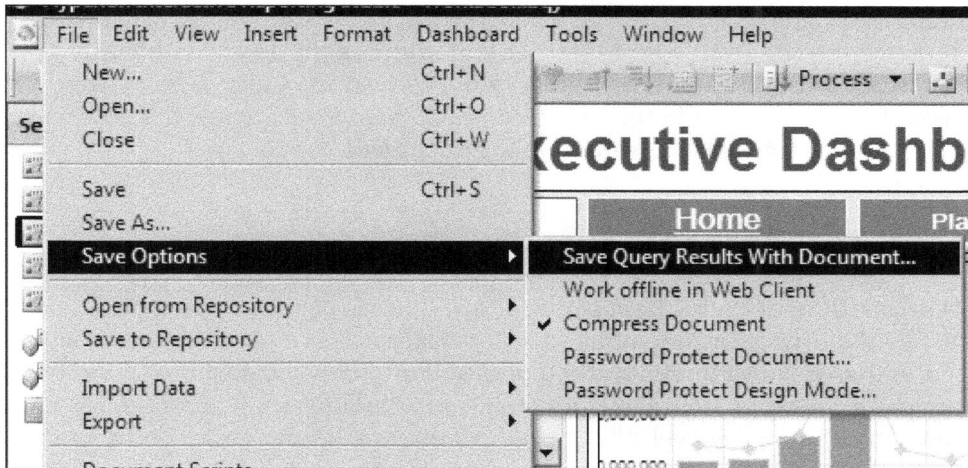

After selecting the **Save Query Results With Document** menu item, the **Save Query Results With Document** window appears as shown in the following screenshot:

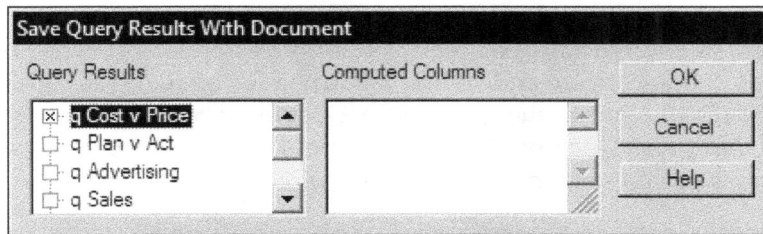

Queries with an x are the queries where the Results section data will be saved when the document is saved. Notice that there is also a setting for **Computed Columns**. The report author may decide to save the data in a Computed Item by keeping the column selected, or may instead force a recalculation of the Computed Item when the document is opened by clicking to remove the x from any of the **Computed Columns**.

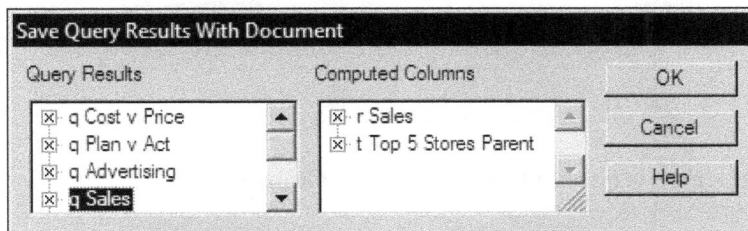

While this setting is used to remove data from the document, the report author may also remove the data from a Results section by running the query with temporary filters that produce no data. This method will produce an empty Results section and will remove all of the data in the Results and dependent sections of the document without having to modify this setting in the document.

Work Offline in Web Client

The **Work Offline in Web Client** setting allows the report developer to create an Interactive Reporting document that does not require server authentication when opened in the Web Client. The method is used commonly for dashboards or reports that are passed around an organization to users without system accounts but with the Interactive Reporting Web Client plugin software. While users cannot process the queries in the document, the user will be able to view or export the data and utilize any dashboards in the document.

Compress Document

The **Compress Document** setting compresses the Interactive Reporting document, making the file size significantly smaller. The compression setting is one of the most useful settings in the software and should be turned on, allowing easier distribution and faster downloading from the Workspace. Document compression is set by selecting the **Compress Document** menu item from the **Save Options** menu located in the **File** menu as shown in the following screenshot:

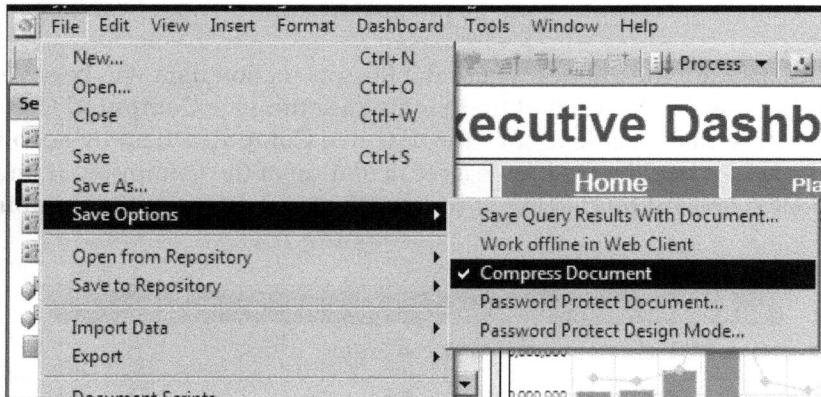

When the check icon is shown to the left of the **Compress Document** menu item, compression is enabled.

Setting Compression by Default

Since document compression is a setting that is commonly used, the default settings of the application can be modified to make sure the document compression setting is enabled for each document created. The default settings for document compression are set by selecting the **Program Options** from the **Options** menu located in the **Tools** menu, as shown in the following screenshot:

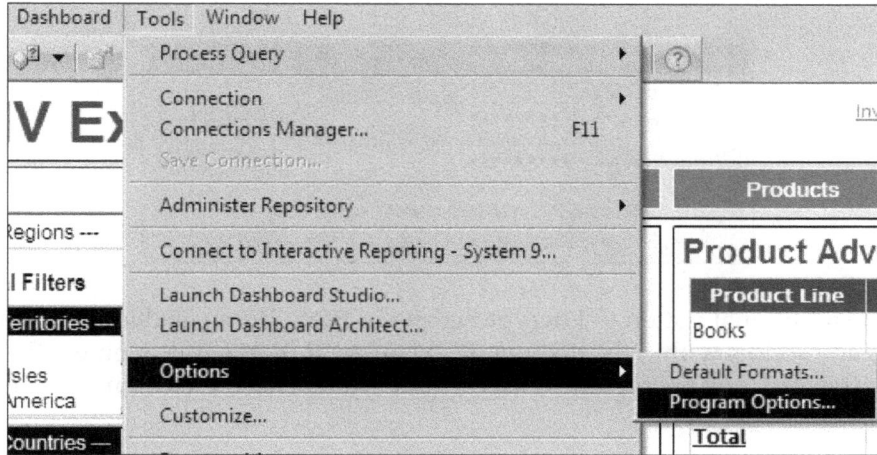

With the **Program Options** window open, check the **Compress All Documents** option to compress all documents saved or check **Create New Document Compressed** to only compress new documents created with the software.

Password Protect Document

The entire document can be password protected using the **Password Protect Document** option. If a document is password protected, a password will be required to open the document. To enable this feature, select the **Password Protect Document** from the **Save Options** menu. When prompted by the **Password Protect Document** window, enter and verify a password as shown in the following screenshot:

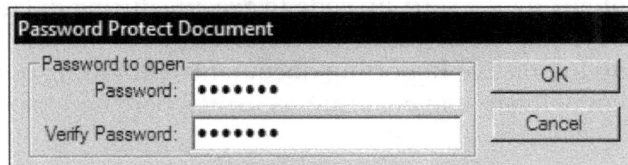

Once set, any user attempting to open the document will be prompted to enter the password.

Password Protect Design Mode

The **Password Protect Design Mode** prevents users from accessing the design mode within a Dashboard section without having the proper password. To prevent users from modifying the Dashboard sections within a document, select the **Password Protect Design Mode** setting from the **Save Options.** Provide and verify the password as requested by the **Password Protect Design Mode** window, as shown in the following screenshot:

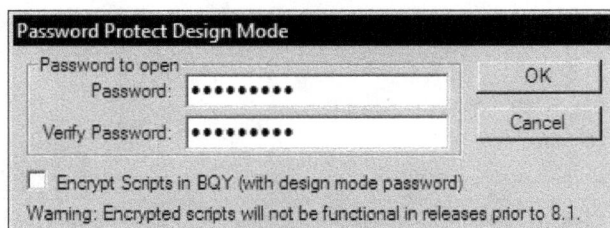

Notice the additional option to **Encrypt Scripts in BQY**. When enabled, this setting encrypts any scripts within the document. When an authorized user enters the proper password, any encrypted scripts are decrypted and the **Design mode** is enabled.

Summary

The goal of this chapter was to introduce the Dashboard Framework and to demonstrate one method to building an effective Dashboard Framework. The chapter started with an introduction to Dashboard Frameworks and the steps for defining a naming convention for sections, variables, functions, and shapes. The chapter continues with the steps to implement the Dashboard Framework, starting first with methods for defining a library of global shapes and global variables. Next, the chapter introduces the steps for organizing all of the start-up code of the document into individual components with specific naming conventions for growth and ease of use. The methods for testing the start-up code are presented and finally the method for the implementation of the Dashboard Framework concludes with instructions for configuring the start-up code to execute during document opening. The final section of the chapter discusses built-in features of the tool for optimizing, securing, and saving Interactive Reporting documents, providing options for improving document delivery and ensuring security where necessary.

6

Advanced Dashboard Techniques

The previous three chapters set a solid foundation for dashboard development and demonstrated a simple approach to building a framework for efficiency and growth. With the framework in place and the dashboard layout determined, the final step in building a dashboard is to add interactivity. Most interactive dashboards provide a method to filter the objects shown on the screen, and advanced dashboards carry that filtering across multiple screens of the dashboard. The goal of this chapter is to introduce and demonstrate an approach to add filtering options to a dashboard, the steps to filter data based on user selections, and the methods for populating filters across dashboard pages. This chapter covers the following content:

- Populating Dashboard Controls with Database-Driven Values
- Applying User Selected Filters to Limit Data
- Synchronizing User Selections across Multiple Dashboards

Populating Dashboard Controls with Database-Driven Values

The values available for selection by an end user in a Drop Down or List Box Control can be populated with custom values by either editing the Values property of the object or through the use of programming to dynamically populate a **List of Values** (**LOV**) from a set of data contained within a Results or Table section in a document. The use of programming allows the displayed LOV in the Drop Down or List Box control to update as the values of the section change without the need to modify the Interactive Reporting document. This section introduces the processes required to use JavaScript code to generate a LOV for a Drop Down or List Box Control from database values.

Querying Available Values

The concept of **Available Values** appears throughout the software when working with filters. The term describes a distinct list of items available for selection, and the distinct list generated is utilized by report authors to generate a custom LOV in Drop Down or List Box Control on a Dashboard section. The list of distinct Available Values is first selected from a data source and then is extracted with JavaScript code to populate the values presented to an end user for selection using objects on a Dashboard section.

When building a dashboard, the report author must decide the filters and filtering methods to present to the users. The next step is to determine the method for obtaining the Available Values for the filter criteria. Obtaining these values depends on the number of queries and the approach used to gather data from the dashboard. Dashboards can consist of one or more queries with small to large results, so the approach to processing the queries and preparing filters plays into the approach for populating and using the LOV to provide customized filters on the Dashboard sections.

When multiple queries are required, best practice in generating the Available Values to populate the LOV is the use of the **Append Query** feature. This feature allows report authors to combine multiple queries in to a single Results section. In addition to cutting down on the number of Query sections required, the single query approach also simplifies the JavaScript code required to populate the dashboard objects. The following sections of the chapter will demonstrate the use of a combined query to generate the Available Values that will populate the LOV used by shapes on a Dashboard section.

Appending Queries

The Append Query feature provides the ability to combine multiple queries to produce a single Results section. Each query shares a single Data Model section, where all of the tables for each query are brought and joined into one model. The query strings are determined by the fields used for each query, so all of the tables do not need to be joined together in the data model.

> It is important to pay close attention to the fields selected for the Request line for each Appended Query, especially if un-joined tables exist in the data model. If unexpected query results appear, the fields used in the Request line should be examined to ensure they are from the desired tables in the model.

When using the Append Query feature, the following options are available for use:

- **Union**: The Union operator combines distinct rows across the joined queries and will not produce duplicate rows if any exist.

- **Union All**: The Union All operator combines all results across all of the joined queries, including duplicate lines.

- **Intersection**: The Intersection operator returns rows that match in both queries.

- **Minus**: The Minus operator returns rows that appear in the first query but not in the second.

A helpful tip when creating an Appended Query, where all of the data from each query is to return in the Results, is to create a custom data identifier field in the Request line of the Query section. The custom identifier field provides information on the query in the Query section and provides the ability to troubleshoot issues in the query output.

The following example continues with the BMV Sales Dashboard example and provides a demonstration of using a single Query section with Appended Queries to generate the LOV for the List Box and Drop Down controls on the Dashboard. The end result is a query with four unions, as shown in the following screenshot:

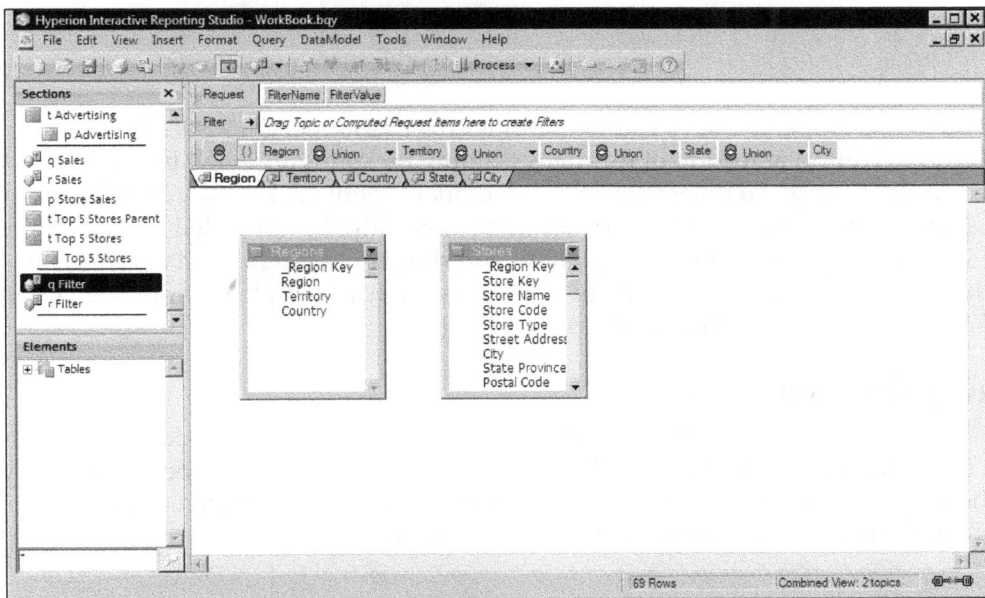

The first step in creating the filter query is to add a new Query section to the document. After adding the Query section to the example, it must be renamed to **q Filter** and the associated Results section to **r Filter** for the purposes of accessing the sections later in the chapter using the example code. The **Regions** and **Stores** tables are used to create all of the appended queries required by this example. Since each table will be used independently of each other in the appended queries, no join is required between the two tables and the tables may be displayed un-joined in the data model.

Each appended query is created using the **Append Query** menu option in the **Query** menu to add an Append Query section, as shown in the following screenshot:

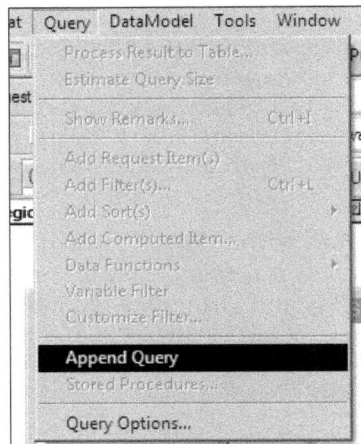

The use of the Append Query feature modifies the traditional Query section interface to display a control at the top of the main window for configuring the behavior between the queries. To rename an appended query, right-click on the query tab with the Append Query name and choose **Rename** to modify the appended section name. The **Union** query operator is set by default and should not be changed to ensure that all distinct rows are retrieved without duplicates. In this example, an appended query will exist for each Drop Down and List Box Control.

Query Request Items

Once the data model is configured and the appended queries are added, the Request line items need to be added for each appended query. In order to process the query without an error, the same number of Request items need to exist in each appended query and the data type of each column must match.

A simple method for generating the LOV for a control on the dashboard is to use two items on the Request line, named `FilterName` and `FilterValue`. The first field, `FilterName`, is a custom Computed Item to represent the name of the filter and should correspond to name of the dashboard Control that will contain the LOV from this query. The second field, `FilterValue`, is a field from the data model and contains the values that will be populated into the LOV for the specific List Box or Drop Down Control represented by the filter name.

Adding the `FilterName` Computed Item is completed by right-clicking on the Request line and choosing **Add Computed Item** as shown in the following screenshot:

Once the Computed **Item Properties** dialog is opened, changing the **Name** property to `FilterName` and entering the filter label name surrounded by single quotes (used specifically to add text to an Oracle query) completes the addition of the custom value. Pressing **OK** will close the dialog box and will add the computed column to the Request line.

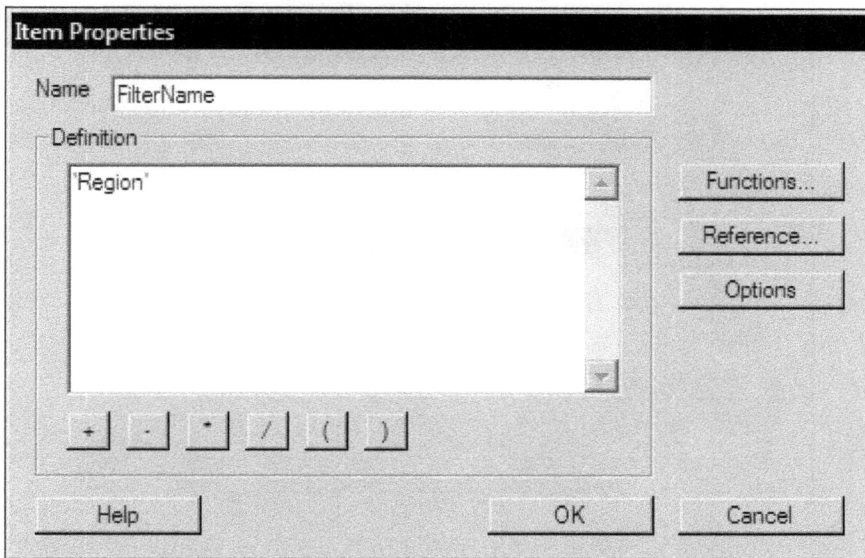

After the Computed Item is added for the filter name, the column containing the filtering values is added to the Request line from the data model. After the column is added to the Request line, the Name property of the column must be changed to **FilterValue** to support the code for populating the dashboard Controls demonstrated later in the chapter. Once completed, repeating the configuration steps for each filter object will complete the Query section for the dynamic LOV.

Staging the Results Set for Code

The FilterName and FilterValue column from each of the appended queries will provide the road map to dynamically populate the LOV within the desired dashboard objects. Once the query with the filter values is processed, a filter is created on the Results section to be accessed by code to allow the report author to segment the results when building filters.

To build this filter, add a filter on FilterName by dragging the FilterName column to the Filter line. Since the values of this filter are programmatically manipulated, it does not matter what value is added. Use an arbitrary value such as 99999 to populate the filter.

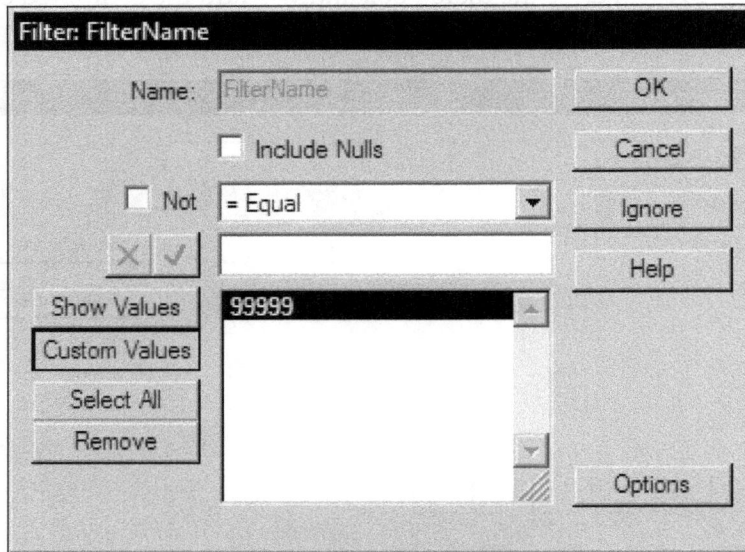

Click on the **OK** button to close the **Filter** dialog box and to apply the filter. The filter now limits the data to show rows where the FilterName column is equal to **99999**. Double click the `FilterName` object on the **Filter** line to open the properties dialog and click on **Ignore** to disable the filter without deleting it.

Scripting the Function

In this section, the code required to script the gfPopulateLOV function is discussed in detail. The purpose of this function will be to add the Available Values from the FilterValue column in the r Filters section to Drop Down and List Box Controls on a Dashboard section. Since this function is a part of the Dashboard Framework established in *Chapter 5, Building the Dashboard Framework*, the JavaScript must be added to a **Text Label** on the **Globals** Dashboard. If the examples in this guide have been followed in order, the **Name** property of the new Text Label should be gf2. Otherwise, the Name property should be gf# where # represents the next number available. The Title property of the Text Label should be set to gfPopulateFilterLOV.

As functions are defined at the global scope and are invoked by objects, testing the functions can be tricky. A handy trick to help facilitate the initial writing of a function is to assign the code to an object that can be clicked, such as a Text Label. To do this, script the function contents outside of the function declaration statement and temporarily define any parameters that will be passed to the function. When the object is clicked, the code will be directly executed using the predefined parameters. Once the function is tested, the additional code used to define the function can be added and the function can be globally declared.

When called, the gfPopulateFilterLOV function will expect parameters for the Dashboard section name and for the name of the Control that will accept the filtering values. Define a sectionName variable to represent the section on which the shape is located and a shapeName variable to refer to the name of the shape calling the script, as displayed below:

```
//---temporary variable for section name
var sectionName = "Home";

//---temporary variable for shape name
var shapeName = "ddRegion";
```

With these two variables defined, the code can be tested by clicking on the Text Label shape during development. The last part of this section describes how to wrap the code written into a function and the steps to supply sectionName and shapeName as parameters, allowing the preceding code to be deleted from the final result.

Determining the vDataName Variable

If the naming suggestions have been followed, the data values in the `FilterName` column of the r Filter section correspond to the Dashboard section shapes to be populated dynamically, with the exception that the shape names have a two-character prefix. When the function that populates the LOVs is called, the name of the shape to be populated and the name of the section to be populated will be supplied as parameters to the function. An additional variable that will equal a value in the `FilterName` column needs to be declared. This is accomplished by using the JavaScript `substring()` method to remove the two-character prefix on the `shapeName` variable.

Substring is a JavaScript method that extracts the individual characters between two values and returns the result as a string. In situations where only one value is assigned, the value defined is the starting point and the ending point is assumed to be the end of the string. The JavaScript below demonstrates using `substring` to remove the first two characters of `shapeName` to define the `vDataName` variable:

```
//---Remove the prefix from the shape name to determine the value of
the FilterName filter on the r Filter section
var vDataName = shapeName.substring(2);
```

If it is assumed that the `shapeName` variable is equal to `ddRegion`, the outcome of the `substring()` method is all characters starting from the third character, R. The reason for this is that the count begins at zero not one, so the number two actually represents the third character. This defines the variable `vDataName` as the string `Region`, allowing report authors to now directly reference the data to be populated in referenced filter control.

Removing All Values from a LOV

Before any values are added to a filtering control object, the existing values must be removed or the LOV presented to the end user will be inaccurate or contain duplicate values. The Drop Down and List Box Controls have a `RemoveAll()` method that will remove all existing values. The following scripting example demonstrates the syntax to remove all values within the referenced shape:

```
//---Remove all existing values from the shape to be populated with
the available values
ActiveDocument.Sections[sectionName].Shapes[shapeName].RemoveAll();
```

Adding a Custom LOV Value

Adding a custom selection item to an object's LOV is a good way to give the end user an option to select all data values to be shown. From a usability standpoint, this option also acts as a very convenient filter label that does not require an additional Text Label graphic to be added for each filter. To ensure the custom 'select all' value is displayed first, this step must occur after the values have been removed from the control but before any other values are added to the LOV of the object. Having standardized the `FilterName` value to be a non-plural value that represents the name of the filter, the addition of an `s` to the `vDataName` value will display a pluralized version of the filter.

The following code demonstrates how to simply add a custom label to a filtering control using the `vDataName` variable to customize the label:

```
//---Add custom value to allow user to select to see all available
data
ActiveDocument.Sections[sectionName].Shapes[shapeName].Add("--All "+
vDataName +"s---");
```

In situations where the name of the filter ends in the letter `y`, the pluralization of the `vDataName` will be incorrect. Adding a logical statement to determine if the `vDataName` ends in `y` will allow the report author to handle these situations separately. The script for the statement to check for a `vDataName` ending is `y` is shown in the following code snippet:

```
// Determine if last character of vDataName is a y to properly
pluralize
if (vDataName.substring(vDataName.length-1)=="y")
{
// Drop y value from vDataName string
var vDataNameTrim = vDataName.substring(0, vDataName.length-1);

// Add ies to end of vDataNameTrim variable
ActiveDocument.Sections[sectionName].Shapes[shapeName].Add("--All "+
vDataNameTrim +"ies---");
}
```

The script uses JavaScript string commands to determine the last character of the `vDataName` variable and then remove that character if it is `y`, allowing for `ies` to be added instead of `s` to pluralize the data label.

The first string command, substring, is combined with a second command, length, to allow the if statement to evaluate the last character of the string. **Length** is a JavaScript method that returns a number representative of the number of characters in a string. For example, if the vDataName variable is assumed to be equal to Country, the following statements would be true:

- The value for vDataName.length-1 would be 6;
- The value for vDataName.substring(6) would be y;
- The value for vDataName.substring(0,6) would be Countr;

The addition of an else statement to handle all situations where the vDataName variable does not end in y, completes the section of code that adds a select all option to the list of available values as shown in the following code snippet:

```
//---Add custom value to select all available data

// Determine if last character of vDataNameis a y
if (vDataName.substring(vDataName.length-1)=="y")
{
// Drop y value from vDataName string
var vDataNameTrim = vDataName.substring(0, vDataName.length-1);

// Add ies to end of vDataNameTrim variable
ActiveDocument.Sections[sectionName].Shapes[shapeName].Add("--All "+
vDataNameTrim +"ies---");
}

else
{
// vDataNamedoes not end with a y so add s
ActiveDocument.Sections[sectionName].Shapes[shapeName].Add("--All
"+vDataName+"s---");
}
```

Customizing Results Section Limits

The remaining values to be populated to the filter control are determined by the values available in the r Filter Results section of the q Filter Query section. To ensure that only the appropriate values are populated in each filter control object, the dummy FilterName filter created earlier in the chapter is modified using JavaScript to limit the data shown in the r Filter section so it displays only one set of values at a time. The following JavaScript code demonstrates the steps to customize the value to be filtered:

```
//---Remove any existing values from the FilterName filter
ActiveDocument.Sections["r Filter"].Limits["FilterName"].
SelectedValues.RemoveAll()
```

```
//---Add the vDataName variable value to the FilterName filter
ActiveDocument.Sections["r Filter"].Limits["FilterName"].
SelectedValues.Add(vDataName);

//---Set the Ignore property of the FilterName filter to false
ActiveDocument.Sections["r Filter"].Limits["FilterName"].Ignore =
false;
```

This JavaScript uses the `RemovalAll()` method of the `FilterName` limit's `SelectedValues` collection to disable any existing selections. The next statement uses the `Add()` method of the `SelectedValues` collection to select the `vDataName` value. The final step is to activate the `FilterName` limit by setting the `Ignore` property to false. The `r Filter` section now displays only the `FilterValues` where the `FilterName` column is equal to the `vDataName` variable.

Adding Values to the LOV Property

The customization of the `FilterName` limit allows a loop statement to be used to first read the value in the `FilterValues` column for each row of the `r Filter` section and then write that value to the shape referenced by `shapeName` and `sectionName`. As shown in the following code snippet, the JavaScript required uses the value of `RowCount` to determine how many times the script included in the loop should be run.

```
//---For each row of the r Filter section
for (var i = 1;  i <= ActiveDocument.Sections["r Filter"].RowCount;
i++)
{
    //Store the current row's data in the FilterValue column
    var vFilterText = ActiveDocument.Sections["r Filter"].
Columns['FilterValue'].GetCell(i);

    //Add the vFilterText to the shape on the desired section
    ActiveDocument.Sections[sectionName].Shapes[shapeName].
Add(vFilterText);
}
```

For each iteration of the loop, the `GetCell()` method of the `Columns` collection is used to first access and then store the data added to the dashboard Control referenced by `sectionName` and `shapeName`. Since the `GetCell()` method expects a numeric value for the row number of the cell to be returned, the incrementing value used in the loop, `i`, is also used to represent the row number.

Each time the loop is run, i will be incremented by 1 and the cell returned is stored as vFilterText. Once vFilterText is populated with a value, the Add() method of the shape is used to add vFilterText to the filter control shape on the Dashboard section represented by the sectionName parameter. When the last row is encountered, as determined by the RowCount property, the loop will end.

Scripting a Default LOV Selection

While the first value in the list of a Drop Down Control is selected by default, the List Box Controls have no default selection and one must be set if desired. In the case of the BMV Executive Dashboard, the first item, 'select all', should be selected by default for all filters. The following code example demonstrates the syntax required to select the first item:

```
// Select the first value in the list as the default selection
ActiveDocument.Sections[sectionName].Shapes[shapeName].Select(1);
```

The Select() method of the shape referenced by sectionName and shapeName expects a numeric value that represents the index value of the item to be selected. Since the item to be selected is the first item in the list of values, the number 1 is supplied and the first item in the list is selected.

Completing the Function

After all of the code is complied and added, the function is tested by clicking on the **gfPopulateFilterLOV** text label. If successful, the **Console Window** is free of errors and the **ddRegions** shape should populate as displayed in the following image:

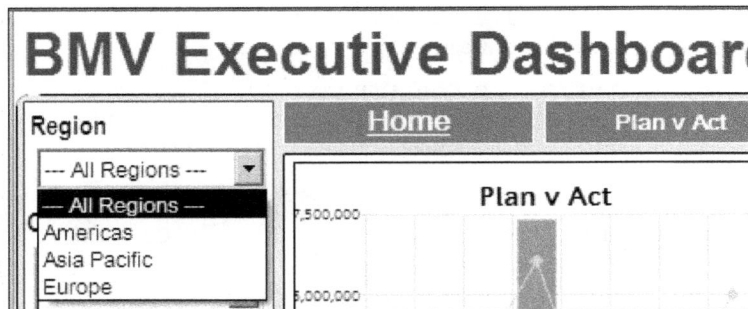

To complete the function, delete the temporary `shapeName` and `sectionName` variable declarations and add the declaration for the function and the opening brace at the top of the script. It is good practice to display the name of the function and define its purpose in comment lines before the function call to assist with maintenance. The comment shown below must be positioned at the top of the code before any other scripts as it is the opening declaration for the function:

```
//------------ function PopulateFilterLOV ------------
//---  This function will populate the filters on Start up
function populateFilterLOV(sectionName, shapeName)
{
```

All other scripts written as a part of this function are contained in the middle and the close brace must be added to the end. The final statement reassigns the function to a global variable making the function accessible throughout the Interactive Reporting document. The following code, which closes the function and then globally defines it, must be added to the end of the existing code:

```
}
gfPopulateFilterLOV = populateFilterLOV;
```

The entire JavaScript code to support the `gfPopulateFilterLOV` global function is displayed in the next code snippet:

```
//------------ function PopulateFilterLOV ------------
//---  This function will populate the filters on Start up
function populateFilterLOV(sectionName, shapeName)
{
  //---Remove the prefix from the shape name to determine the value of
  the FilterName filter on the r Filter section
  var vDataName = shapeName.substring(2);

  //---Remove all existing values from the shape to be populated with
  the available values
  ActiveDocument.Sections[sectionName].Shapes[shapeName].RemoveAll();

  //---Add custom value to select all available data
  // Determine if last character of vDataName is a y
  if (vDataName.substring(vDataName.length-1)=="y")
  {
    // Drop y value from vDataName string
    var vDataNameTrim = vDataName.substring(0, vDataName.length-1);

    // Add ies to end of vDataNameTrim variable
    ActiveDocument.Sections[sectionName].Shapes[shapeName].Add("--All
      "+ vDataNameTrim +"ies---");
  }
```

```
  else
  {
    // vDataName does not end with a y so add s
    ActiveDocument.Sections[sectionName].Shapes[shapeName].Add("--All
    "+ vDataName +"s---");
  }

  //---Remove any existing values from the FilterName filter
  ActiveDocument.Sections["r Filter"].Limits["FilterName"].
    SelectedValues.RemoveAll()

  //---Add the vDataName variable value to the FilterName filter
  ActiveDocument.Sections["r Filter"].Limits["FilterName"].
    SelectedValues.Add(vDataName);

  //---Set the Ignore property of the FilterName filter to false
  ActiveDocument.Sections["r Filter"].Limits["FilterName"].Ignore =
    false;

  //---For each row of the r Filter section
  for (var i = 1;  i <= ActiveDocument.Sections["r Filter"].
    RowCount; i++)
  {
    //Store the current row's data in the FilterValue column
    var vFilterText = ActiveDocument.Sections["r Filter"].
      Columns['FilterValue'].GetCell(i);

    //Add the datavalue to the shape on the desired section
    ActiveDocument.Sections[sectionName].Shapes[shapeName].
      Add(vFilterText);
  }
  // Select the first value in the list as the default selection
  ActiveDocument.Sections[sectionName].Shapes[shapeName].Select(1);

}
gfPopulateFilterLOV = populateFilterLOV;
```

Calling gfPopulateFilterLOV

When called, the gfPopulateFilterLOV function expects a sectionName and a shapeName parameter. The syntax to invoke the gfPopulateFilterLOV function to populate the ddRegion object on the Home Dashboard section is displayed below:

```
//Call gfPopulateFilterLOV
gfPopulateFilterLOV('Home','ddRegion');
```

In addition to referencing parameters as strings, parameters can also be referenced as variable objects. With regard to the BMV Executive Dashboard example, the ddRegion shape exists on more than one Dashboard section so the above call will not work to populate ddRegion on all sections. Leveraging a for loop statement and the length property of the gDashboardArray object allows report authors to populate the LOVs for all ddRegions across the defined Dashboards. Modifying the Activation shape on the Globals dashboard to include the array of multiple sections is displayed as follows:

```
//Populate Dashboard filter controls
for (var i=0; i<gDashboardArray.length; i++)
{
    var sectionName=gDashboardArray[i];
    gfPopulateFilterLOV(sectionName,'ddRegion');
    gfPopulateFilterLOV(sectionName,'lbTerritory');
    gfPopulateFilterLOV(sectionName,'lbCountry');
    gfPopulateFilterLOV(sectionName,'lbState');
    gfPopulateFilterLOV(sectionName,'lbCity');
}
```

For each loop iteration, the string indexed at value i of gDashboardArray[i] is stored as sectionName. The gfPopulateFilterLOV function is then called for each of the dashboard shapes to populate the objects with values. With the abstraction of the parameter representing sectionName, the addition or removal of Dashboard sections to the dashboard array will not affect the effectiveness of this code.

When combined with the Dashboard Framework already in place, the example code will populate the dashboard filters on all Dashboard sections defined in gDashboardArray each time the document is opened. Clicking on the **startUpEvents** shape on the Globals Dashboard section will test the document's onStartupscript activities. When completed, the list of values for the **Region**, **Territory**, **Country**, **State**, and **City** filters are populated as shown in the following image:

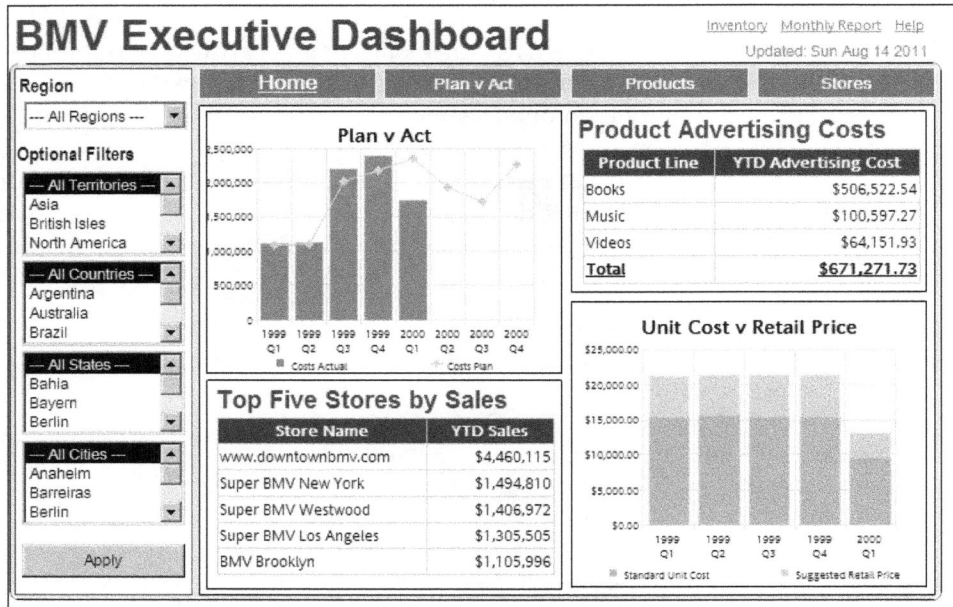

Applying User-Selected Filters to Limit Data

Once the filtering options are set on the dashboard, the next step is to configure the application of the filter across all of the dashboard pages within the document. These filters are applied locally to the data in the Results or Table sections or to the desired Query section based on the data refresh strategy. The following sections discuss an efficient approach for applying user-selected local filters in both Drop Down and List Box Controls throughout dashboard pages in a document.

Preparation for Dynamic Limits

The term **Dynamic Limits** refers to Query or Results filters that are controlled by end user interactivity. These types of limits can be handled a couple of different ways using JavaScript. The most straightforward option is to have any limits that the user can control already positioned on the Results sections as filters, and then to use JavaScript to modify the limit's properties. Another option, which would provide more flexibility but involves considerably more JavaScript code, would be to create the filter limits on the fly. This technique would be well suited for enterprise-level solutions that leverage frameworks that extend beyond the Interactive Reporting document.

In the BMV Executive Dashboard, the filters required are unlikely to change, so pre-positing the limits and using JavaScript to modify the properties of the predefined limits is well suited for this example. The process is similar to the process used to modify the `FilterName` limit used on the `r Filters` section. The process requires any Table or Results sections affected by the end user limits have the filters already applied to the required columns, so the filter selections can then be added with minimal JavaScript code.

Modify the Global Variables Shape

The first step in preparing the dashboard for dynamic filtering across sections is to create an array containing the sections of the document that will be filtered. The array approach is similar to the array created for accessing Dashboard sections and cuts down on repetitive code that would have to be maintained throughout the Dashboard if an array is not used. The following code, added to the Global Variables shape of the Globals dashboard, demonstrates adding an array containing the names of the Results sections for filtering:

```
//---Array of Results Sections to be limited by user selections
gResultsArray =[];
   gResultsArray[0]="r Plan v Act";
   gResultsArray[1]="r Advertising";
   gResultsArray[2]="r Sales";
```

In the BMV Executive Dashboard example, the **Cost v Price Results** section is not filtered based on location, since the data contained within the **Cost v Price** sections are company-specific and not affected by region. Therefore, the **r Cost v Price** section is not included in the above `gResultsArray` and is not filtered by user selections.

Modifying the Query and Results Sections

The next step after creating the global Results section array is to verify that all columns that can be filtered are added to the Filter line in all of the sections contained in gResultsArray. Additionally, to take advantage of the Dashboard Framework, the names of the columns in each section must conform to the names previously defined as FilterName and should be non-plural. In the BMV Executive Dashboard example, **q Plan v Act**, **q Advertising**, and **q Sales** must all include **Region**, **Territory**, **Country**, **State**, and **City** columns as shown in the following screenshot:

Applying Local Filters with JavaScript

The process for modifying the local filters with JavaScript, based on the user's selections from the dashboard is very similar to the process used to manipulate the FilterName local filter to load the dashboard objects. However, in this situation, the user controls the limit values and interacts with the filter controls.

While the processes required to read user selections to manipulate local filters from List Box and Drop Down Controls are similar, each Control must be handled separately. If the framework naming standards are followed, the shape types are easily differentiated using the two-character prefix, which denotes type of shape by name. Shapes prefixed with dd are Drop Down Controls and shapes prefixed with lb are List Box Controls. While the code example assumes use of the framework naming convention defined in *Chapter 5, Building the Dashboard Framework,* the shape type can also be identified using the **BqShapeType** constant if defined standards are not followed.

While the logic required to apply the local filters could very easily be contained within a single function, the next section will demonstrate the creation of multiple functions to handle various tasks so each function can be accessed independently. Since all of these functions are global, the declaration order is not important.

Applying a Drop Down Control Selection to a Local Filter

The first of three functions will apply a value selected from a Drop Down Control to a local filter on the Results section. Using the BMV Executive Dashboard example, add a new Text Label Graphic shape to the **Globals** Dashboard and set the **Name** property to gf3 and the **Title** to gfApplyDDFilters.

When the function is called, shapeName and sectionName will represent parameters passed to the function. As demonstrated earlier, temporary variables can be defined to make testing easier. Define shapeName and sectionName as shown below to create temporary variables if desired:

```
//---Temporary Variables
var shapeName = "ddRegion";
var sectionName = "Home"
```

The code below demonstrates using the substring() function to remove the prefixing value on the shapeName variable, dynamically defining vLimitName to represent the name of the column to be filtered.

```
//Define the limit name from the shape name
var vLimitName = shapeName.substring(2);
```

Selecting All Values with a Drop Down

If the custom **Select All Values** item is chosen from the control, the end user is requesting all values to be shown. Logically, the request to show everything is the same as ignore, so the filter represented by vLimitName should be ignored. If the user selects an item other than the first item, the selected item represents the value to be added to the filter to show data only for that specific selection.

To accommodate the Select All Values selection, a conditional statement is used to determine if the first item is selected. In the case of a Drop Down Control, the SelectedIndex property is equal to the numeric value that indicates which item is selected. If the first item is selected, the SelectedIndex property is equal to 1 and the ignore property of the filter must be set to true to ensure all data is displayed.

The code required to ignore a filter upon the selection of the first item is shown in the following code snippet:

```
// Is the selected the first item selected?
if(ActiveDocument.Sections[sectionName].Shapes[shapeName].
SelectedIndex == 1)
{
 //Set the limit ignore property to true for all sections
 for (var i=0; i<gResultsArray.length; i++)
 {
  //determine the vActiveResults  from the Results Array
  var vActiveResults = gResultsArray[i];

  //set the ignore property of the limit collection to true
  ActiveDocument.Sections[vActiveResults ].Limits[vLimitName]
.Ignore=true;
 } //close loop
}// close if
```

The addition of the `for` loop to cycle through the values defined in the `gResultsArray` ensures that the filter represented by `vLimitName` is modified on all of the sections defined in `gResultsArray`.

Selecting Filters with a Drop Down

If the first item is not selected, then the user has selected a value that must be added to the filter for each of the required Results sections to limit the data displayed. Since Drop Down Controls allow the selection of only one item at a time, the filter is set by retrieving the value from the Drop Down control on the Dashboard section and then applying that value to the items corresponding filter on each of the Results sections in `gResultsArray`. The following code demonstrates the steps to apply the selected Drop Down value to the Results section filters using JavaScript:

```
else //the selected item is not the first value
{
 //Access and store selected value
 var vLimitText = ActiveDocument.Sections[sectionName].
Shapes[shapeName].Item(ActiveDocument.Sections[sectionName].
Shapes[shapeName].SelectedIndex);

 //For all table sections in the ResultsArray
 for (var i=0; i<gResultsArray.length; i++)
 {
  //Store the results array reference to the active section
```

```
    var vActiveResults = gResultsArray[i];

    //Remove all values from the custom values collection
    ActiveDocument.Sections[vActiveResults ].Limits[vLimitName].
CustomValues.RemoveAll();
    //Add the user selected value stored as vLimitText from the
    Dashboard section to the Custom Values collection
    ActiveDocument.Sections[vActiveResults ].Limits[vLimitName].
CustomValues.Add(vLimitText);
    //Add all values in the Custom Values collection to the Selected
    Values Collection
    ActiveDocument.Sections[vActiveResults ].Limits[vLimitName].
SelectedValues.AddAll();
    //Set the Ignore property of the filter to false to activate the
    filter
    ActiveDocument.Sections[vActiveResults ].Limits[vLimitName].
Ignore=false;
    }// close the loop for results array
}// close the else conditional reaction
```

Since the check for the first value has already been completed, the `else` statement at the beginning of the preceding code executes only when a user selects a value other than the first value in the list. The selected value in a Drop Down Control is accessed by passing the **Item** control to the **Selected Index** of the Drop Down Control. The Selected Index is a numeric value that represents the item selected based on the order the items are added to the Drop Down Control. For example, if the Drop Down Control representing months has the first value, **January**, selected, the Selected Index of the value is `1`. If the tenth item, **October**, is selected, the value of Selected Index is `10`. When the Items property of a Drop Down or List Box control receives a number as a parameter, it returns a string that represents the value stored. In keeping with the months comparison example, if the value `10` was provided to the Items property of a Drop Down Control, the value `October` would be returned.

By leveraging the Selected Index and Items properties of the Drop Down Control, the string value of the item selected by the end user is stored as **vFilterText** if the selected item is not the first value in the list. The `vFilterText` value is then added to the Custom Values collection of the appropriate limit on the currently active Results section, represented by **vActiveResults**. The code then adds the custom value to the Selected Values collection of the filter, and sets the `Ignore` property of the limit to `false`, which activates the limit. This script executes once for each item in `gResultsArray`.

Completing the Function

Upon completion of testing, replace the temporary `shapeName` and `sectionName` variable declarations with the declaration for the function and the opening brace at the top of the script as shown:

```
//----------- function ApplyDDFilters ------------
//--- This function will apply user selections to local results
filters from drop down Dashboard objects
function applyDDFilters(sectionName, shapeName)
{
```

Add the close brace and globalization of the declared function at the bottom of the script:

```
}
gfApplyDDFilters = applyDDFilters;
```

The code for the function in its entirety is displayed below:

```
//----------- function ApplyDDFilters ------------
//--- This function will apply user selections to local results
filters from drop down Dashboard objects
function applyDDFilters(sectionName, shapeName)
{

//Define the limit name from the shape name
var vLimitName = shapeName.substring(2);

// Is the selected the first item which denotes all values?
if (ActiveDocument.Sections[sectionName].Shapes[shapeName].
SelectedIndex == 1)
{

 //Set the limit ignore property to true to ignore the filter which
will show ALL values for all table sections
 for (var i=0; i<gResultsArray.length; i++)
 {

   //determine the vActiveResults   from the Results Array
   var vActiveResults = gResultsArray[i];

   //set the ignore property of the limit collection to true for the
active section
   ActiveDocument.Sections[vActiveResults ].Limits[vLimitName]
.Ignore=true;

 } //close loop for results array
}// close if statement reaction

else //the selected item is not the first value
{
```

```
  //Access and store selected value
  var vLimitText = ActiveDocument.Sections[sectionName].
Shapes[shapeName].Item(ActiveDocument.Sections[sectionName].
Shapes[shapeName].SelectedIndex);

  //For all table sections in the ResultsArray
  for (var i=0; i<gResultsArray.length; i++)
  {

    //Store the results array reference to the active section
    var vActiveResults = gResultsArray[i];

    //Remove all values from the custom values collection
    ActiveDocument.Sections[vActiveResults ].Limits[vLimitName].
CustomValues.RemoveAll();

    //Add the user selected value stored as vLimitText from the
Dashboard section to the Custom Values collection
    ActiveDocument.Sections[vActiveResults ].Limits[vLimitName].
CustomValues.Add(vLimitText);

    //Add all values in the Custom Values collection to the Selected
Values Collection
    ActiveDocument.Sections[vActiveResults ].Limits[vLimitName].
SelectedValues.AddAll();

    //Set the Ignore property of the filter to false to activate the
filter
    ActiveDocument.Sections[vActiveResults ].Limits[vLimitName].
Ignore=false;

  }// close the loop for results array
}// close the else conditional reaction

}
gfApplyDDFilters = applyDDFilters;
```

Applying List Box Selections to a Local Filter

While the process for assigning user-input values for a List Box Control to a local
filter is a similar process to a Drop Down Control, the List Box Control object allows
the user to select more than one contiguous or non-contiguous value.

Continuing with the BMV Executive Dashboard, add a new Text Label Graphic
shape to the Globals Dashboard section and set the **Name** property to **gf4** and the
Title to gfApplyLBFilters.

With the `gfApplyLBFilters` shape selected, open the Script Editor. If desired, add temporary variables to reference a specific shape on a specific section to test the function, as shown below:

```
//---Temporary Variables
var shapeName = "lbTerritories";
var sectionName = "Home"
```

Use the `substring()` method to define `vLimitName` from the `shapeName` variable, as shown below:

```
//Define the limit name from the shape name
var vLimitName = shapeName.substring(2);
```

With the first two characters of `shapeName` removed, the resulting variable, `vLimitName` now represents the name of the Results section limit to be modified.

Selecting All Values with a List Box

Similar to the Drop Down, the List Boxes in the example contain an option to **Select All Values**. If selected, the filter must be ignored. To determine if an end user has selected the **Select All Values** option, the code simply needs to check if the first item in the list is selected. If the first item is selected, the `Ignore` property of the filter represented by the `filterName` variable on each of the results sections must be set to `true`. By setting the property to `true`, the filter is ignored and all values are shown.

The following code demonstrates the conditional statement and steps to ignore the filter if the first entry in the List Box is selected:

```
//is the first item in the list a selection?
if (ActiveDocument.Sections[sectionName].Shapes[shapeName].
SelectedList.Item(1)==ActiveDocument.Sections[sectionName].
Shapes[shapeName].Item(1))
    {
    //Set the limit ignore property to true to ignore the filter
which will show ALL values for all table sections
    for (var i=0; i<gResultsArray.length; i++)
        {
        //Ignore filter for active results section
        var vActiveResults = gResultsArray[i];
        ActiveDocument.Sections[vActiveResults].Limits[vLimitName].
Ignore=true;
        }
    }
```

The preceding code first determines if the first item is selected by comparing the string value of the item, represented by `selectedList.Item(1)`, to the string value of the first item in the LOV, represented by `Item(1)`. If the values match, the code recognizes that the end user has chosen the first item and steps through `gResultsArray` to set the `Ignore` property of the filter to `true`.

Selecting Filters with a List Box

If the first item is not selected, then the user has selected one or more values to filter the data. For each selection, the selected value must be added to the Results filter that is represented by the `filterName` variable for each Results section represented in the `gResultsArray` variable. The following code demonstrates the steps to apply the selected List Box values to a Results section filter using JavaScript:

```
else
{
 //for all table sections
 for (var i=0; i<gResultsArray.length; i++)
 {
  //Store variable to denote active results section
  var vActiveResults = gResultsArray[i];

  //Remove all values from the custom values collection
  ActiveDocument.Sections[vActiveResults].Limits[vLimitName].
CustomValues.RemoveAll();

  //for each selection up to the total number of selections
  for (var k=1; k<=ActiveDocument.Sections[sectionName].
Shapes[shapeName].SelectedList.Count; k++)
  {
   //store the current selected value as filter text
   var vLimitText = ActiveDocument.Sections[sectionName].
Shapes[shapeName].SelectedList.Item(k);
   //Add the user selected value stored as vLimitText from the
Dashboard section to the Custom Values collection
    ActiveDocument.Sections[vActiveResults].Limits[vLimitName].
CustomValues.Add(vLimitText);
  }
  //Add all values in the Custom Values collection to the Selected
Values Collection
   ActiveDocument.Sections[vActiveResults].Limits[vLimitName].
SelectedValues.AddAll();

  //Set the Ignore property of the filter to false to activate the
filter
```

```
    ActiveDocument.Sections[vActiveResults].Limits[vLimitName].
Ignore=false;
  }
}
```

Since this code immediately follows the code used to determine if the user has selected the first item, the first statement is an `else` statement. This means the preceding code will be executed only when the first item is NOT selected. This code executes two for loops: one to iterate through the `gResultsArray` to apply the selections on all appropriate sections and the other to iterate through the items the end user selected in the List Box and add the selections to the appropriate filter.

The first part of this statement is shown in the following code snippet:

```
//for all table sections
 for (var i=0; i<gResultsArray.length; i++)
 {
   //Store variable to denote active results section
   var vActiveSection = gResultsArray[i];

   //Remove all values from the custom values collection
   ActiveDocument.Sections[vActiveSection].Limits[vLimitName
].CustomValues.RemoveAll();
```

This section of the code first stores the active Results section, defined as `gResultsArray[i]`, to the `vActiveResults` variable. This code then removes any existing custom values from the limit, represented by the `vLimitName` variable. The `CustomValues` property of the filter represents values to be limited by the filter. The user-selected values are written to the this property, so any existing values must be cleared in the event a user is revising a previous selection.

The second for loop is shown in the next code snippet. This loop steps through every value in the SelectedList collection of the List Box control and adds the string value of each collection member to the `CustomValues` property of the filter represented by `filterName`. Since the loop is contained, or nested, within the first loop, this `for` loop will be executed for every item within the first `for` loop. More specifically, the loop will run once for each section represented in `gResultArray`.

```
//for each selection up to the total number of selections
   for (var k=1; k<=ActiveDocument.Sections[sectionName].
Shapes[shapeName].SelectedList.Count; k++)
   {
     //store the current selected value as filter text
     var vLimitText = ActiveDocument.Sections[sectionName].
Shapes[shapeName].SelectedList.Item(k);
```

```
    //Add the user selected value stored as vLimitText from the
Dashboard section to the Custom Values collection
    ActiveDocument.Sections[vActiveSection].Limits[vLimitName].
CustomValues.Add(vLimitText);
    }
```

The above section section of the code uses k to increment through each of the values in the SelectedList collection one at a time. The value currently being assessed, as represented by SelectedList[k], is first stored as the vLimitText variable and then added to the CustomValues collection of the filter using the Add() method.

The final statements of the loop are as shown in the following code snippet:

```
    //Add all values in the Custom Values collection to the Selected
Values Collection
    ActiveDocument.Sections[vActiveResults].Limits[vLimitName].
SelectedValues.AddAll();

    //Set the Ignore property of the filter to false to activate the
filter
    ActiveDocument.Sections[vActiveResults].Limits[vLimitName].
Ignore=false;
```

These statements first use the AddAll() method of the filter's SelectedValues collection to select all of the values displayed in the Custom Values collection. Then, the Ignore property of the filter is set to false, to activate the filter.

Finalizing the Function

Upon successful testing of the function, replace the temporary shapeName and sectionName variable declarations with the declaration for the function as shown in the following code snippet:

```
    //----------- function ApplyLBFilters -----------
    //--- This function will apply user selections to local results
filters from drop down Dashboard objects
    function applyLBFilters(sectionName, shapeName)
    {
```

Add the close brace and globalization of the declared function at the bottom of the script:

```
    }

    gfApplyLBFilters = applyLBFilters;
```

The code for the function in its entirety is displayed below:

```
//----------- function ApplyLBFilters ------------
//--- This function will apply user selections to local results
filters from drop down Dashboard objects
function applyLBFilters(sectionName, shapeName)
{
    //is the first item in the list a selection?
   if (ActiveDocument.Sections[sectionName].Shapes[shapeName].
SelectedList.Item(1)==ActiveDocument.Sections[sectionName].
Shapes[shapeName].Item(1))
    {
        //Set the limit ignore property to true to ignore the filter
which will show ALL values for all table sections
        for (var i=0; i<gResultsArray.length; i++)
        {
            //Ignore filter for active results section
            var vActiveResults = gResultsArray[i];
            ActiveDocument.Sections[vActiveResults].Limits[vLimitName].
Ignore=true;
        }
    }
    else
    {
        //for all table sections
        for (var i=0; i<gResultsArray.length; i++)
        {
            //Ignore filter for active results section
            var vActiveResults = gResultsArray[i];

            //Remove all values from the custom values collection
            ActiveDocument.Sections[vActiveResults].Limits[vLimitName].
CustomValues.RemoveAll();

            //for each selection up to the total number of selections
            for (var k=1; k<=ActiveDocument.Sections[sectionName].
Shapes[shapeName].SelectedList.Count; k++)
            {
                //store the current selected value as filter text
                var vLimitText = ActiveDocument.Sections[sectionName].
Shapes[shapeName].SelectedList.Item(k);
                //Add the user selected value stored as vLimitText from
the Dashboard section to the Custom Values collection
                ActiveDocument.Sections[vActiveResults].
Limits[vLimitName].CustomValues.Add(vLimitText);
            }
```

```
        //Add all values in the Custom Values collection to the
Selected Values Collection
        ActiveDocument.Sections[vActiveResults].Limits[vLimitName].
SelectedValues.AddAll();

        //Set the Ignore property of the filter to false to activate
the filter
        ActiveDocument.Sections[vActiveResults].Limits[vLimitName].
Ignore=false;
      }
    }
}
gfApplyDDFilters = applyDDFilters;
```

Calling Functions with a Function

The final function used to apply filters from Drop Down and List Box Controls on a dashboard is the function called directly by the **Apply** button from the dashboard. This function simply determines the shape type of each filter being assessed and determines whether to call the gfApplyDDFilters function or the gfApplyLBFilters function.

To script this function, add a new Text Label Graphic to the Globals Dashboard section. Set the **Name** property to **gf5** and the **Title** to gfApplyFilters. The JavaScript for this shape is shown in the following code snippet:

```
//------------ function ApplyFilters ------------
//---  This function calls the ApplyFilters functions after the shape
type has been determined
function applyFilters(sectionName, shapeName)
{
    //---Determine shape type by using 2 character shape prefix
    var vShapeType = shapeName.substring(0,2);

    // Is the shape a drop down object?
    if (vShapeType == "dd")
    {
      // Call the gfApplyDDFilters function
      gfApplyDDFilters(sectionName, shapeName)
    }
    // Is the shape a list box object?
    else if(vShapeType == "lb")
    {
      // Call the gfApplyLBFilters function
      gfApplyLBFilters(sectionName, shapeName)
    }
```

```
}
// make the function globally accessible
gfApplyFilters = applyFilters;
```

This function first uses `substring` to determine the first two characters of the shape name. If the recommended naming convention is used, the resulting value is either `dd` or `lb`. The function then uses conditional logic to determine if the resulting two character value, represented as `vShapeType`, is `dd` or `lb`. Depending on the result, the `gfApplyDDFilters` or the `gfApplyLBFilters` function is called appropriately.

Set the Function to the Dashboard Filter Object

When a user has finished making selections, the user clicks on the **Apply** button to set the event in motion, which applies the selections to the filters. The code required to call the main function, the `gfApplyFilters` function, is placed in the `onClick` event trigger of the **Apply** button. The call to the function must be made for each filter to be applied and the `sectionName` and `shapeName` parameters must be supplied. The following code demonstrates calling the `gfApplyFitlers` function for each of the items to be filtered when the user clicks on the **Apply** button on a Dashboard section:

```
// Call the Apply Filter global function for each of the filters to be
applied
// Add the Region Selection
gfApplyFilters(ActiveSection.Name, "ddRegion");

// Add the Territory Selection
gfApplyFilters(ActiveSection.Name, "lbTerritory");

// Add the Country Selection
gfApplyFilters(ActiveSection.Name, "lbCountry");

// Add the State Selection
gfApplyFilters(ActiveSection.Name, "lbState");

// Add the City Selection
gfApplyFilters(ActiveSection.Name, "lbCity");
```

The value `ActiveSection.Name`, which denotes the Name property of the current section, and the string value of the Shape the user selections have made are passed as the expected `sectionName` and `shapeName` parameters.

Synchronizing User Selections across Multiple Dashboards

Synchronizing user selections across Dashboard sections is completed by taking the user selections on one section and applying the selections across all of the Dashboard sections in the document. While the there are many approaches that can be used to execute the synchronization, this section demonstrates one efficient and effective procedure for keeping List Box object selections in sync across multiple dashboards.

The first step in executing the synchronization is to unselect any prior selections for the control across all Dashboard sections. With this approach, of the Controls are now consistent across the sections and are ready for the adding of filter selections. The second step to keeping the filters consistent across the dashboard is to obtain the selected values from one particular dashboard and propagate the selections to consistent controls in the other dashboards.

Synchronizing List Box Controls

The List Box is one the most common Controls used for filtering on a dashboard. List Boxes are more complicated than many other Controls, due to the need to keep track of multiple selections that can be made inside the Control. This section of the chapter provides an in-depth view of the code necessary to keep List Boxes synchronized between Dashboard sections. While the chapter does not detail similar steps for Drop Down Controls, the approach and code displayed in this chapter can be easily modified to perform Drop Down Control synchronization.

The first step in synchronizing a List Box Control across multiple Dashboard sections is to make sure that the number of available values and the order in which the available values are stored is identical across the Dashboard sections. Any mismatch in the number or order of the values displayed in the List Box Controls will display a flawed result when the synchronizing functions are executed.

Similar to the other global JavaScript functions discussed in this chapter, the functions used to synchronize List Box Control selections must be declared during the document start-up processes to become globally available. Add a Text Label to the Globals Dashboard section to leverage the Dashboard Framework staged in *Chapter 5, Building the Dashboard Framework*. Set the name property to gf5 and the title property to gfSyncLBFilters. The three functions, gfUnselect, gfSetBox, and gfSyncLBFilters will all be tied to the OnClick event trigger of this Text Label.

Unselecting Values

To ensure that the synchronization functions apply consistent values on execution, unselect all of the values from any correlated List Box Controls across the Dashboard sections. While selected values can be compared from one dashboard to another for matches, it is far easier to program and more efficient to simply unselect all the objects that are synced. This function will be called only when the filters change, so it makes sense to baseline all of the values in the List Box Controls across dashboard sections.

When working with List Box Controls, there is no method to remove all of the selected values from the Selected collection in a single command. With this limitation, a `for` loop must be used to step through all the values in the List Box and unselect one value at a time. The following code demonstrates the removal of the selected items from a List Box on a dashboard:

```
//--------- function Unselect ---------
//--- This function unselects all shape selections
function unselect(sectionName, shapeName)
{
   for (var i=1; i<=ActiveDocument.Sections[sectionName].
Shapes[shapeName].Count; i++)
   {
       ActiveDocument.Sections[sectionName].Shapes[shapeName].
Unselect(i)
   }
}gfUnselect = unselect;
```

The first line of the `unselect` function uses a `for` loop, which steps through the full list of values in the List Box Control. As each item is encountered, the `unselect()` method is used to unselect each item from the List Box where `i` is the index or numeric value of the items in the List Box.

The `unselect` function also accepts the `sectionName` and `shapeName` parameters, allowing report authors to use this function to unselect the values of any List Box Control on any Dashboard section.

Selecting Values

Once the values in the List Box are unselected, the new filters are ready to be added to each Dashboard section. The approach used to setting the filters in the function below is a bit different than the steps to set the selected values in a simple dashboard. The following function takes two arguments, the first for the name of the shape on the dashboard and the second for the position number or index of the item in the selected list for the selection.

```
function setBox(shapeName,numList)
{
    for (var k=0; k<gDashboardArray.length; k++)
    {
        var vSectionName = gDashboardArray[k];
        ActiveDocument.Sections[vSectionName].Shapes[shapeName].
Select(numList)
    }
}
gfSetBox=setBox;
```

While the function in the previous section looped through all of the values in a single List Box and unselected each item, the `select` function loops through all of the Dashboard sections and applies the selected values to each specified List Box on each dashboard. The first line in the function is a loop that is used to enumerate through all the Dashboard sections that are specified in the dashboard array. Notice that the `for` loop in this function starts with a value of `k=0`. Also notice that the next argument in the `for` loop for specifying the number of iterations has the syntax of `gDashboardArray.length`, where the `length` syntax is a property of an array and is used to provide the number of entries in the array.

Synchronizing Selections

The final step is building a synchronization function to serve as the single function called to execute all of the processing for the synchronization, where all the operations and other dependent functions are referenced and the items executed. The following function references the previous functions for selecting and unselecting values while providing the additional processing necessary to provide the arguments to both functions:

```
function syncLBFilters(sectionName, shapeName)
{
    var itemCount = ActiveDocument.Sections[sectionName].
Shapes[shapeName].SelectedList.Count;
    for (var i=0; i<gDashboardArray.length; i++)
```

```
    {
        var vSectionName = gDashboardArray[i];
        if (vSectionName != sectionName)
        {
            gfUnselect(shapeName, vSectionName);
        }
    }
    for (var i=1; i<= itemCount; i++)
    {
        var index = ActiveDocument.Sections[sectionName].
Shapes[shapeName].SelectedList.ItemIndex(i);
        gfSetBox(index, shapeName)
    }
}
gfSyncLBFilters=syncLBFilters;
```

The function above takes two arguments similar to the other two functions, where the name of the shape or Control and the section name are passed in. The first line of the function creates a variable `itemCount` and sets the value to the number of selected items in the List Box of the Dashboard section. The names of the List Boxes and Dashboard section are provided in the arguments of the function. This `itemCount` variable now holds the total number of selections that need to be made in each List Box for each dashboard. The second line of the function specifies a `for` loop to unselect all of the selected items in every Dashboard section in the document, taking into account logic to skip the section that was provided in the argument of the function, to make sure that the filters made on a specific Dashboard sections are retained after the unselect has occurred. The implementation of this logic is demonstrated in the fourth and fifth line of the function, where a new variable `vSectionName` is set to the name of the section currently selected by the loop through the array, as demonstrated by the code `var vSectionName = gDashboardArray[i]`. The fifth line of the function then compares the section provided in the argument of the function to the section that is currently set during the loop. If the section names do not match, then the function is allowed to continue and the final step is to call the `Unselect` function with the name of the control or shape and the section name as arguments. Once all of the sections in the Dashboard array are looped through, all list boxes in the document across all Dashboard sections will contain no selected values, except for the one where the user made the filtering selections in the first place.

Once all of the List Boxes are unselected, the next step is to populate all of the List Boxes throughout the document with the values selected by the user on the filtered Dashboard section. Line 11 of the preceding function contains a `for` loop that loops from one through the total number of selected items in the List Box. This loop does not specify the actual index or number of the particular items that are selected, but rather just specifies the total count of items. The next line of code begins with setting the variable `index` to the numerical position of the selected item in the list box where the user filtered. The statement is executed through using the `SelectedList.ItemIndex(i)` code, which provides the numerical position of the selected item for a value in the List Box. In the code, this is denoted by the variable `i`, which is assigned its value from the `for` loop and is configured to iterate through the total selected items in the List Box. The final step in the function is to call the `Selection` function and set the selected item from the filtered List Box to all of the other Dashboard sections, where the index of the item to select in the List Box as well as the section name is provided to the `Selection` function as an argument. Once the loop has completed iterating through the total selected items in the filtered List Box, the function completes and the list boxes across Dashboard sections are synchronized.

Calling the Functions

With the supporting functions in place, the `gfSyncLBFilters` function must be called using JavaScript. The function is called using `gfSyncLBFilters(shapeName, sectionName)`. This code is only called during a user-driven event, such as a button click, and is always the last step of the filter application process.

With regards to the BMV Executive Dashboard example, this function is called from within the `gfApplyFilters` global function located on the Globals Dashboard:

```
//------------ function ApplyFilters ------------
//--- This function calls the ApplyFilters functions after the shape
type has been determined
function applyFilters(sectionName, shapeName)
{
   //---Determine shape type by using 2 character shape prefix
   var vShapeType = shapeName.substring(0,2);
   // Is the shape a drop down object?
   if (vShapeType == "dd")
   {
     // Call the gfApplyDDFilters function
     gfApplyDDFilters(sectionName, shapeName);
```

```
    }
    // Is the shape a list box object?
    else if(vShapeType == "lb")
    {
        // Call the gfApplyLBFilters function
        gfApplyLBFilters(sectionName, shapeName);

        // Call the gfSyncLBFilters function
        gfSyncLBFilters(sectionName, shapeName);
    }
}
// make the function globally accessible
gfApplyFilters = applyFilters;
```

In the preceding example, shapeName and sectionName are the same sectionName
and shapeName variables received by the gfApplyFilters global function. Since
the gfSyncLBFilters function is called only when the script has determined if the
shape is a List Box shape, this function is only executed for List Box objects.

Summary

The goal of this chapter was to introduce and demonstrate an approach to add
filtering options to a dashboard, the steps to filter data based on user selections,
and the methods for populating filters across dashboard pages. The chapter began
with the steps to populate Dashboard section Controls with values from a database.
The method of using available values is introduced and the approach to loading all
of the dashboard filters from a single Results section is demonstrated. The chapter
continues with an overview of the steps to add user-selected filters to the data
sections of an Interactive Reporting document to filter dashboard content from Drop
Down and List Box Controls. The method to select all filter values was presented
as was the positioning of code within the Dashboard section and Dashboard
Framework. The chapter concludes with the advanced steps to synchronize
dashboard filter selections across multiple dashboards. Each section of the chapter
included information to add the code to the Dashboard Framework, and the chapter
along with the previous three chapters provide a solid foundation for building
advanced dashboards.

7
Advanced Data Analysis

One of the key aspects of business intelligence is the ability to analyse and manipulate content for reporting or to gain insight into data. Many business users prefer to use Microsoft Excel to perform data analysis due to their comfort with the software. While Microsoft Excel provides many excellent tools for performing data analysis, Interactive Reporting provides very strong data analysis capabilities including the ability to filter, add computations, leverage data sets, build functions, leverage variables, and manipulate millions of records.

While many business intelligence products on the market today provide the ability to perform analysis, some of these tools are limited in their ability to handle the number of records that Interactive Reporting can handle, thanks to the browser-based Interactive Reporting Web Client. While the Web Client plug-in introduces additional overhead in managing the software throughout the enterprise, it provides the ability to quickly perform analysis on a large set of information. The goal of this chapter is to provide an in-depth explanation of the options available in Interactive Reporting for manipulating data throughout the document.

This content in this chapter covers the following analysis topics:

- Building Queries for Analysis
- Computed Items
- Leveraging Built-in Functions and Calculations
- Using JavaScript

Building Queries for Analysis

Data analysis in Interactive Reporting starts with the configuration of the query. Since Interactive Reporting provides the user with flexibility to perform manipulations on the data returned to the document, the user building the query must determine the level of detail, filtering, and manipulation to apply before the results are returned from the database. While this sounds trivial, there are reasons for building a simpler query and retrieving more data into the Results section than needed for analysis. When making decisions on building queries, query performance as well as data volume must be taken into account when designing the query. The best practice approach to determining the best query design is to find the most efficient balance between the data volume (taking into account the level of detail needed for analysis) and query speed. Since Interactive Reporting provides the ability to effectively filter and perform computations on data after it is returned from the query on the local machine, it is important to identify the filters needed on the query and the filters that can be performed on the data results.

Interactive Reporting contains many presentation sections of the document where data returned from the query is manipulated and presented to the user. In these sections, sorting, filtering, and leveraging custom computations can be used in concert along with other sections to transform and prepare reports. The following sections of this chapter walk through the common data manipulation procedures available in Interactive Reporting.

Computed Items

Once the query is configured and data is returned into the Results section, the user has the ability to leverage the standard features of the Results section for filtering, grouping, totalling, and sorting. The user can also leverage a feature called **Computed Items**, introduced in *Chapter 1, Advanced Hyperion Interactive Reporting Techniques*, to perform custom computations using the set of results. These custom computations provide the ability to manipulate, calculate, enhance, and build filter criteria into the data results. While the ability exists to leverage custom computations in the Query section, Computed Items in the other Interactive Reporting sections provide additional flexibility that is helpful when conducting analysis.

Building Advanced Computed Items

When adding Computed Items to a document, the Computed Item window appears as shown in the screenshot below. *Note: The Computed Item window is used in every section except for the Report section, which contains its own section specific Computed Item window. Report section Computed Items are described later in this chapter.*

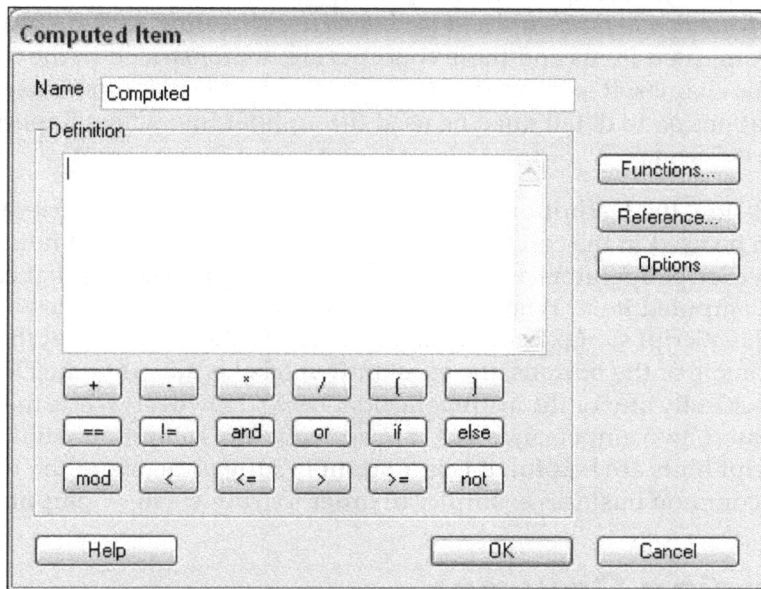

The text box at the top of the window is used to set the name of the Computed Item, which will become the name of the column in the section. The name of the Computed Item must be unique to the section. If another Computed Item exists with the same name, the name of the new item is automatically appended with a numerical value to ensure uniqueness. For example, if a column named Total Sales exists and a Computed Item is added to the section with the name Total Sales, Interactive Reporting will use the name Total Sales2 as the column name. To overcome the automatic addition to the name, blank spaces can be added after the name of the column allowing more than one column to display the same name. While the names will appear the same, it is important to note that the new column is referenced with an _ for each space added. In this case, the Totals Sales column with one space after the column name will appear as Total_Sales_ as the actual column reference.

Building the Definition using JavaScript

The **Definition** text box is the location for entering the logic for the Computed Item. All Computed Items leverage one or a combination of built-in functions, data columns, and JavaScript to construct a Computed Item. *Chapter 2, Introduction to JavaScript and the Interactive Reporting API*, provides an overview to logical programming with JavaScript in Interactive Reporting. The concepts described in *Chapter 2, Introduction to JavaScript and the Interactive Reporting API*, are heavily used in creating Computed Items and these concepts are demonstrated in the following sections of this chapter. It is important to note again that JavaScript is **case sensitive** and specific attention to detail must be used throughout Interactive Reporting when leveraging JavaScript.

The buttons below the **Definition** text box are resources to assist the user with the logic that can be used in the column definition. It is important to first note that the displayed JavaScript operators are not the only JavaScript operators that can be used in the Computed Item. When an operator button is pressed in the window, the appropriate JavaScript syntax is inserted into the Definition window at the cursor location. For some of the buttons, the exact button label is added to the Definition window (specifically any of the arithmetic operators). However, when the **and** button is pressed, two ampersands (&&) are added to the Definition window. While these JavaScript hints are helpful, it is important to fully understand the use of these operators in common business examples in order to truly master Computed Items.

Referencing Columns

A column (data element) from the section can be typed into the Definition window or the user can leverage the **Reference** button to the right of the Definition box. It is important to note that the name of the column used in a definition may be different than the name of the column in the section. The Definition window requires that a column name not contain spaces or special characters when used in Computed Items so an underscore (_) is used in the place of either a space or a special character when referencing a column name. It is important to note that the column names are case-sensitive and an error will occur if the data element name is not entered properly.

While the reference to a column name could be typed directly into the Definition box, the Reference button is especially helpful when selecting a long column name or when attempting to reference a column with special characters in the column name. When the Reference button is pressed, a **Reference** window appears allowing the user to select the item to insert into the **Definition** window. Upon selecting the column and pressing the **OK** button, the column name will appear in the Definition window at the point of the cursor location.

Functions

Interactive Reporting comes with a number of built-in functions to support data analysis and manipulation. These functions are similar to functions found in Excel and databases and can be used in concert with JavaScript enhance content displayed in the software. Functions are either typed into the **Definition** window or the user can leverage the **Functions** button on the right of the Computed Item window. When the **Functions** button is pressed, the **Functions** window appears as shown in the following screenshot:

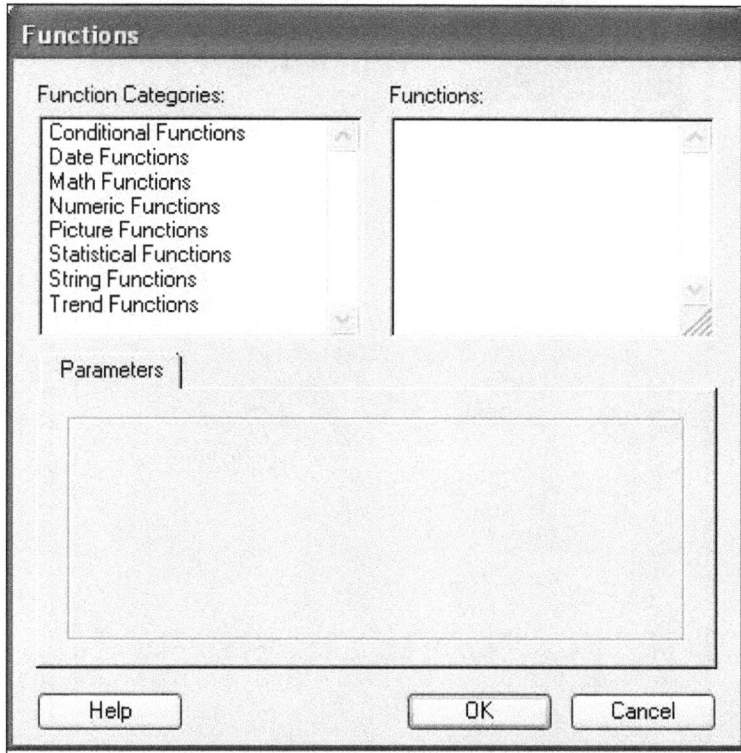

Since a large number of functions exist, the functions are segmented into several categories by function type. Upon pressing one of the **Function Categories**, the **Functions** window is populated with the functions available in the selected category. Upon selecting one of the functions, the parameter segment of the window becomes populated with a brief description of the function and the required and optional arguments. The following screenshot displays the **Functions** window open to the **Date Functions** category with the **ToChar** function selected.

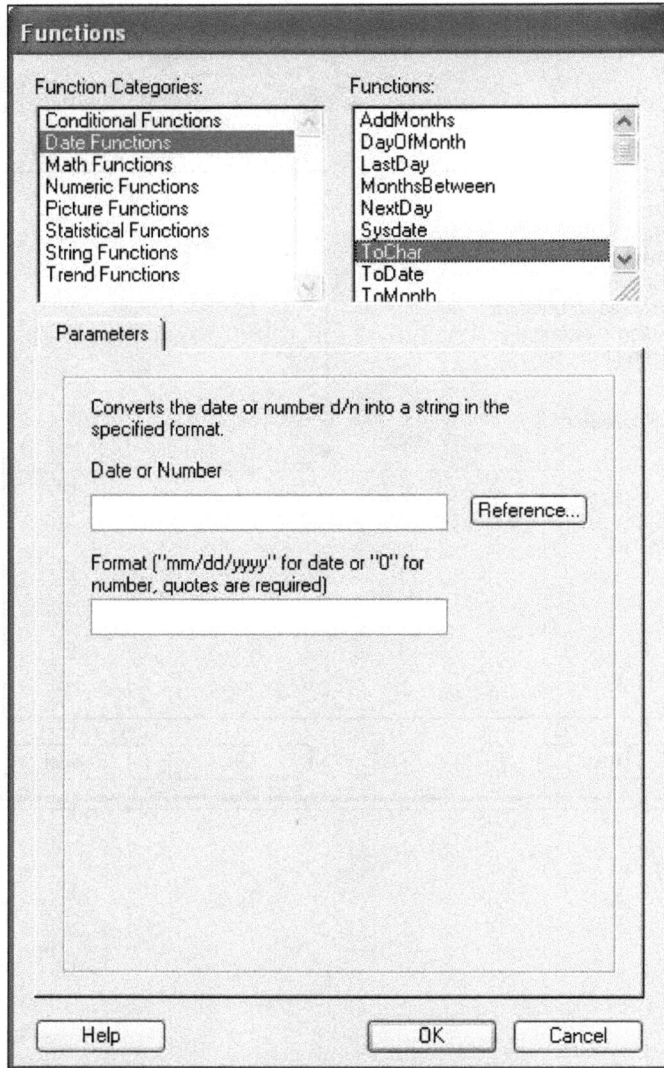

The required and optional parameters may allow for the use of data elements (columns), text, or specific formatting information. When a data element is a possible argument value, the **Reference** button is provided next to the input box to allow the user to easily insert a column name into the specific argument. In the example above, the **ToChar** function allows for a date or number as the primary argument and the format to display the data as the second argument.

Function Formatting Arguments

Formatting functions and custom Computed Items in Interactive Reporting requires the user to enter specific text to provide instructions for formatting a set of data. These instructions are specific to Interactive Reporting and the instructions must be accurately specified for the function to correctly translate the data. Format instructions are predefined and the easiest place to locate many of these instructions is the **Number Format** menu, which provides the syntax and many examples of different formatting types. Right-clicking on a column in a section and selecting the **Number** menu item will open a **Properties** menu, providing the **Number** formatting options for the column. The **Number Properties** window is shown in the following screenshot:

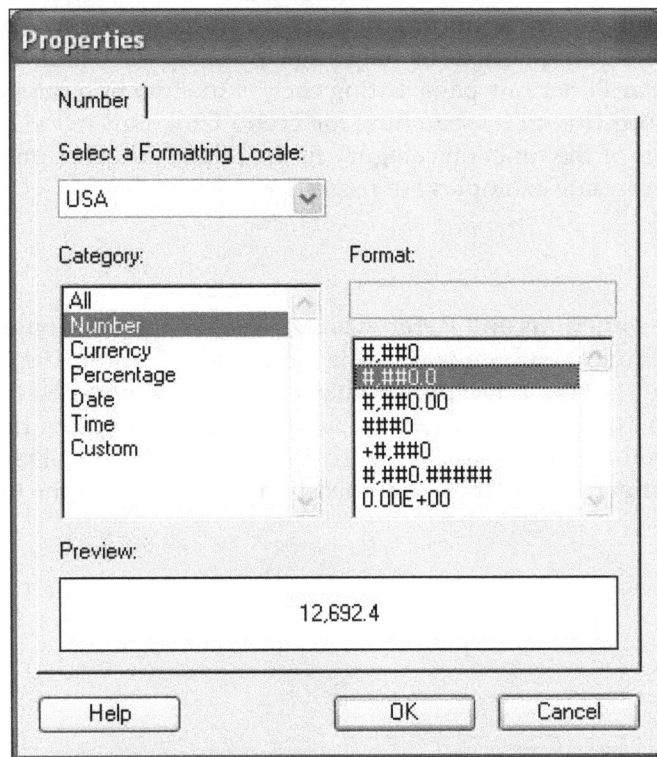

The formatting options are grouped into categories by formatting type, including **Number, Currency, Percentage, Date,** and **Time.** Clicking on the category will provide a list of standard formatting options available for each category. When clicking on one of the formatting options, the **Preview** window will update to demonstrate the formatting option selected. The syntax displayed in the **Formatting** window can be used in the software where formatting is required. For example, using the formatting #,##0.0 in a Computed Item provides a number with a comma after every third character and one number after the decimal. Similarly, using the formatting mmmm dd, yyyy in the **ToChar** function will convert a date into a string with a full month name, two-digit day, a comma, and a four-digit year. The formatting window only lists the common formatting types but custom combinations of the formatting syntax can be utilized to create a desired format. Using custom combinations is very common and provides the ability to transform data into a wide variety of formats.

Additional Help

While the documentation provided in the parameter area of the **Functions** window is brief, the **Help** button at the bottom left of the screen can be clicked to obtain additional documentation on each function contained in the software. Upon pressing the **Help** button, Interactive Reporting will open a web browser to a page on using functions. From the **Using Functions** help page, pressing the **Scalar Functions** link will open the **Scalar Functions** page, listing each of the function categories for all but the **Trend Functions** (found by searching for Trend Functions in the Help material). Upon pressing one of the function category links, a detailed description of each function and appropriate examples are presented.

Options

In addition to the **Functions** and **Reference** buttons, the final button on the right-hand side of the Computed Item window is the **Options** button. The **Options** button provides the ability to select the specific datatype for the Computed Item. This option allows the user to override the **Automatic** datatype selection, providing the ability to select the desired data definition for the column from the Drop-Down menu. The following screenshot displays the Computed Item window with the **Options** feature open.

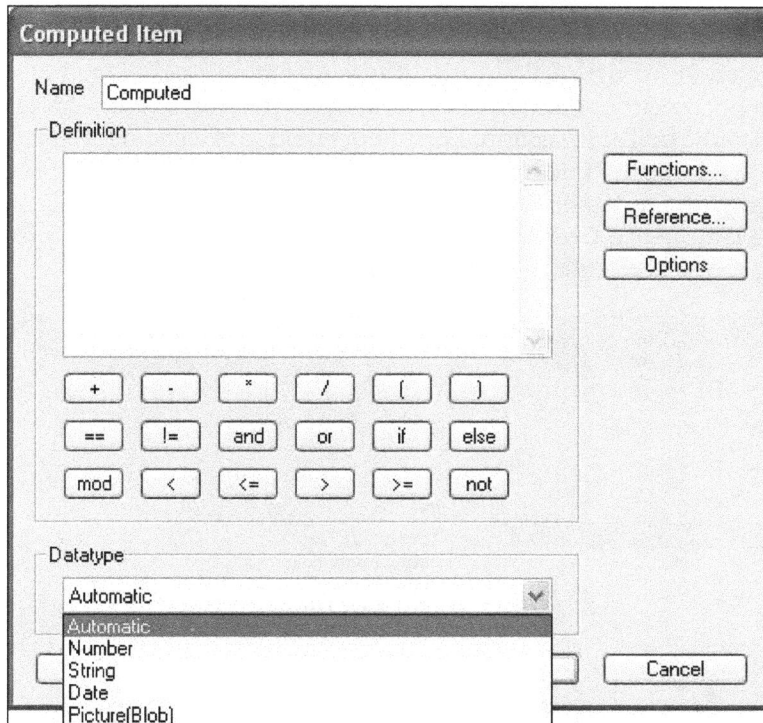

Deleting Computed Items

Computed Items are deleted from each section by highlighting the column and pressing the DEL key or by selecting one of the **Remove** menu items from the section-specific menus or right-click menu. If the column is not referenced by another column or section in the document, the Computed Item will be removed without a warning message. If the column is referenced in another section or if the column contains a dependency with another column, an alert will appear alerting the user to the section or other Computed Item dependency and will prompt the user to accept the desired change.

Report section Computed Items

Computed Items in Report sections are different from other sections of the document. Report sections contain objects called Report Tables that display data similar to a Results or Table section. Each Report Table is a separate object inside the section and each Report Table may contain a unique set of Computer Items which are not shared with any other Report Table in the report. The following screenshot provides an example of a Computed Item inside a Report Table. In this example, the Advertising Expenses Column is divided by 1000.

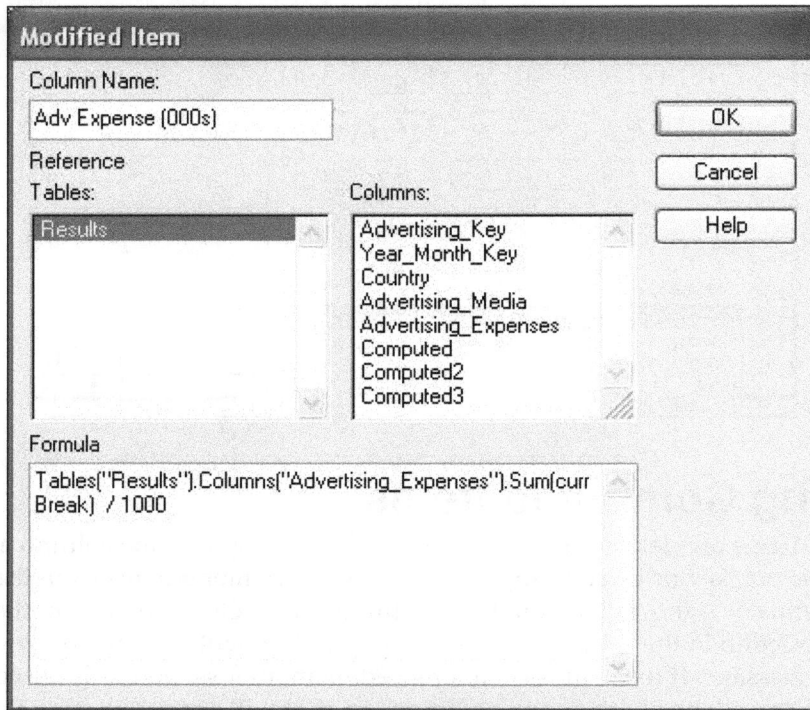

Computed Items in a Report section provide the ability to combine elements across multiple Results and Table sections. Each expression references the section of the document, the column, and finally the data function to use on the item of data. Notice the final value assigned in the data function is the word currBreak. The currBreak identifier is used by Interactive Reporting to identify the level of detail to split out the data in the report, where the Break value is determined by the location of the table within the section (whether the table is located within the Body or inside a Report Group causing data aggregation).

Built-in Functions and Calculations

While most users creating a Computed Items will choose to leverage the built-in Interactive Reporting functions to write calculations, it is important to completely understand the functionality provided within each built-in function. Once fully understood, the functions provide the gateway for building computations, filtering data, and preparing data for other presentation sections. The following content in this section breaks down each built-in function and provides examples of commonly used functions.

Conditional Functions

Conditional Functions in Interactive Reporting are specific to replacing content of a field based on a set of conditions. There are only two functions that exist in the Conditional Function grouping. The functions are **Nvl** and **Decode**. The **Nvl** function is used to replace null values with a defined value. The first argument of the function is the column of data and the second argument is the replacement string. `Nvl(PRODUCTS, "No Product Name")` will yield the result `No Product Name` in the Products field of the results set for each null value.

The **Decode** function is used to replace a value in a field with a different value. The Decode function takes a minimum of three arguments. The first argument in the function is the data column, the second is the value identified for replacement, and the third is the value to use for replacement. The second and third arguments may be repeated for as many values as desired. A final argument may be included to serve as the default value for all items that are not defined for replacement. If the final column is omitted, the values in the column not identified for replacement will be blank. To resolve the columns from showing blank, the field used in the first argument can be specified as the final argument to populate all of the values in the column not identified for replacement with the initial value. The example, `Decode(Calendar_Month_Number, '01', 'January', '02', 'February', '03', 'March', 'Other')` will yield the result `January` for all instances of `01`, `February` for all instances of `02`, `March` for all instances of `03` and `Other` for any other values outside of `01`, `02`, or `03`.

Date Manipulation

Interactive Reporting provides a set of **Date Functions** that can be used to manipulate date and time values. While Interactive Reporting provides a large number of date manipulation functions, a number of commercial database products provide a more robust set of tools for manipulating dates. Before attempting complex date computations in Interactive Reporting, try to identify if the relational database containing the data has functions to manipulate date and time values.

Current Date & Time

One of the most popular date functions is **Sysdate**. Sysdate provides the current date and time and is commonly used to obtain the days between a set date and the current date and time.

Adding Time

The **AddMonths** function is used to add or subtract time from a date. This function takes two arguments, where the first argument is the date to adjust and the second argument is the number of months to add or subtract. This function is very useful and is commonly used to convert calendar dates to fiscal dates. For example, AddMonths("01/01/2008", 3) yields the result 04/01/2008. Entering a negative date subtracts time from the entered date. For example, AddMonths("01/01/2008", -3) yields the result 10/01/2007.

Identifying Specific Days

Three functions exist in Interactive Reporting for identifying a specific day from a date. The **DayOfMonth** function takes a single argument and provides the day of the month. For example, DayOfMonth("01/15/2008") yields the result 15. The **LastDay** function takes a single argument and provides the last day of the month for the date provided, and the function also takes into account leap years. For example, LastDay("02/12/2008") yields the result 29. The **NextDay** function takes two arguments and provides the next occurrence of the day of the week specified in the second argument. For example, NextDay("01/01/2008", "Monday") yields the result 01/07/2008.

Date Conversion

Dates are commonly converted to character strings in various formats for presentation. The most common function for date conversion is the **ToChar** function. This function takes two arguments, where the first argument is the date to convert and the second argument is the format to display the date. For example, `ToChar("01/01/2008", "mmm")` yields the result `Jan`. The inverse of the ToChar function is the **ToDate** function, which provides the user with the ability to convert a character string into a date. The ToDate function in Interactive Reporting takes only a single argument, which is the string to convert. After transformation, the character string will display and behave as a date in the document.

Three other date conversion functions exist for converting a date. The functions **ToMonth**, **ToQtr**, and **ToYear** take a single argument and convert the specified value into a month, quarter, or year respectively.

Leveraging Mathematical Operations with Dates

Dates, similar to numbers, can be manipulated using math operators. Date fields are commonly subtracted to determine the time between two dates and date fields are commonly manipulated by adding or subtracting values from the date to obtain a desired value. For example, the addition of 1 to a date field adds a single day to the date. The subtraction of `"01/15/2008"` and `"01/10/2008"` yields the result `5`, and the function MonthsBetween calculates the number of months between two dates. For example, `MonthsBetween("01/15/2008", "04/10/2008")` yields the result `2.83871`.

Mathematical Operations

Interactive Reporting provides built-in **Math Functions** for performing manipulations on numbers. Commonly used functions such as Abs, Ceil, Floor, Mod, Max, Min, and Sign can be nested and leveraged inside other functions in order to facilitate the appropriate manipulation of numbers into the document. The following provides information on each of the common functions:

- The **Abs** function applies an absolute value calculation on the value in a column, which is used to convert negative numbers into positive numbers. The function takes a single argument and is commonly used in calculations where a positive number difference between two numbers must be calculated. For example, he `Abs(-1)` will return the value `1`.

- The **Ceil** function takes a single argument and rounds the number **up** to the nearest whole number. The function is commonly used in date calculations to round fractions of a date to the next day. The `Ceil(2.781)` returns the value 3.

- The **Floor** function takes a single argument and rounds the number **down** to the nearest whole number. This function is used to round fractions of any value down. The `Floor(2.781)` returns the value 2.

- The **Mod** function takes two arguments and performs a modulus calculation, returning the remainder produced when the first argument is divided by the second. The modulus function is very powerful and can be used to segment data and identify numbers that divide evenly, in addition to many other operations. The `Mod(10,2)` returns the value 0 and the `Mod(10,4)` returns the value 2.

- The **Max** function takes two arguments and returns the maximum of the two values. The `Max(2,5)` returns the value 5.

- The **Min** function takes two arguments and returns the minimum of the two values. The `Min(2.5)` returns the value 2.

- The **Round** function takes two arguments and returns the first value rounded to the decimal place specified in the second argument. The `Round(5.63,1)` returns the value 5.6 and `Round(5.63,0)` returns the value 6.

- The **Sign** function takes a single argument and is used to determine whether a value is positive, negative, or zero. The Sign function returns a -1 if the value is less than zero, a 1 if the value is greater than zero, or a 0 if the value is equal to zero. The `Sign(-5)` returns the value -1.

There are many other math functions in addition to the ones identified in the section above. These math functions are very common to basic math operations and range from leveraging exponents, logarithms, and trigonometric functions.

Numeric Operations

Interactive Reporting separates a number of functions from the math category into a category called **Numeric Functions**. Unlike the math functions, which only allow the user to look at one value at a time, the numeric functions provide the user with the ability to perform a calculation across a set of data in the results. For example, the **Sum** function can be used to calculate a total from the sum of numbers in a column. Most functions in the Numeric Functions section also provide the user with the ability to **break** on a column. The break feature allows the function to look at subsets of the dataset, providing the user with the ability to calculate multiple sub-computations across the set of results. The following provides an overview of each Numeric function:

- The **Avg** and **AvgNonNull** functions are used to calculate the average across a column of data, where the **AvgNonNull** function excludes the null values in the column. The **Avg** and **AvgNonNull** functions allow for the addition of a break column or value.

- The **ColMax** and **ColMin** functions are used to select the maximum or minimum value across a column of values. The **ColMax** and **ColMin** functions allow for the addition of a break column or value.

- The **Count**, **CountDistinct**, **CountNonNull**, and **CountNull** functions are used to perform counting operations across a column of values. The counting functions allow for the addition of a break column or value. The **Count** function counts all of the values inside the column, including repeats and null values. The **CountDistinct** counts each distinct value as only one item in the count calculation. The **CountNonNull** function counts all of the values in a column with the exception of the null values. The **CountNull** function counts all of the null values in a column of data.

- The **Sum** function provides the ability to create a summation of all of the values in a column of data. The **Sum** function allows for the addition of a break column or value.

- The **Cume** function provides the ability to create a cumulative summation across the values in the column. When creating a cumulative summation, sorting is necessary to align the data in the order to perform the calculation. The **Cume** function allows for the addition of a break column.

- The **Next** and **Prior** functions provide the ability to grab the value of data before (**Prior**) or after (**Next**) a value in a column. These functions are very useful when determining whether or not there are duplicate values across a column and are commonly used with section sorting. The **Next** and **Prior** functions take a single argument and do not allow for any break columns or values. These functions are commonly used with conditional logic to flag repeats in a data set, such as a key identifier. When using the syntax if(Prior(COL) == COL) {1} else {0} in a Computed Item, where COL is a column of data and the data results are sorted by COL, a 1 will be displayed for every repeating value in the column COL.

- The **Chr** function is very different than the other functions in the section where it takes an ASCII value for the argument and returns the character value associated with the supplied ASCII value.

It is important to note that Numeric functions, also referred to as **aggregate functions,** produce a result based on a set of values within the section instead of a single value. Since the calculation spans the entire set of data, Computed Item columns containing Numeric functions cannot be filtered directly in the section where the function is calculated. Attempting to filter on an aggregate function will produce the error message shown in the following screenshot:

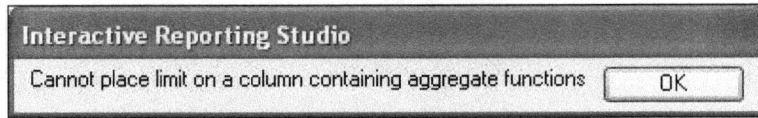

Interactive Reporting Studio

Cannot place limit on a column containing aggregate functions   OK

To overcome the error, a Table section can be added to the document and the field containing the aggregate calculation can be filtered in the new section. This feature is especially important as Computed Item fields with aggregate functions are used to create flags for filtering a set of results.

Note: The Next, Prior, and Cume functions are not available for use in the Pivot section.

String Manipulation

Interactive Reporting provides **String Functions** to perform   string manipulations and translations such as changing the case of a string or trimming characters from a string. The following is an overview of the String Functions available in Interactive Reporting:

- The **Concat** function takes two arguments and concatenates the two string values provided together. The Concat("A", "BC") returns the result ABC. Note: Strings in Computed Items can also be concatenated using the + operator, which is also demonstrated in JavaScript in earlier chapters of the book.

- The **Initcap** function takes a single argument and sets the first letter in each word of the string to uppercase and all other letters in the word to lowercase. This function is especially useful with name fields as the function Initcap("firstname lastname") returns the result Firstname Lastname.

- The **Lower** and **Upper** functions take a single argument and are used to change a string to all lowercase letters or all uppercase letters. The Lower("Name") returns the result name and the Upper("Name") yields the result NAME.

- The **Ltrim** and **Rtrim** functions expect two arguments and are used to trim off a set of characters from the left or right of the string. The functions are commonly used to trim the white space from the left or right of a value. When trimming the white space, the second argument in the function can be omitted. The `Rtrim("value    ")` returns the result of `value` without any spaces.

- The **Substr** function is used to create a subset of a string from a string value. The function takes three arguments, where the first argument is for the value of the whole string, the second argument is for the starting position to begin the substring, and the third argument determines the length of the substring. The `Substr("First Last", 1, 5)` returns the result `First`. String properties, such as length, can also be combined with the substring function to dynamically calculate the starting position and/or number of characters to for the substring.

- The **Length** function takes a single argument, which is the string to be evaluated, and is used to identify the number of characters within the supplied string. For example, the statement `Length("Test")` yields the result `4`.

- The **Instr** function expects four arguments and is used test for the existence of a value within the supplied string. The Instr function returns the numeric position of the value in the tested string. The first argument in the Instr function is the string value, the second argument is for the value to identify, the third argument is the starting position for where to start searching in the string, and the fourth argument is used to select the occurrence of the value in the string. A simple demonstration of the Instr function is `Instr("test", "s", 1, 1)` which returns the result `3`. In the example, the Instr function is looking for the first occurrence of the letter `s` in the string starting from the first character of the string.

- The **Replace** function is used to replace a set of characters in the string with a new set of characters. This function takes three arguments: the first argument is the string, the second argument is a set of characters to find in the string to replace, and the third argument is the set of replacement characters to put into the string. `Replace("string", "st", "b")` returns the result `bring`.

- Similar to the Replace function, the **Translate** function is used to replace a single character with another character and, multiple characters can be replaced inside one translation. The Translate function takes three arguments: the first argument is the string to translate, the second argument is the string of characters to replace, and the third argument is the set of characters to use for the replacement. `Translate("143281", "12", "97")` returns a result of `943789`, where every instance of the number 1 is replaced with a 9 and every instance of the number 2 is replaced with a 7.

Statistical and Trending Operations

Interactive Reporting provides a set of function to perform statistical and trending calculations to address the more complicated needs of reporting users performing statistical analysis and data trending using Interactive Reporting. With the exception of the Rank and RankAsc functions, the functions contained within this section serve a specific analytical purpose and are rarely used beyond the realm of statistical analysis. As a whole, the Statistical and Trending group of functions behave similarly to Numerical functions in that these functions aggregate values within the dataset and allow users to define a break column.

Ranking

The **Rank** and **RankAsc** functions provide the rank of a value in a set of data. The Rank function ranks the data with the largest value in the column set to the value one of 1, the next largest to 2, and so on. The second function, RankAsc, provides similar functionality but the smallest number in the dataset is set to the value of one, the second smallest is set to 2, and so on. Ranking functions are especially useful to generate rank based data groupings, such as Top 5 Sales reports.

Using JavaScript

Computed Items support the use of JavaScript which allows users to leverage functions beyond those supplied by Interactive Reporting to include the use of conditional logic, variables, and functions. Additionally, Computed Items can access globally defined variables or functions already declared within the document. These features provide users with enhanced flexibility to dynamically modify data presented to the user in a set of results.

Variables and Functions in Computed Items

One very useful feature in Interactive Reporting is the ability to use both functions and variables defined with global scope in Computed Items. The functionality allows a user to write a custom code to apply modifications to data returned from a query. For example, the following simple code can be specified to run when the document is opened:

```
function STRFUNC(val1)
{

  return val1 + 10;

} strfunc = STRFUNC;
```

The function above expects a single value and then increases the value specified by 10. The `return` statement returns the value with the increase to the place that it is used in the code. Once the function is initialized by opening the document, the function can be used in a Computed Item. For example, `strfunc(Col2)` where `Col2` is a numerical column of data from a Results section will return each numerical value in the results `Col2` increased by 10 in the new column. Similarly, a variable can be defined and then added to a Computed Item in the same manner to provide similar flexability.

Math Functions

One JavaScript component key to Computed Items is the **Math** object. The Math object has a number of functions assigned to it that allow users to perform complicated arithmetic. For any supported calculations, the Math object is supplied the required parameters, performs the desired calculation, and returns the resulting value. For example, the Math object can determine the absolute value of a number using the `Math.abs()` function. If the value -3 is supplied to the function, the result of the statement `Math.abs(-3)` is 3. Additional code samples of other Math object functions are found using a simple web search for JavaScript Math functions.

Random Number Generation

Generating random numbers is very useful for randomly splitting a data set into subsets. Since Interactive Reporting does not contain a random function, the `Math.random()` object function is very useful for generating a random number for each row in a column. This function can be used together with the Rank and Ceil functions to create random buckets of data. For example, creating a Computed Item called **Rand** with the `Math.random()` will create a random number for each row in the column. Then creating the Computed Item named **Grouping** with the logic `Ceil(Rank(Computed2)/10)` will create random buckets of 10 rows in the data results. Creating a Table section under this section will allow for the filtering and additional calculations on the **Grouping** column.

Summary

The goal of this chapter was to provide an in-depth explanation of the options available in Interactive Reporting for manipulating data throughout the document. The chapter starts with an overview of structuring a query for data analysis, where the concept of data volume versus query performance is presented. The chapter continues with an overview of the Computed Item interface and the interface specifically for Report sections. The chapter continues with an in-depth view into a majority of the functions that exist in Interactive Reporting. The chapter details both an explanation and examples of functions from each function group and provides information on obtaining additional material from the system documentation. The chapter concludes with material on using JavaScript in Computed Items with information on adding functions and variables. The content presented in the JavaScript section provides a brief guide into the vast functionality that can be performed using custom JavaScript programming. Leveraging knowledge from this chapter and other chapters of the book should serve as a solid foundation for creating custom computations for advanced analysis.

8

Creating Briefing Slides and Executing Batch Exports

Interactive Reporting provides many options for exporting information and deliverables to different file formats. Users commonly struggle with the best and most appropriate method for creating a data or formatted export, with most users overlooking some of the most effective and efficient exporting methods. In addition to searching for the best export format, many users express interest in exporting information from Interactive Reporting into a Microsoft PowerPoint presentation. While the Hyperion SmartView product can be used to refresh objects in Microsoft Office documents, another exporting technique can be executed using the native functionality of Interactive Reporting and does not require the use of an additional piece of software.

Another less commonly known feature in Interactive Reporting is the ability to add custom code to generate batch exports of deliverables. The use of a simple programming approach to exporting allows the user to save significant time and effort when exporting multiple slices of information from the same document.

The goal of this chapter is to educate the advanced user on the methods and features most commonly used for exporting information from Interactive Reporting. The chapter will focus on the native software export features, leveraging custom programming to perform simple and complex exports, and simple steps for configuring a Report section to produce briefing slide content.

This chapter covers the following topics:

- Exporting Interactive Reporting sections
- Exporting sections with custom code
- Creating briefing slides from a report section
- Creating and executing batch exports

Exporting document sections

Interactive Reporting provides many formats for exporting information to Adobe PDF, Microsoft Excel, images, HTML, and text formats. Each section of the document allows for different export options, and some sections provide more export flexibility than others. While there are many options, three formats are commonly used to produce deliverables from objects in the document. These three options are the PDF, JPEG, and MHTML formats.

Many users of the product are not familiar with and do not commonly use the **MHTML (Microsoft Office Web Archive)** export option. The **MHTML** export option provides users with the best method for exporting a section for use in Microsoft Excel, where the formatting of the section is retained and the export is not limited at 65 thousand rows allowing for a larger export to the newer version of the Excel software. When exporting a section to the **MHTML** format, the **MHTML** document is created as a single page, unlike the regular HTML option, which provides a page and a folder of objects referenced in the HTML document. Once exported, the **MHTML** document can be opened in Internet Explorer by default or in Microsoft Excel through opening the file through the application or by changing the file extension from .mhtml to .xlsx.

Exporting natively

A section is exported natively from the document by accessing the section and selecting one of the export options from the **File** menu. The **File** menu includes three options available for exporting sections, including **Section**, **Document as Web Page**, and **HTML Wizard**. The following screenshot depicts the export options from the File menu:

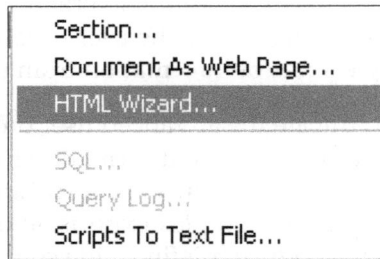

The first and most frequently used export option, **Section**, allows the user to export one section of information into one of the default file types. The export is executed by selecting the **Section** menu item from the **File | Export** menu. Upon selecting the option, a dialog box appears to allow the user to set the filename, export location, and export file type of interest. Upon completion, the system writes the file in the desired export format to the specified location.

> Some sections in Interactive Reporting will not export into every available file type. These sections show a smaller subset of file types in the file type drop-down of the **Export** window.

The second option, **Document as Web Page**, provides the user the ability to export multiple sections of the document into a web page. When this export option is selected, a window appears allowing for the selection of the sections in the document to export, as shown in the following image:

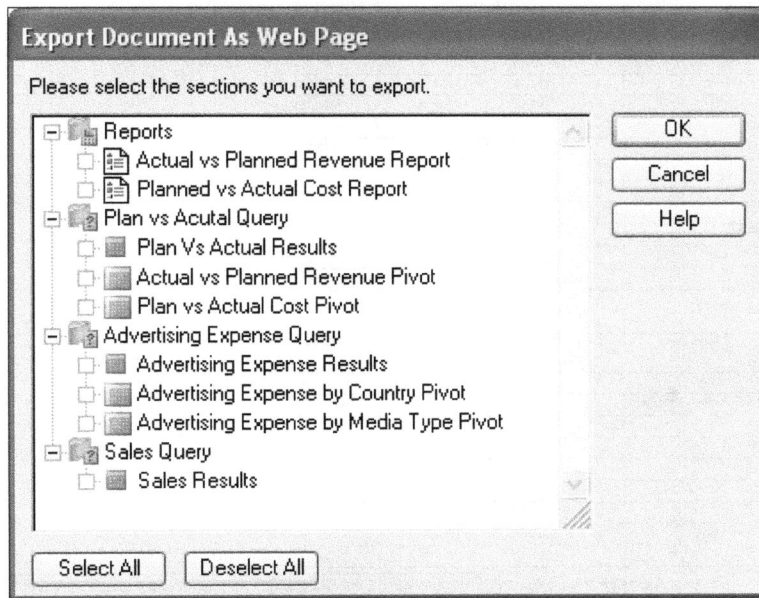

After selecting sections and pressing the **OK** button, a dialog box appears to configure the name of the document. Only two file types can be selected as the export file type with the **Document as Web Page** export method. The first option is the default HTML option, and the section option is MHTML file type. When the document is exported to HTML or MHTML, the user is provided with a formatted result where each exported section is displayed as a page with tabs at the bottom of the document to allow user to navigate between the different pages or sections. While both of these documents provide the same output, the MHTML format of the document is stored in a single page and is more manageable to distribute. The following screenshot displays the exported document open in the web browser:

A key benefit of this feature is that both the HTML and MHTML objects can be opened in Microsoft Excel for viewing and editing. Each tab on the web page is converted into sheets in the Microsoft Excel document. Content can be easily modified, formatting can be easily changed, and the document can be saved into a native Microsoft Excel file type. The following screenshot provides an example of the document open in Excel:

	A	B	C	D	E	F	G	H
1	Franchise							
2								
3	**Store Name**	**Actual Revenue**	**Planned Revenue**	**Actual vs Planned Revenue**				
4	BMV Anaheim	1,359,465	2,200,943.	-841,478				
5	BMV Barreiras	731,976	1,203,267.	-471,291				
6	BMV Brooklyn	7,245,879	11,514,980.	-4,269,101				
7	BMV Buenos Aires	692,300	2,745,819.	-2,053,519				
8	BMV Cologne	1,015,927	1,760,616.	-744,689				
9	BMV Dublin	3,159,783	7,038,655.	-3,878,872				
10	BMV Hiroshima	442,379	925,754.	-483,375				
11	BMV Lyon	4,674,077	7,740,650.	-3,066,573				
12	BMV Osaka	2,599,912	4,135,881.	-1,535,969				
13	BMV Oslo	1,627,859	2,641,901.	-1,014,042				
14	BMV Perth	691,960	1,382,702.	-690,742				
15	BMV Santos	365,131	736,354.	-371,223				
16	**Total**	**24,606,649**	**44,027,522.**	**-19,420,873**				
17	Superstore							
18								
19	**Store Name**	**Actual Revenue**	**Planned Revenue**	**Actual vs Planned Revenue**				
20	Super BMV London	1,605,290	2,608,136.	-1,002,846				
21	Super BMV Los Angeles	6,315,562	11,125,960.	-4,810,398				
22	Super BMV Munich	1,102,433	1,669,873.	-567,440				
23	Super BMV New York	7,266,260	15,502,870.	-8,236,610				

Actual vs Planned Revenue Repor / Planned vs Actual Cost Report / Plan Vs Actual Resul / Actual vs Planned Revenue Pivot / Plan vs

The final export option is the **HTML Wizard**. This feature is specifically used for exporting the document into an HTML layout. Used less frequently than the other features, the HTML Wizard is primarily focused on publishing content for the Web.

Exporting a single section (code)

While Interactive Reporting provides the ability to easily export sections of the document natively in the interface, the software also provides the ability to export sections of the document using simple JavaScript code statements. Two features exist for exporting a single section of the document. The first method, **Export**, is commonly used to export a single section of the document from the Interactive Reporting Web Client. The second export method, **ExportToStream**, is used with the iHTML client or to improve exporting performance.

The following is the Oracle documented syntax of the Export method:

```
Export( [optional] Filename As String, [optional] FileFormat As
BqExportFileFormat, [optional] IncludeHeaders As Boolean, [optional]
Boolean Prompt, [optional] BqEncoding Encoding)
```

The following is the Oracle documented syntax of the ExportToStream method:

```
ExportToStream([optional]String Filename, [optional]BqExportFileFormat
FileFormat, [optional]Boolean IncludeHeaders, [optional]Boolean
DataStreaming, [optional]Boolean Prompt, [optional]BqEncoding
Encoding)
```

The syntax of these methods may appear odd compared to other JavaScript code methods described in this book, since all of the arguments of the method are optional. If the methods are used without setting any arguments, a dialog box will appear prompting the user to set a filename, file type, and encoding when the export methods are executed. While the dialogue box allows the user to customize the export settings at the time of export, the developer configuring the document may want to preset some of the settings. The following is a breakdown of the arguments for both methods:

- The **Filename** [optional] argument allows the user to set the filename and/or path for the export.

- The **FileFormat** [optional] argument sets the file type of the document and accepts an Interactive Reporting constant from the `BqExportFileFormat` set of constants.

- The **IncludeHeaders** [optional] argument set the export to include section headers (specific to sections that allow page headers and page footers from the Insert menu).

- The **DataStreaming** [optional] argument is specific to the `ExportToStream` method and is used to toggle data streaming on and off.

- The **Prompt** [optional] argument sets the dialog box to display when the method is executed.

- The **Encoding** [optional] argument is used to specify the document encoding for the export and accepts a constant from the `BqEncoding` set of constants.

> The `BqExportFileFormat`, `BqEncoding`, and entire set of constants with descriptions are found in the Script Editor by expanding the **Constants** list of values.

Export examples

The following examples demonstrate the use of the Export method to export a Report section of a sample Interactive Reporting document. The first example, Export Example 1, exports the *Planned vs. Actual Cost Report* section without any arguments providing the user the ability to specify the file path, filename, file type, and file encoding at runtime. The second example, Export Example 2, prompts the user to export the *Planned vs. Actual Cost Report* section into a PDF file format in the `c:` directory.

Export Example 1:

```
/* Prompts the user to set the file name, file type, and encoding at
   Runtime */
```

```
ActiveDocument.Sections["Planned vs Actual Cost Report"].Export()
```

Export Example 2:

```
// Predefines all of the arguments for the user
```

```
ActiveDocument.Sections["Planned vs Actual Cost Report"].
Export("C:\\Cost Report.pdf", bqExportFormatPDF, false, true, bqEnc_
WesternEuropean_Windows)
```

> Note the use of two backslashes (\ \) in Export Example 2 when specifying the location C : \ \. Two slashes are required when specifying a file path in Interactive Reporting.

ExportToStream examples

The following examples demonstrate the use of the ExportToStream method to export a Pivot section of a sample Interactive Reporting document. The first example, ExportToStream Example 1, exports the *Advertising Expense by Country Pivot* section without any arguments, which allows the user to specify the file path, filename, file type, and file encoding at runtime. The second example, ExportToStream Example 2, prompts the user to export the *Advertising Expense by Country Pivot* section into a MHTML file format in the C: directory.

ExportToStream Example 1:

```
/* Prompts the user to set the file name, file type, and encoding
at Runtime */
ActiveDocument.Sections["Advertising Expense by Country Pivot"].
ExportToStream()
```

ExportToStream Example 2:

```
// Predefines all of the arguments for the user
ActiveDocument.Sections["Advertising Expense by Country
Pivot"].ExportToStream("C:\\Advertising Pivot.mhtml",
bqExportFormatOfficeMHTML, false, true, true, bqEnc_
WesternEuropean_Windows)
```

Exporting multiple sections (JavaScript code)

In addition to exporting a single section of the document through custom programming, Interactive Reporting provides the ability to export multiple sections of the document together in one HTML or MHTML file. This export is not completed at the section level but rather at the document level, using an Export method of the ActiveDocument object. This custom programming export functionality mimics the native **Documents as Web Page** export feature, and these HTML or MHTML documents can be opened and edited with Microsoft Excel, similar to other exports.

> While Interactive Reporting appears to allow the user to set a file in any of the export formats, setting the file format to a value other than HTML or MHTML would generate the following error when the code is executed:
>
> ```
> Error Code: Script(x):uncaught exception: Export
> format not supported
> ```

While the exporting of multiple sections functionality is limited in export format, it is extremely important when leveraging the batch feature, described later in this chapter. If there is an interest in exporting multiple sections of an Interactive Reporting document into one export format while running a batch process, the Export method of the ActiveDocument object must be utilized. The ActiveDocument object contains three different methods utilized when exporting multiple sections:

- The AddExportSection method is used to add sections of the document into the export queue. This method accepts one argument, which is the name of the section to export.

- The RemoveExportSections method is used to clear out all sections from the export queue.

- The Export method is used to generate the multi-section export. While the Export method appears to be similar to the method described in exporting a single section, the ActiveDocument version of the **Export** method is limited to the HTML and MHTML file types. Additionally, the path of the file must be specified, as this specific **Export** method will not prompt the user to save the file, but will write the file directly to the specified file path.

The following example highlights the use of the ActiveDocument Export method to export two Report sections to the C:\Temp directory:

```
/* The AddExportSection statement must be unique for each
Section */
ActiveDocument.AddExportSection("Planned vs Actual Cost Report");
```

```
ActiveDocument.AddExportSection("Actual vs Planned Revenue
Report");

/* Code use to generate the export to the specified file location
on the drive as an MHTML file type. */
ActiveDocument.Export("C:\\Temp\\Revenue and Cost Report.mhtml",bq
ExportFormatOfficeMHTML);

// Removes all sections from the export queue.
ActiveDocument.RemoveExportSections();
```

> If the Temp file folder does not exist on the machine running the export, the following error message will be written to the **Console** window:
> **Error Code 2: Script(x):uncaught exception: Unable to open output file: 'Revenue and Cost Report.mhtml'**

Briefing slides

Many users are interested in using Interactive Reporting to create briefing slides for Microsoft PowerPoint documents. While there is no native export feature in Interactive Reporting to export a section to Microsoft PowerPoint, Hyperion created a tool called SmartView to integrate the different products of Microsoft Office with Interactive Reporting. While this product fills the void of integrating the Microsoft Office suite with Hyperion Interactive Reporting, there are additional custom methods that can be used to generate briefing slide content.

Report sections in Interactive Reporting can be exported to a JPEG file type, where each page of the Report section is saved as an individual image file. This image export feature from a Report section provides a convenient and easy to use approach for generating slide content for Microsoft PowerPoint presentations, where the content of the Interactive Reporting document can be segmented and arranged on a report with Report Groups with defined page breaks to create quality slide content.

Microsoft PowerPoint contains two different methods for importing files. The first method is used to import image files into a document. When the image files are imported into the document, the file is copied into the document and any changes to the original file do not impact the file displayed in the slide deck. This method can be used to import images from an Interactive Reporting document, but the images in the PowerPoint document must be exported from Interactive Reporting re-imported and reconfigured each time the data in Interactive Reporting is refreshed.

A second option exists for linking images into a PowerPoint document through the addition of an object to the PowerPoint document. Microsoft PowerPoint recognizes the bitmap file type as one of the default objects in the software, where bitmap images can be linked into PowerPoint documents from a specified file location. When the source bitmap image is updated, the image in the PowerPoint document is updated when the document links are refreshed (the update setting is configurable in Microsoft PowerPoint). This feature is very effective and can be used together with the exported images from Hyperion Interactive Reporting to create updatable PowerPoint slideshows. However, there is a manual step that is necessary when using this feature. Interactive Reporting only exports files into the JPEG file type and Microsoft PowerPoint does not recognize the JPEG file type as one of the default object formats. Therefore, the files exported from Interactive Reporting will have to be renamed from the .jpg extension to the .bmp extension. Once the file extensions have been adjusted, the source bitmap files can be overwritten with the newly renamed files from the Interactive Reporting export. The next time the linked objects from the Microsoft PowerPoint document are updated, the new image files will automatically appear in the document.

Building the report for a briefing slide export

A Report section created for an image export should differ significantly from a Report used as a static report. Since each Interactive Reporting Report section page will be exported to a single image when the image export is utilized, each page of the Report section should be designed to support a single slide of the slideshow. Since the Report Groups feature of the Report section splits the content into subsections of data, the Report section provides an easy method to segment pivots and charts into grouped content for briefing slides. Once the content of the report is configured, a few Report section options are available to help prepare the report for export to image files. The following screenshot displays a Report section configured to display two Charts sections and one Report Group:

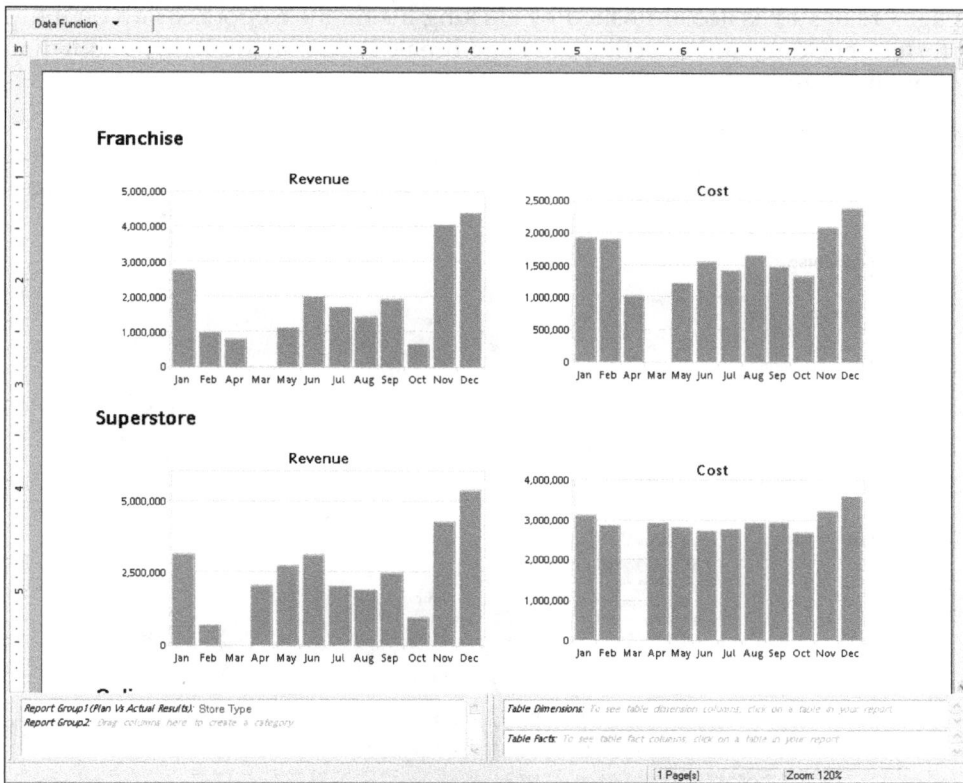

In the screenshot above, notice that the groups of information are listed on the same page of each report, which makes the document difficult to segment into multiple pages. However, the default Report Group display settings can be modified to split each Report Group heading onto a separate page.

The page break step is accomplished by clicking inside the Report Group on the report, right-clicking, and selecting the **Page Break Before** menu item as shown in the following figure:

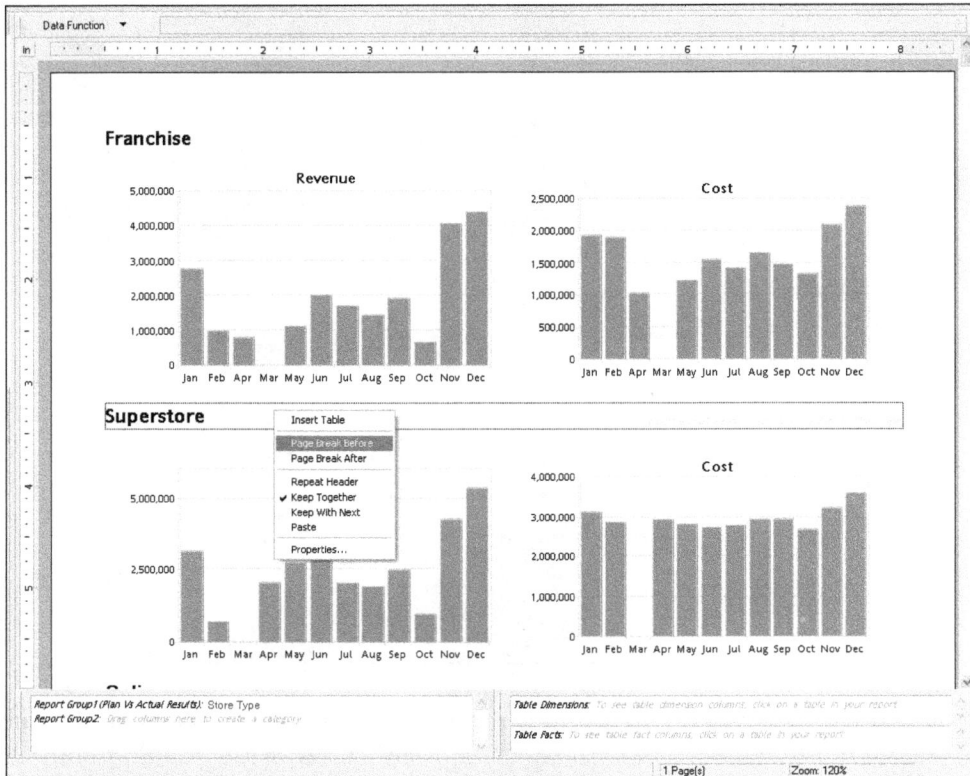

Since each Report Group is now on a separate page, the briefing content for each content area appears in a single image. However, when the images are exported from the report with the default report page size, the images contain a large portion of white space at the bottom of each image.

The second important feature of the Report section is the ability to change the report page size to better fit the information on each page of the report. The report page size is adjusted by selecting the **Report Setup** menu item from the **Report** menu. The **Report Page Setup** window opens to the **Page Size** tab with the default setting to use the dimensions of the printer (configured by the **Page Setup** options of the **File** menu). The report can be set to a custom page size by switching the **Page Size** radio button to use custom dimensions. Setting the custom dimensions is completed by clicking on the **Custom Dimensions** radio button and entering the width and height of the desired page size in the Report section.

> To identify the best dimensions for the Report section size, the rulers
> may be turned on by selecting the **Rulers** menu item from the **Report**
> menu. In the same **Report Page Setup** window, the margins tab may
> also be utilized to adjust the margin sizing as desired.

Once the page sizing has been modified, the report will appear as shown in the
following screenshot and will export to image sizes that are appropriate for the size
of the report pages. The following screenshot shows the initial example with the
Page Break setting of the Report Group configured and the report page resized:

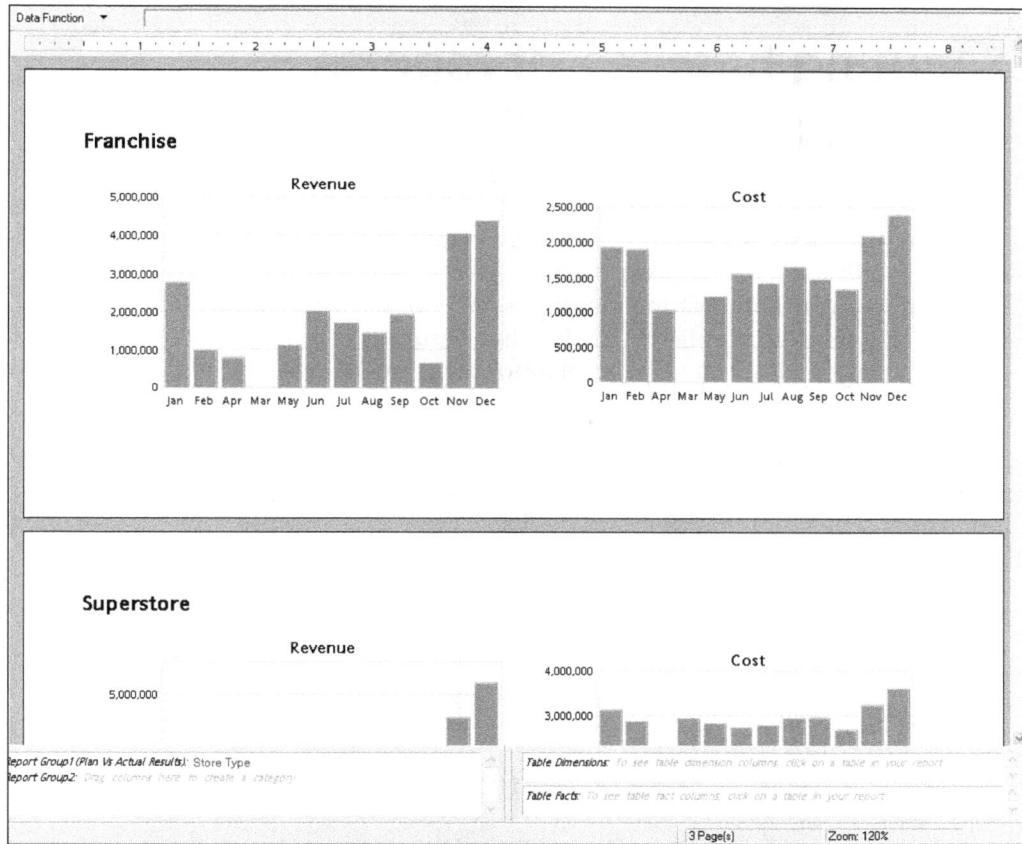

Export code for briefing slides

The majority of work in creating briefing slides for the image export is completed in the formatting of the Report section and the setup and configuration of the Microsoft PowerPoint document. While the Report section is easily exported natively in the product by exporting the section to JPEG format, the Report section can also be exported using custom code. The following code example showcases the ability to export the PowerPoint example Report section into JPEG format:

```
ActiveDocument.Sections["PowerPoint Example"].Export("C:\\Cost
Report", bqExportFormatJPEG, false, true)
```

Executing batches of reports

Users frequently express interest in creating an Interactive Reporting document that processes one or more queries and exports one or more reports for a set of input criteria. Interactive Reporting has a job scheduler utility allowing the user to perform batch processing features. However, many environments do not allow users to access the job scheduler feature. The Interactive Reporting Web Client does not natively contain the ability to batch process in the software. However, custom programming can be used to create similar functionality to the job scheduler by running a query and producing an export multiple times. This feature is extremely effective and can be easily leveraged to save a significant amount of time and effort.

While there are many different methods for creating batches in Interactive Reporting, the most common approach is to create a set of code to loop through input criteria, process the required queries of the document, and produce the export for each input criteria value. The following diagram depicts a high-level process flow for the batch approach:

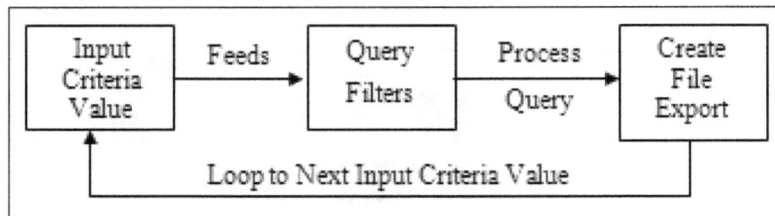

Batch processing example

The following example is a demonstration of the methods for creating a PDF report of *Actual Revenue vs. Plan Revenue* by store type and store name for each month of each year from the sample data model. The input criteria are all of the month and date combinations stored in the month dimension. The following screenshot displays the different sections of the sample Interactive Reporting document:

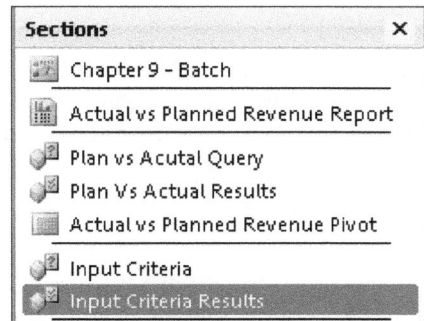

Notice that a Dashboard section, a Report, and two Query sections with Results and one Pivot section exists in the document. The Dashboard section contains a button for executing the batch process and, upon pressing the button, the program will execute the batch process and will start producing exports.

The input criteria in the example are derived from the **Input Criteria Query**, which selects all of the distinct year and month combinations from the **Month Dimension**. Each record from the input criteria Results section will result in one PDF document created for the specified criteria. When executed, the program will start with the first record of the input criteria and will loop sequentially to the last record. At each iteration of the process, the year and month number from input criteria will be applied to the year and month number filters of the **Planned vs. Actual Query**. The **Planned vs. Actual Query** will be processed and a PDF export will be written to the c:\ directory with the year and month criteria included in the file name to distinguish each file.

> Sorting the Results section of the input criteria query will present an ordered output of the batch and may assist with troubleshooting errors.

Batch processing code

```
/* Process the Input Criteria Query to obtain the distinct list of
input criteria values. The query properties are configured to
return unique rows and the Results section is sorted by row and column
*/


ActiveDocument.Sections["Input Criteria"].Process();



/* For loop iterating through all of the values in the input criteria
Results section.  The loop starts with the first value and
continues through each record up to the total values of the  results
section (denoted  by the row count). */


for(var i=1; i<=ActiveDocument.Sections["Input Criteria Results"].
RowCount; i++)
{
    /*   Variable Set to reduce the need to repeat the query string
definition multiple times */


MainQry = ActiveDocument.Sections["Plan vs Acutal Query"];


    /*    Remove all of the values selected in the Year and Month
    Number filters of the Plan vs Actual Query  */


  MainQry.Limits["Year"].SelectedValues.RemoveAll();
MainQry.Limits["Month Number"].SelectedValues.RemoveAll();


    /*    Grab and set the input criteria Year and Month number
results to a variable.   */


  InputYear = ActiveDocument.Sections["Input Criteria
Results"].Columns["Year"].GetCell(i);
  InputMonth = ActiveDocument.Sections["Input Criteria
Results"].Columns["Month Number"].GetCell(i);


    /*    Sets the input criteria value for the month and year into
the month and year filters of the Plan vs Actual Query */


  MainQry.Limits["Year"].SelectedValues.Add(InputYear);
  MainQry.Limits["Month Number"].SelectedValues.Add(InputMonth);


    //      Process the Plan vs Actual Query for the specified values
```

```
MainQry.Process();

    /*      Allows the processor to complete the processing of the
events in the statement.  The addition of this method prevents
the application from failing during the export by requiring the
application to complete events before moving onto the next step.  */

Application.DoEvents();

    /*      Specifies the path and creates a unique filename for each
file.  Leverages the InputYear and InputMonth variables declared in
the previous statement to mark the file name with the appropriate year
and month combination.  */

FileName = "C:\\Revenue Report " + InputYear + "-" + InputMonth;

    /*      Exports the document to the specified file path with dynamic
file name.  Notice the prompt export setting is
set to the off position so the program runs seamlessly
without interruption.  */

ActiveDocument.Sections["Actual vs Planned Revenue Report"].
Export(FileName, bqExportFormatPDF, false, false, bqEnc_
WesternEuropean_Windows)

    /*      Repeated to make sure the program completes the export
before moving forward with processing the next set
        of input criteria.  */

Application.DoEvents();

/*      Once the file export is completed, the program moves to the
next set of input criteria until all of the documents
        are completed.  */


}
```

After the batch processing script completes, the directory configured to contain all of
the export of files will be populated with a PDF document for each set of
input criteria.

Refining the batch code to remove empty results sections

Many times, situations arise where specific input criteria values do not yield a result when processed in the main query. Since users are typically interested in ignoring empty reports of information, adding a conditional statement to the export statement to ignore exporting empty reports is an efficient way of handling this situation. Replacing the export script statement in the batch export example above with the following statement (shown below), provides the specific logic to *not* export a Report section in instances when the main query has an empty results section:

```
/*      Exports the document to the specified file path with the
name specified above provided the results section of the
document contains information.  Notice the prompt export setting
is set to the off position so the program runs seamlessly without
interruption.  */

if(ActiveDocument.Sections["Plan vs Acutal Results"]) {

ActiveDocument.Sections["Actual vs Planned Revenue Report"].
Export(FileName, bqExportFormatPDF, false, false, bqEnc_
WesternEuropean_Windows)
}
```

After the refined batch processing script completes, the directory specified to receive the export of files will display the list of files where data existed for the input criteria.

Summary

The goal of this chapter was to demonstrate new and innovative approaches for using Interactive Reporting to generate deliverables and briefings as well as the methods and features most commonly used for exporting information from the software. The chapter began with an introduction to the native export functionality provided by Interactive Reporting, including exporting an individual section to different file formats and exporting multiple sections of the document to a web page at one time. Once an explanation of the native tool features was discussed, an in-depth view of the code used to generate an export of information using custom programming was presented, which included basic section exporting and the process to export multiple sections at a time. The chapter continued with an innovative approach to using the Interactive Reporting Report section as a means of generating content for a Microsoft PowerPoint slideshow through the use of image files. The chapter then concluded with an approach to creating multiple custom deliverables by creating a custom process and using the export functionality to run multiple queries without manual intervention. At the end of this chapter, the advanced user should have a solid understanding of the export functionality provided in Interactive Reporting, and the user should have the knowledge needed to begin using the briefing slide and batch approaches to support daily efforts.

The Central Code Repository

9

One challenge that advanced users encounter with Interactive Reporting's report-centric model is the tracking and maintenance of heavily customized dashboard reports, especially in enterprise-level implementations where code is used repetitively and transparently across multiple documents. Given the common and straightforward practice of storing similar JavaScript code within each document in an enterprise, it is incredibly difficult and infeasible to individually identify, track, and edit changes across documents.

One simple and invaluable methodology is to store report customization scripts in an accessible database table within the enterprise environment. This script table, referred to as the **Central Code Repository (CCR)**, is an external reporting library that allows code to be quickly pushed into some or all documents in an enterprise. This centralized repository provides the capability for agile responses to ongoing business changes and code maintenance without modifying the consuming reporting documents. In addition to providing an efficient code update capability, the CCR drastically reduces development and testing man-hours since the code can be tested and vetted independently from the reporting document.

The goal of this chapter is to educate advanced users on both the theory and processes for creating a CCR. This chapter covers the following topics:

- Understanding the CCR
- Preparing code statements and implementing the CCR
- Querying and executing the CCR
- Creating the CCR Global Code Dashboard
- Scripting the Document Startup Event
- Advanced application concepts

Understanding the Central Code Repository

The Central Code Repository (CCR) is a database model created for Hyperion Interactive Reporting that allows the storage, management, and implementation of a centralized code base. The repository is purely a custom developed database table or set of database tables created by development and business users to effectively leverage and maintain JavaScript code statements and variables across multiple Interactive Reporting documents. The tables are maintained by the development and user community, and the table must exist in a centralized location that is accessible by the Interactive Reporting documents using code from the developed solution. Below is a conceptual diagram of the use of the CCR across multiple Interactive Reporting documents:

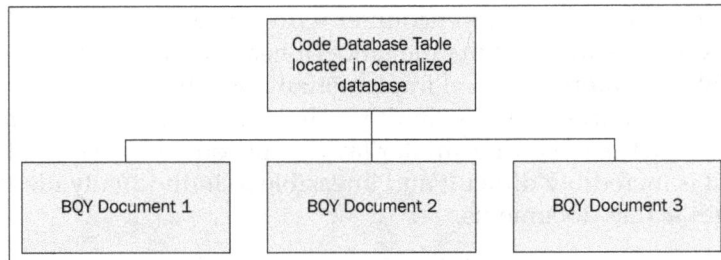

```
                    ┌──────────────────────┐
                    │  Code Database Table │
                    │  located in centralized │
                    │      database        │
                    └──────────────────────┘
        ┌───────────────────┼───────────────────┐
┌───────────────┐   ┌───────────────┐   ┌───────────────┐
│ BQY Document 1 │   │ BQY Document 2 │   │ BQY Document 3 │
└───────────────┘   └───────────────┘   └───────────────┘
```

Changes made to the code database tables are efficiently managed within the CCR, and when changes are enacted the code updates globally across BQY documents. As business requirements evolve or even drastically change, the CCR will provide developers, managers, and advanced users with tremendous flexibility for global or partial report code management.

Preparing the JavaScript code

In order for the CCR to work properly in all database environments, the JavaScript code must be stripped of all comments and carriage returns. The removal of carriage returns from the code requires that the JavaScript deployed in the CCR adhere to strict coding standards including using semi-colons at the end of statements. These single lines of code are stored in the CCR code database table to be queried, evaluated, and then utilized by the individual BQY documents.

Table structure

Since the CCR is a custom-developed solution, the repository can be flexible to accommodate many needs of the user community. The rest of the chapter discusses using a single table as the CCR for simplicity in demonstrating the capabilities of the feature. When building the CCR with a single table, the CCR table should be structured with at least the three columns as shown in the following table:

	A	B	C
1	**Number**	**Name**	**Code**
2	1	Debug Messages	function debugMessage (vMes
3	2	Execute Batch Process	function batchProcess (gInput
4	3	Execute Refined Batch Process	function refinedBatchProcess(

- **Number**: The Number field will determine the order in which the function is executed, which is especially useful for functions that perform document actions that have a hierarchy to them, such as Document Startup scripts
- **Name**: The Name field is used to provide a title for the code provided
- **Code**: The Code field stores the formatted JavaScript code used in the Interactive Reporting documents

As specified in the previous sections, additional columns or tables to manage content including report names, categories, or groupings, can be added to enhance the organization and management of Interactive Reporting documents in the enterprise. Using these additional components will allow developers and advanced users to minimize the amount of JavaScript coding declared as a part of the start-up process through the use of modifying the code query to obtain only the specific functions for each Interactive Reporting document.

Configuring the CCR code table and query

With the report code now stored in the CCR code table in the database, BQY documents can query the table and then evaluate the code that is stored in the table. The image below shows the CCR workflow within the Interactive Reporting document.

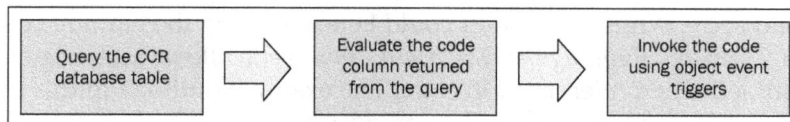

When the document is first opened, the query to retrieve the code from the CCR code database is processed during the document start-up process. Once the query results are retrieved, the results from the code column are then looped through the JavaScript `eval()` function to declare the functions and variables or to execute code statements.

[🔅 Store any code statements commonly used in user interface
modifications, including hiding or unhiding toolbars, menus, and
other interface components in the CCR.]

Querying the Central Code Repository (CCR)

Each Interactive Reporting document using code from the CCR requires a Query
section to return the contents of the CCR database table into the specific document.
The results of the code query will be read during the document start-up process
using code described in the section above and demonstrated throughout the rest of
this chapter.

Creating the Query section

The first step in using the CCR is to add a new Query section to the document. The
new query must have access to the CCR database table. There is no harm in storing
the database table with the other tables in a common production database, nor is
there harm in allowing the table to be accessed by the OCE connection containing
the production data set utilized by the user community. However, there are
implementations where development teams like to separate the code tables along
with other metadata, remarks, and other reference materials used by Interactive
Reporting. This is also perfectly acceptable and requires the selection of the proper
OCE connection with access to the CCR table.

Renaming the Query and Results sections

The names of the Query and Results sections are important because these sections
are directly referenced by the code to read the contents of the table. The naming
of the Query and Results sections should be consistently applied throughout the
document and code. While any names could be used, using the naming convention
described in *Chapter 5, Building the Dashboard Framework*, allows section types to be
easily determined when referenced in code. The example outlined in this chapter
specifies that the Query section must be named q Code and the Results section must
be named r Code.

Buidling the code DataModel

Once the new Query section is added to the database and renamed, expand the tables in the Elements Section by right clicking on the + sign to access the database and locate the CCR table. Bring the CCR table into the main window of the Query section to begin building the code query:

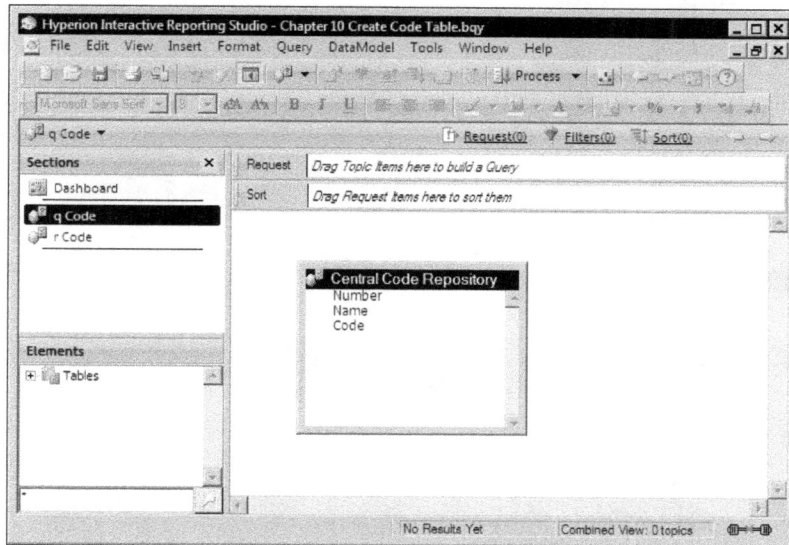

Building the code query

Once the table is moved into the main window of the document, add all columns of the CCR code table to the Request line to bring in all of the data from the table into the Interactive Reporting document. Additionally, add the Number field to the Sort line to sort the query in ascending order. Sorting the document will ensure that the code is read in the proper order.

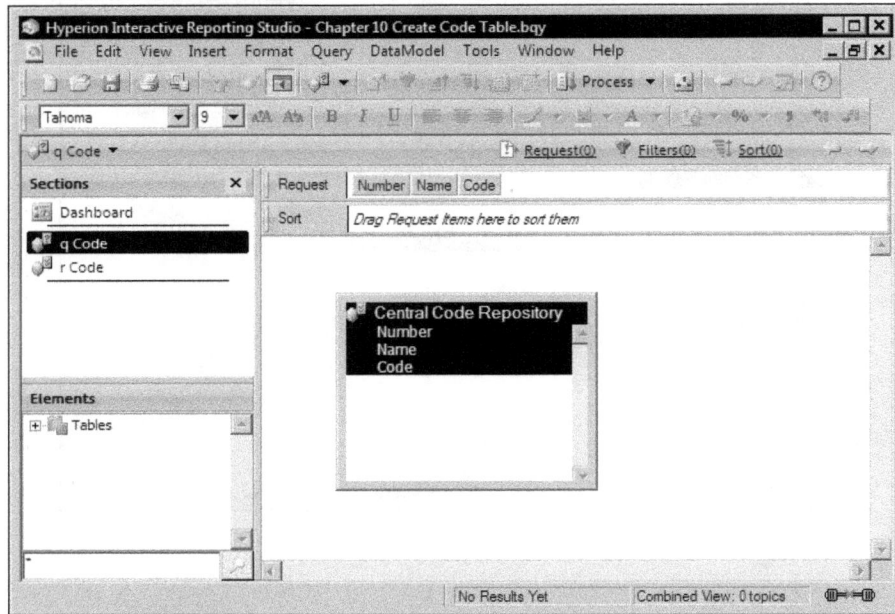

Building the Global Code Dashboard

In order for any section of the Interactive Reporting document to access functions stored in the CCR, the functions need to be globally declared as part of the document start-up process. If the necessary code was directly assigned to the document object's `OnStartup` event, the code would be run when the document was opened before any other actions were performed by the client. While this would ensure the functions are declared before any report object attempts to call them, code errors, such as an infinite for loop, will cause the document to become unstable and irrevocably corrupt. To avoid this hazard, use the techniques explained in *Chapter 5, Building the Dashboard Framework* to alternatively mange the document start-up processes.

Creating the Global Code Dashboard

Once the query is configured, the next step in the process is to create a Global Code Dashboard to prepare all of the code for use in the document. Add a **New Dashboard** to the document using the Insert menu.

In the Sections window, click and activate the newly created Dashboard section. Rename the section and change the section label from `Dashboard` to `Global Code Dashboard`.

Once a new dashboard is added, renamed, and active, set the dashboard in Design Mode to begin adding controls and JavaScript code to the dashboard. While in **Design Mode**, add a **Command Button Control** to the dashboard. Click to select the command button and then right-click to open the menu. Choose the **Properties** option to view the object properties. Change the Name of the command button from `CommandButton1` to `cbDocumentStartupScripts` and change the Title of the button from `CommandButton1` to `Document Start up Scripts`. Once complete, click **OK** to close the dialog box.

> Any dashboard control or dashboard graphic with an `OnClick()` event method can be used in place of the command button control.

Select the command button again and right-click to open the right-click menu. Choose the **Scripts** menu option to open the **Script Editor**. Add the following code to process the code table and then loop through and evaluate each line of code returned to the Results section:

```
/* Process the Code Query to retrieve the records in the Central Code
Repository table */
ActiveDocument.Sections["q Code"].Process();

/* Store the row count from the query results. */
var vRowCount = ActiveDocument.Sections["r Code"].RowCount;

/* For each row in the r Code section, perform the enclosed code and
increment the i variable by 1 until the i variable is more than the
row count in the r Code Section */
for (var i=1;i<= vRowCount; i++)
{
```

```
/* The GetCell method returns the value of row number i in
the code text column of the r code section. The eval() function
executes the contents of that cell as JavaScript statements. */
  eval(ActiveDocument.Sections["r Code"].Columns["code"].GetCell(i));
}
```

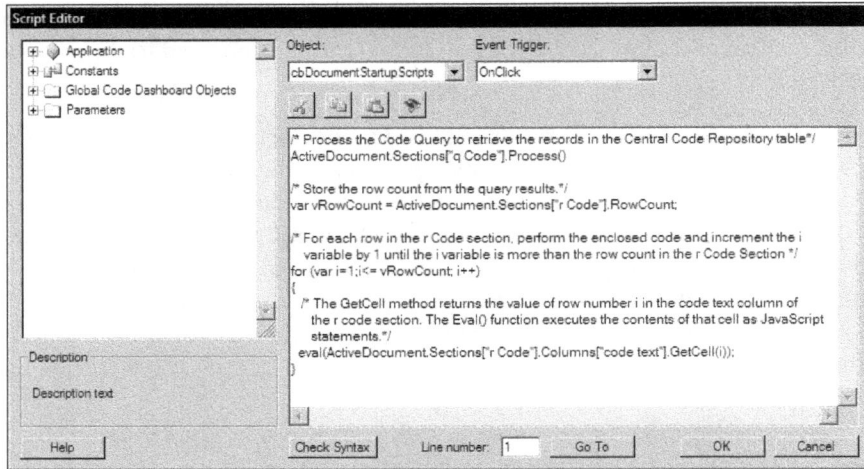

Click **OK** to close the Script Editor and return to the **Global Code Dashboard** section. The following image shows the dashboard after the command button modifications and code steps are complete:

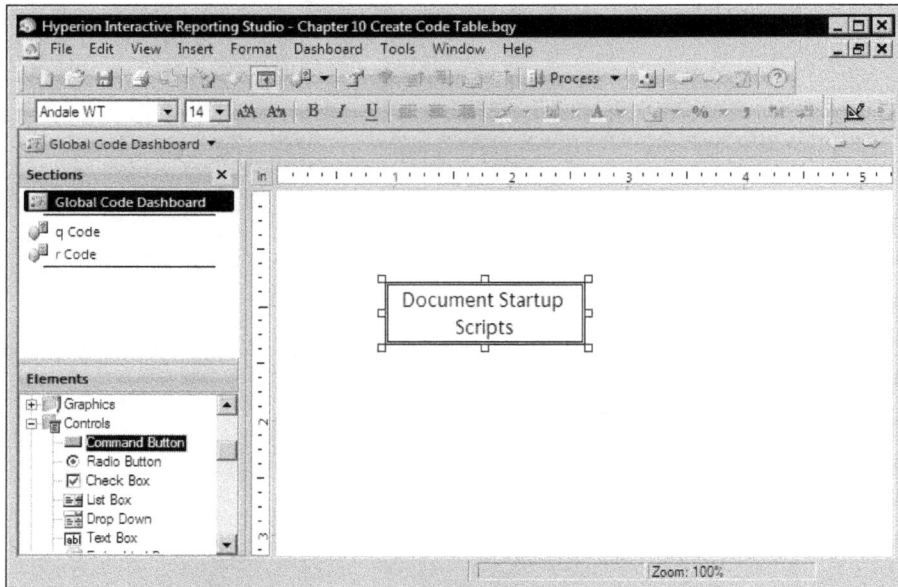

By assigning code to the `OnClick` event trigger of the button, the code can be invoked by either manually clicking the command button or programmatically clicking it by calling the execution of the `OnClick` event through using code. Manually clicking the button allows the code to be tested without risking document corruption before the button is programmatically executed by the Document `OnStartup` event.

Now with the dashboard configured, switch the dashboard to Run Mode. With the dashboard now active and actionable, monitor the Console Window for any errors.

The Console Window is very helpful for debugging sections of code or for testing conditional statements. The Console Window is opened by selecting **Console Window** from the **View** menu as shown in the following image:

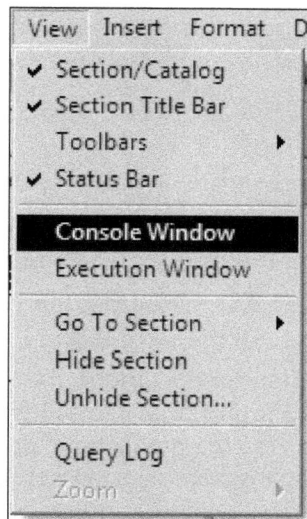

Use the code statement `Console.Writeln("<message>");` in any block of code to display a message in the Console Window, where <message> is the message to be displayed. For example, `Console.Writeln("Hello World!");` would display Hello World!.

The following screenshot shows the dashboard ready to be executed. Click the **Document Startup Scripts** command button to test the code and to check for errors:

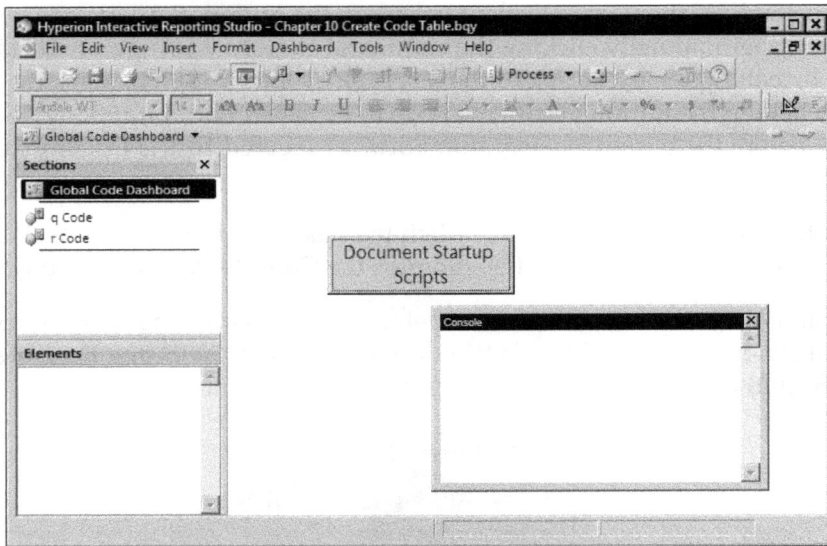

Once the button is clicked, the Console Window should appear blank without errors, as shown in the screenshot above.

Applying the code to objects

Once the code is processed using the `eval()` statement, the functions become globally available to objects within the document. Accessing functions from the Central Code Repository is no different than accessing functions centrally contained within the document. If the `eval()` statements have not occurred or the function is no longer in the CCR code table, any objects referencing the unavailable function will output a scripting error to the Console Window as the function will not be recognized by Interactive Reporting.

Scripting the Document Startup Event

The final automation of the dashboard requires that the Document Startup Scripts command button be executed when the document opens. Now that the Document Startup Scripts are tested and ready for implementation, the final step is to invoke the `OnClick()` method of the Document Startup Scripts button on the `Global Code Dashboard` during the document's `OnStartup` event process.

In the **File** menu, click **Document Scripts** to open the document level Scripts Editor window:

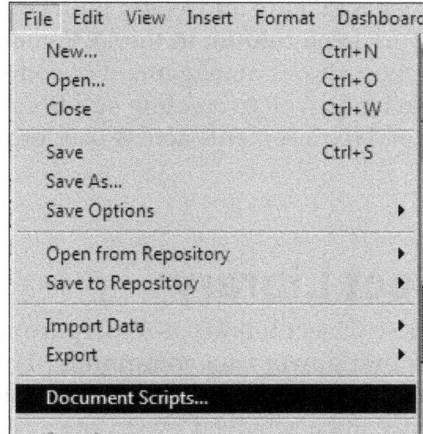

Add the following code to the main section of the Document Script Editor to invoke the OnClick() method of the cbDocumentStartupScripts shape on the Global Code Dashboard section:

```
/*Invoke the OnClick() Method of the cdDocumentStartupScripts shape on
the Global Code Dashboard section */

ActiveDocument.Sections["Global Code Dashboard"].Shapes["cbDocumentSta
rtupScripts"].OnClick()
```

Click **OK** to close the Document Script Editor and use save the document. The next time the document is opened, the document OnStartup() event trigger will be called and the code will be executed.

Advanced concepts

With an understanding of the concepts discussed and the demonstration of the simple example, the following topics are ideas for how the Centralized Code Repository can be enhanced in an enterprise implementation.

Report Type Grouping

Different report types such as ad-hoc, dashboard, or canned typically have vastly different business requirements that are addressed with code unique to the report type. The addition of a Report Type column in the CCR code table and a Report Type filter on the CCR Query section allows management of code within a subsection of reports. This concept also lends well to creating sub-libraries by a business unit to address differing functional requirements across user groups in an enterprise implementation.

Enterprise Object Library

The idea behind an Enterprise Object Library is to prepare code and training for users outside the developer and power user community. This implementation would allow even beginner business users to create customized dashboards easily. Creating an Enterprise Object Library can be achieved by storing a series of standardized dashboard functions in the CCR code table. Business users can then be trained to attach simplistic function calls that resolve to code stored and maintained by the development team in the code table.

Batch Report Creation

Adding an additional column to the code table that denotes one-time use functions and code blocks to be accessed by blank documents is the bridge between combining the concepts described in *Chapter 8, Creating Briefing Slides* and *Executing Batch Exports* to automate the process of creating BQY documents. This is especially useful when creating multiple integrations of an existing Interactive Reporting document with minimal variances between the documents.

Summary

The goal of this chapter was to provide the developers and users of Interactive Reporting with an approach to creating a Central Code Repository to programmatically push code into Interactive Reporting documents. The chapter began with an introduction to the concepts of the CCR, where the approach and configuration of the repository and database tables were discussed. The chapter continued with a simple example implementation, where the configuration of the query, dashboard, and code was demonstrated to provide the steps to implement the repository in an environment. Topics including best practices in code placement and error checking through the Console Window were discussed to assist with reducing failures and troubleshooting the implementation. Finally, advanced concepts for enhancing the CCR were introduced to describe other more advanced techniques and applications in the enterprise. An effective implementation of the CCR will provide both users and developers a stable environment with a significant reduction in document maintenance.

10
Optimizing and Merging

The Interactive Reporting Web Client or Studio developer utility provide the user significant flexibility in using software, but these products do not allow two critical functions commonly needed by users and developers. The first function is the ability to merge sections of two or more documents together, and the second function is the ability to reorder sections in the document. While many users believe this functionality does not exist in the software, the Interactive Reporting Studio developer utility is bundled two developer tools that are essential to the environment. The two software products are the Dashboard Studio and the Dashboard Studio Optimize software. These products complement the Studio developer software and allow developers to merge, modify, and fix Interactive Reporting documents.

The goal of this chapter is to educate the developer and user on additional software products that provide benefits outside the normal development tools. This chapter details the features of the Dashboard Studio and Dashboard Studio Optimize Utility for managing document content.

This chapter covers the following topics:

- An overview of the Dashboard Studio Merge Utility
- Merging two or more Interactive Reporting documents
- An overview of the Dashboard Studio Optimize Utility
- Changing the parent section of a Pivot, Chart, or Table
- Fixing corrupt Interactive Reporting documents

The Dashboard Studio

The **Dashboard Studio** is an Interactive Reporting product packaged with the Interactive Reporting Studio developer software installation for developers. The software was created and is commonly used as a utility for developers to quickly implement dashboards from a well-defined template. While this book is focused on creating dashboards using a customized programming approach, developers can use this product to create dashboards in a more automated fashion. While the Dashboard Studio provides the functionality for creating dashboards, these dashboards must follow a rigid set of requirements, and customizing these objects is often more complicated than programming the dashboards from a blank document. Additionally, the dashboard developer must have the Dashboard Studio utility on their local machine to create a dashboard. It is easier and just as effective for the user to use the Interactive Reporting Web Client program to create a simple customized dashboard.

Dashboard Studio: Merging sections

While the Dashboard Studio provides the ability to create custom dashboards, another lesser-known feature of the product allows the user to merge sections from one or more documents into a new document. The merge document feature is extremely useful for merging and sharing preconfigured sections from one document to another. This merging cannot be achieved through the Interactive Reporting Studio or Interactive Reporting Web Client and is specific to the Dashboard Studio product. As this product is a developer-specific product, users will need to contact a member in their organization with the Dashboard Studio to execute the merging of the documents into a single document. While this feature is not available to the general user community, it is important for users to understand that this feature exists and that this feature can be easily leveraged to merge content from multiple Interactive Reporting BQY documents into a single document.

Merging sections example

The Interactive Reporting Dashboard Studio Merge Utility is a very simple and easy-to-use software feature. The Merge Utility is accessed from inside the Interactive Reporting Dashboard Studio client tool, which is opened from the `Reporting and Analysis` folder of the `Oracle EPM` system folder in the **Start Menu**. The following screenshot displays the shortcut for the product:

🪟 Interactive Reporting ▶	
🪟 Utilities and Administration ▶	🔧 Dashboard Architect Update Utility
📇 Dashboard Architect	📇 Dashboard Studio Inspector Utility
📇 Dashboard Studio	📇 Dashboard Studio Optimize Utility
📇 Financial Reporting Studio	📇 Dashboard Studio Update Utility

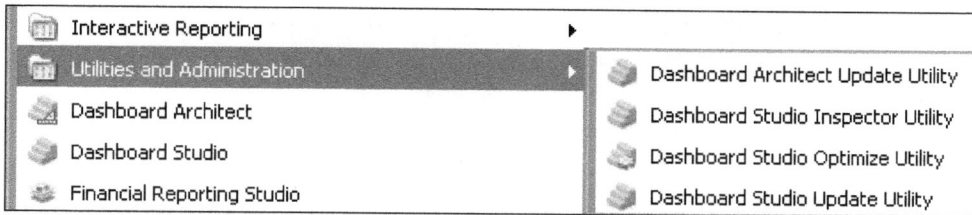

When the **Dashboard Studio** is opened, a splash screen is displayed and then the product progress to the main window of the **Dashboard Studio**. This main window does not contain the title **Dashboard Studio**, but rather denotes the first step in building a dashboard with the title of the window as **Select a Framework Template**, as displayed in the following screenshot:

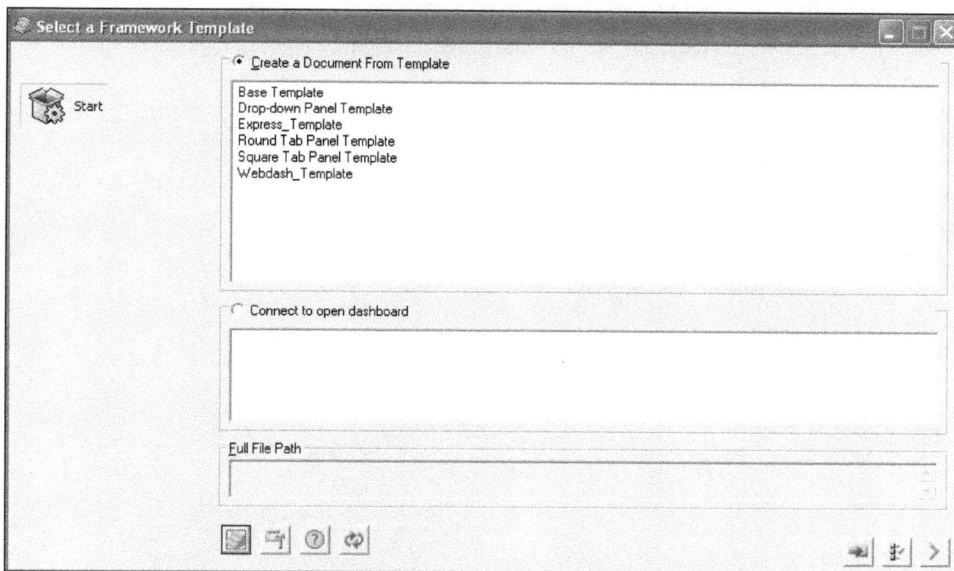

Notice that there is no reference to the **Merge Utility** on this screen. However, many buttons are displayed at the bottom of the window which are used for executing features and setting options in the product. While many of the buttons are focused on options and utilities for the **Dashboard Studio**, the button at the bottom right-hand side of the screen is used to execute the **Merge Utility**.

The following image shows the **Merge Utility** execution button:

When the **Merge Utility** button is pressed, the Dashboard Studio product opens a new window with the title **Dashboard Studio Merge Utility** in the product header. The following screenshot displays the **Dashboard Studio Merge Utility** main window:

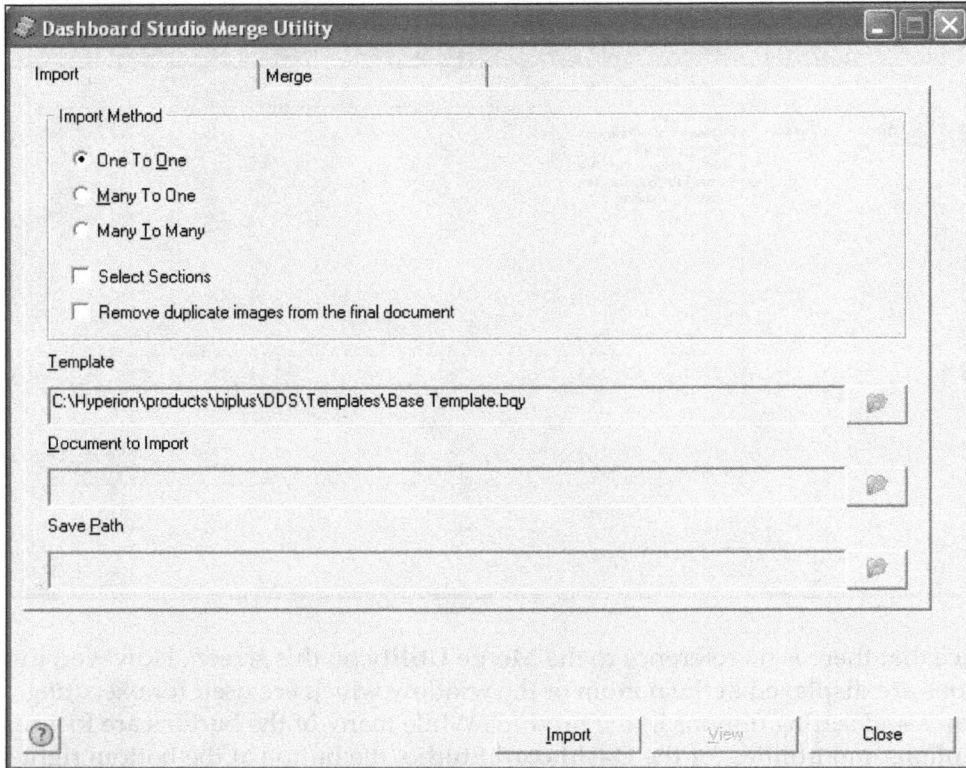

The **Merge Utility** contains two tabs at the top of screen. The first tab is for importing and the second tab is for merging. The **Import** option is used to import sections of a document into a standard **Dashboard Development Studio Template**. This feature is not used to merge sections of two or more custom documents together, but is specific to importing documents into a Dashboard Studio dashboard template.

The second tab at the top of the screen is the **Merge** tab. It is used for merging sections of Interactive Reporting documents together into a single document. The following screenshot displays the **Merge Utility** screen open to the **Merge** tab:

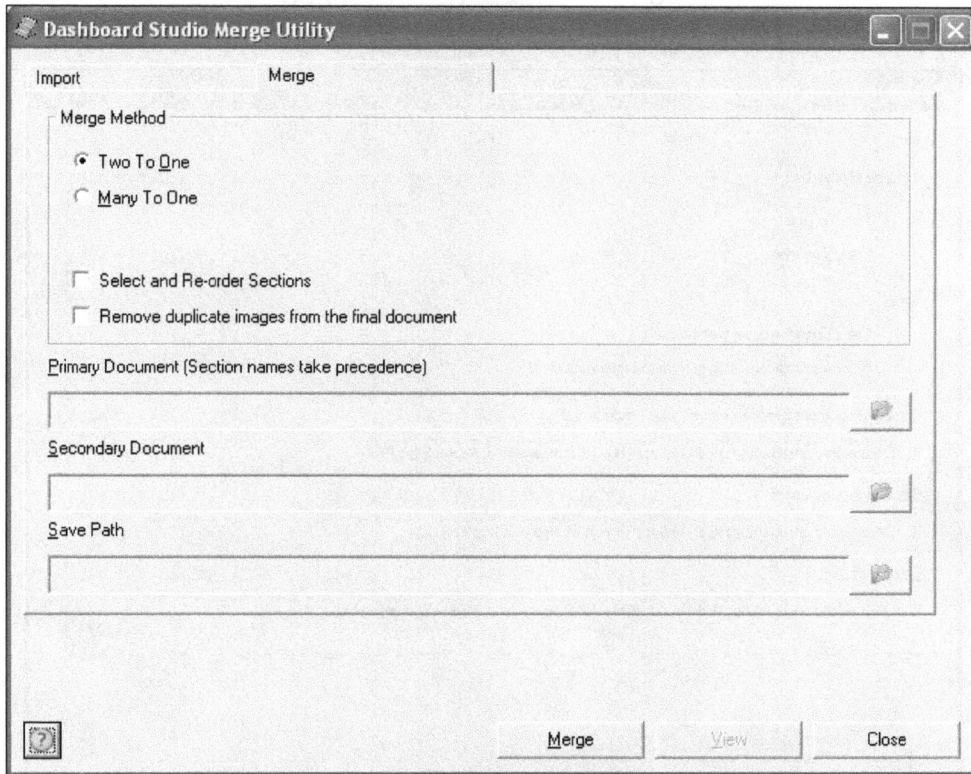

Merging two documents into one

The default **Merge Method** is set to the **Two To One** option. This option is the most common merge method as most requests are for merging the sections of two documents together. The **Two To One** option requires the user to define a **Primary Document** and a **Secondary Document** for the merge process. The **Primary Document** is defined as the document that accepts the new sections, and the **Secondary Document** is the document supplying the new sections. Both the primary and secondary documents, as well as the output for the merge (denoted by the label **Save Path**), are configured at the bottom of the **Merge** window. These features are executed by clicking on the folder icons to the right of the text boxes to bring up a file browser window, allowing the user to navigate to the document of interest.

After selecting the primary and secondary documents, the final merged document, referred to as the **Save Path**, is automatically populated with the location and filename of the primary document, but with the text _merged appended to the end of the filename. The following screenshot displays the Merge Utility configured with two files selected:

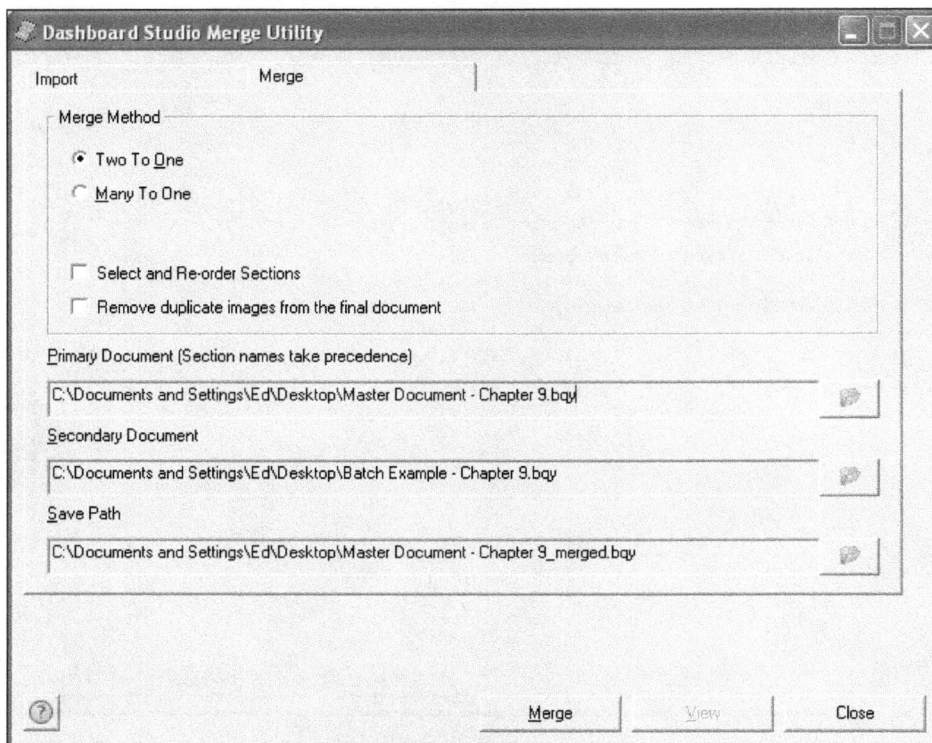

The textboxes displayed in the previous screenshot containing the file path names are read-only. The filenames must be selected using the file browsing window and cannot be edited by typing. Similar to selecting the **Primary** and **Secondary** documents, the filename and path of the final merged document in the **Save Path** textbox is edited by pressing the folder button to the right of the textbox and by specifying the filename in the file browser window.

In addition to the configuration of the path and filename for the primary, secondary, and final merged document, the user is presented with two other features to enable through checkboxes on the main screen. The first checkbox is the **Select and Re-order Sections** option. When the **Select and Re-order Sections** option is checked, the Merge Utility displays a window allowing the user to select the sections of interest from the secondary document to import into the primary document. If the **Select and Re-order Sections** option is not checked, the Merge Utility will import all of the sections from the **Secondary Document** into the **Primary Document**. The second checkbox on the screen is named **Remove duplicate images from the final document**. When this feature is checked, all consistent images that match between the primary and secondary documents are set to the image in the primary document to reduce the size of the file. The following screenshot displays the Merge Utility configured to run a merge between two documents with the **Select and Re-order Sections** and **Remove duplicate images from the final document** options selected:

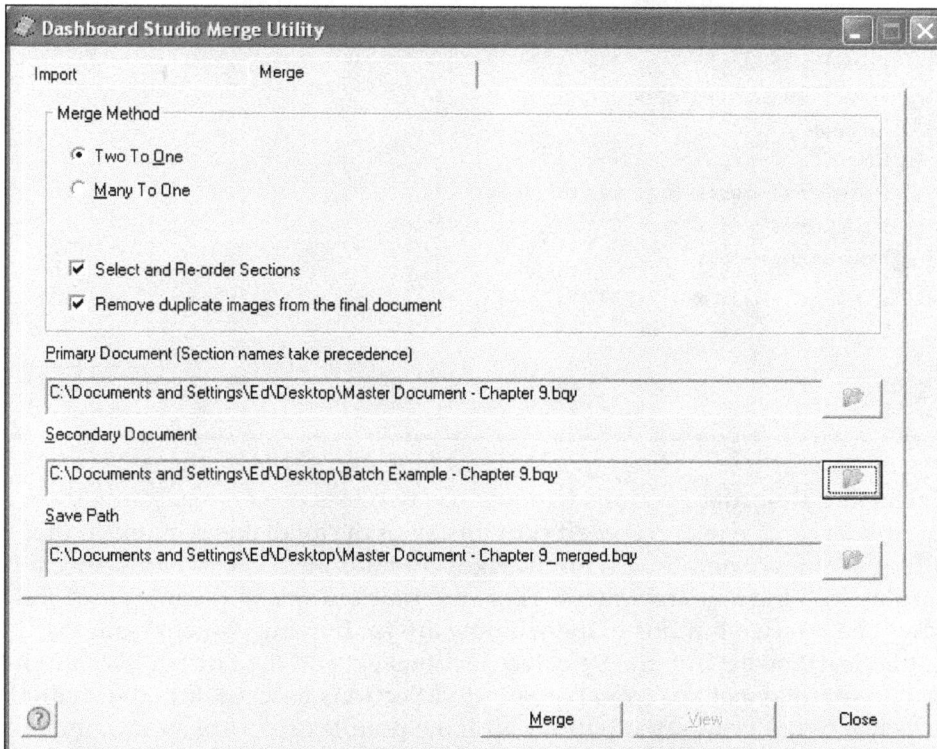

The final step in executing the merge is to press the **Merge** button at the bottom of the **Merge Utility** window. Upon pressing the **Merge** button, the **Select and Re-order Sections** window appears, providing the ability to select the sections of the secondary document for merging into the final document. The following screenshot displays the **Select and Re-order Sections** window:

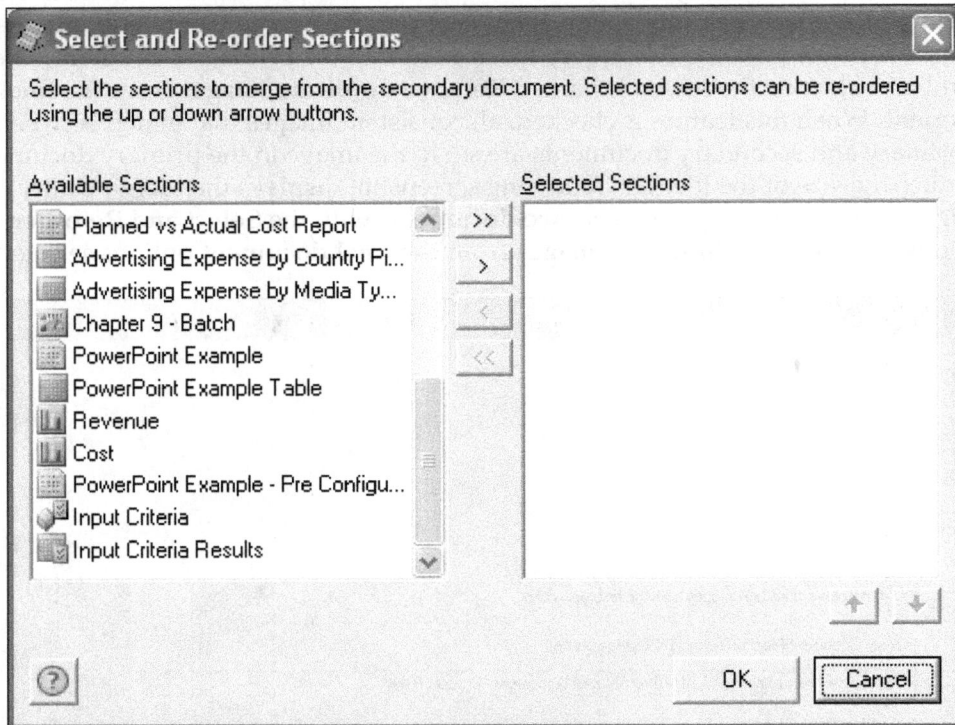

The **Select and Re-order Sections** window has two lists used for selecting the content to merge. The list on the left contains all of the available sections in the secondary document and the list on the right contains all of the sections selected for merging into the final document. There are four buttons in the middle of the window. The top two buttons in the window are for moving content from the **Available Sections** list into the **Selected Sections** list and the bottom two buttons are used to remove sections from the **Selected Sections** list back into the **Available Sections** list. In both cases, the buttons with the double carets are used to move all of the sections into or out of the **Selected Sections** list and the single caret buttons are used to move a single item at a time.

It is important to note the order of the sections in the **Available Sections** window. The order of the **Available Sections** is not the order that the sections are displayed in the Interactive Reporting document, but rather the order that the sections are assigned by the Interactive Reporting software product. The ordering of the sections is discussed further in the *Dashboard Studio Optimize Utility* section of this chapter.

As items are added into the **Selected Sections** list, these items are reordered by selecting a single section and pressing the up and down buttons at the bottom of the **Selected Sections** list to move the selected section up or down in the list order. The following screenshot shows items moved from the **Available Sections** list into the **Selected Sections** list:

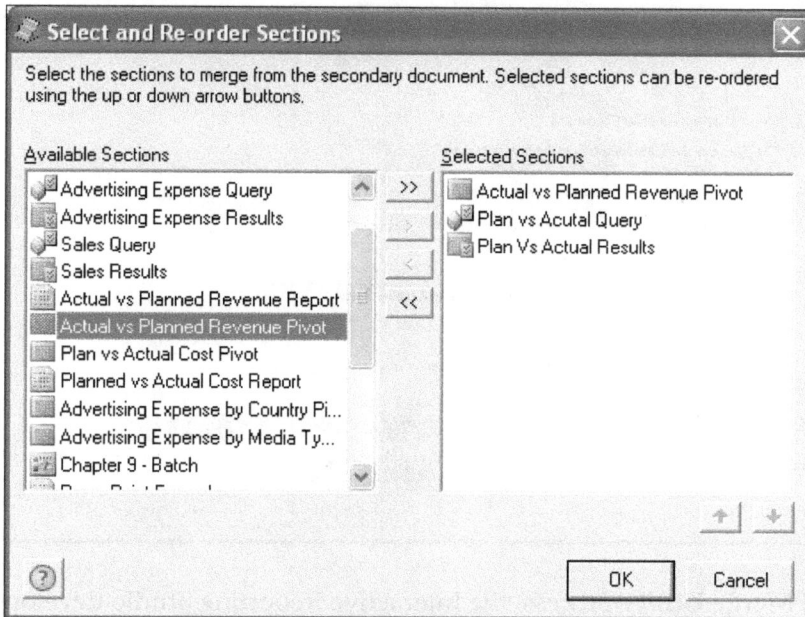

In the previous screenshot, the **Planned vs Actual Query** and the **Planned vs Actual Results** were automaticity selected when the *Actual vs. Planned Revenue Pivot* section was moved into the Selected Sections list. The reason these additional sections moved with the pivot is because the Pivot section is dependent on the Query and Results sections to supply the pivot with data. These dependent sections are referred to as **Parent sections**. Parent sections will be discussed later in the *Dashboard Studio Optimize Utility* section of this chapter.

After all of the desired sections are added to the **Selected Sections** list, the next step in executing the **Merge Utility** is to press the **OK** button at the bottom of the **Select and Re-order Sections** window. Upon pressing the **OK** button, the screen reverts to the **Dashboard Studio Merge Utility** window with two status bars shown at the bottom of the screen, providing information on the status and progress of the merge process. The following screenshot shows the two status bars and related information at the bottom of the **Dashboard Studio Merge Utility** window:

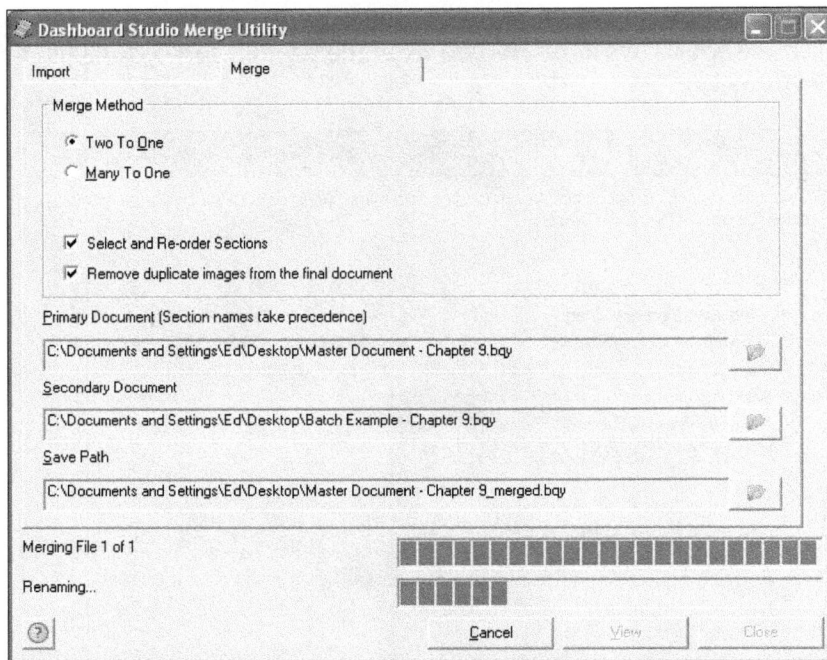

During the **Merge Utility** process, the Interactive Reporting Studio developer utility is active and performing operations. The Interactive Reporting Studio is used by the **Dashboard Studio Merge Utility** to perform the section merging and manipulation. When the **Merge Utility** completes the merge process, the **Report** window appears and displays a full log of the activities that took place during the merge process. Any change that took place in the document is highlighted in blue text and a full text description provides an explanation of the changes. The **Report** is closed by pressing the **OK** button. The **Report** can also be saved into an HTML file by pressing the **Save** button. The following screenshot shows the **Report** window that appears when the **Merge Utility** has completed (the **Report** window in this example has been scrolled to the bottom to display the merge changes):

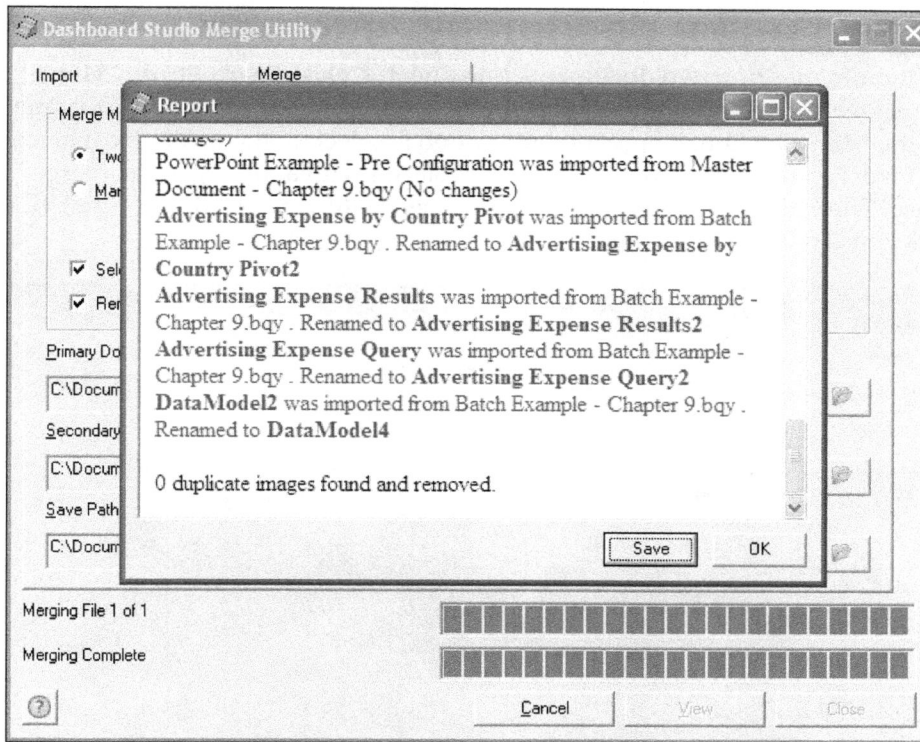

After the merge process is complete, the final document may be opened and the sections merged into the document will be displayed at the bottom of the list of documents sections.

Merging many documents into one

In addition to merging two documents into one, the **Dashboard Studio Merge Utility** allows for the merging of multiple documents together into one document. When the **Many To One** merge method option is selected, the flexibility that existed in the **Two To One** merge method is now replaced with a more generic merge interface. The following screenshot displays the **Dashboard Studio Merge Utility** set to the **Many To One** merge method:

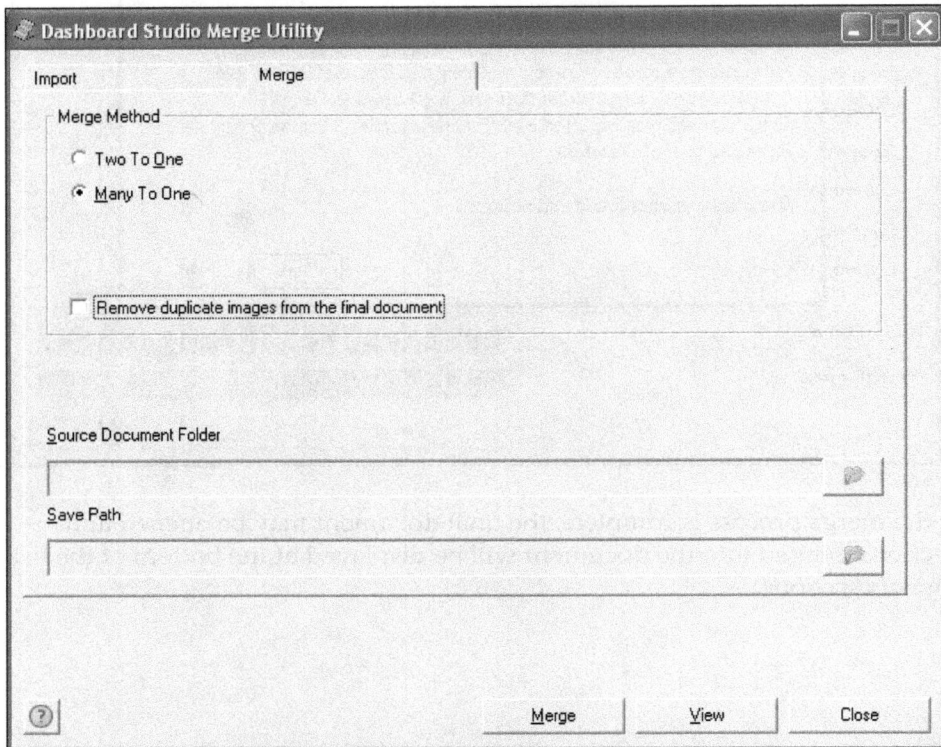

The **Many To One** interface does not provide the ability to select and reorder sections, and the ability to select a primary and secondary document is removed and replaced with a **Source Document Folder**. The **Source Document Folder** option is used to select a folder containing multiple Interactive Reporting documents and not individual files. Upon selecting the folder icon to the right of the **Source Document Folder** option, the **Browse for Folder** window appears for selecting the desired folder. After a folder is selected, the **Save Path** for the document must be manually specified. The **Save Path** is set by clicking the **folder** icon to the right of the **Save Path** textbox and by browsing to a folder and providing a filename for the final merged document.

The following screenshot shows the **Many To One** merge method window populated and ready for merging:

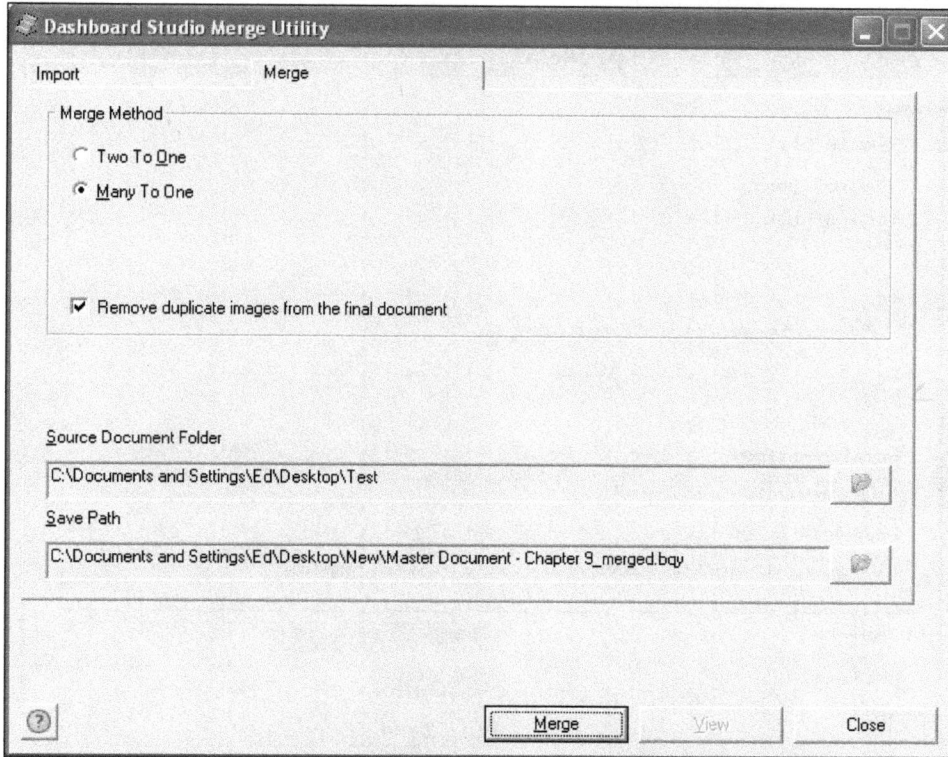

Once the merge process is executed, the software merges all of the documents together into the final file. The following screenshot shows the **Merge Utility** during the **Many To One** merge execution:

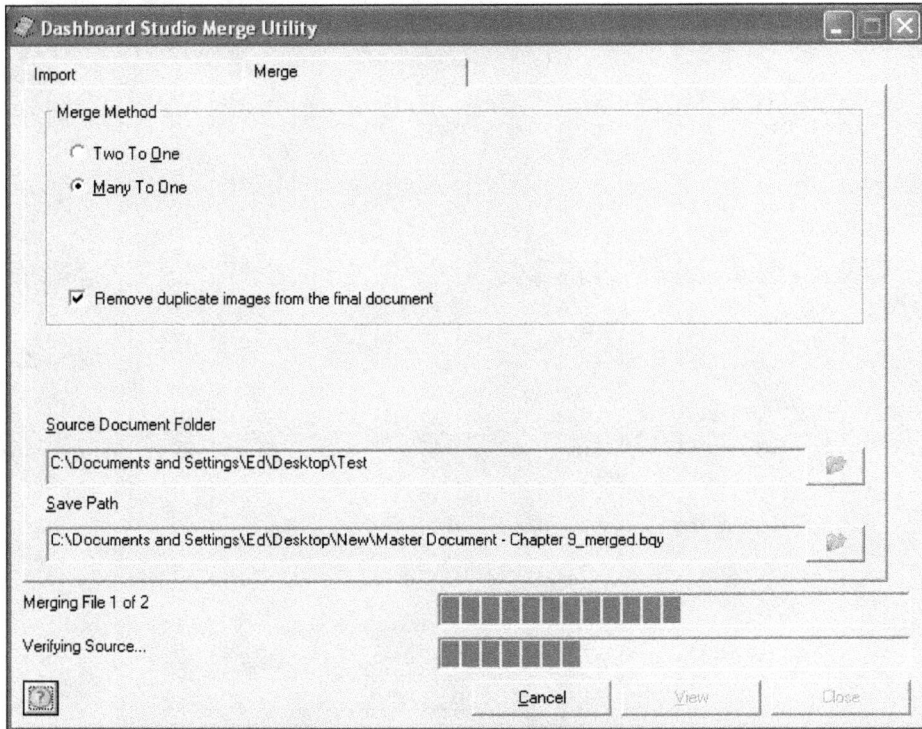

Similar to the **Two To One** merge method, the **Merge Utility** creates a merge report after the **Merge Utility** completes. The following screenshot shows the **Report**:

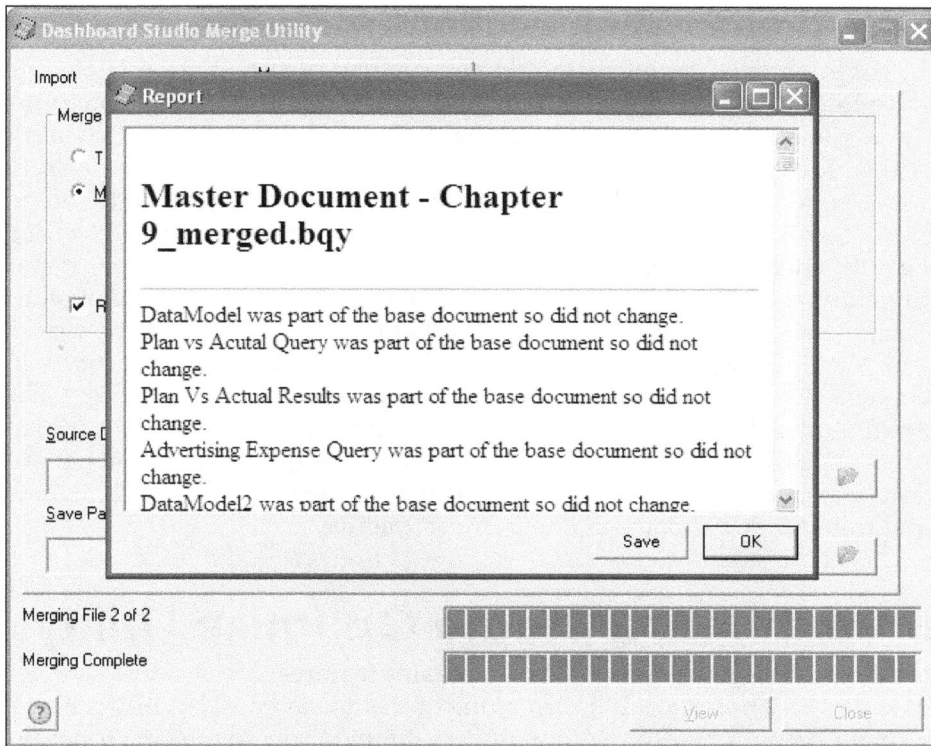

Merging documents for users

As Interactive Reporting allows users to save documents locally with a saved connection to the server, it is important to note the impact of using the Merge Utility on documents saved locally and run by users from their desktops. When the Merge Utility is executed on a set of documents, the final document produced will allow the queries from the primary document to continue to be processed against the server. However, any query that is merged from the secondary document into the final document will not have a connection for processing. When users attempt to run a query merged in from a secondary document, the query will fail. To re-establish a connection between the document and the server for processing, the final document from the merge process must be posted to the Oracle EPM Workspace and the query connections made.

Merging presentation sections for users

In many environments, the interest to share formatted presentations sections across Interactive Reporting files exists. As detailed Pivot, Chart, Dashboard, and Report sections are time-consuming to produce, the ability to merge the formatted sections into another document and then switch the objects to use a different Query section would save significant time in the development process. The Dashboard Studio Merge Utility in concert with the Dashboard Studio Optimize Utility can be used to execute the sharing of presentation sections across documents. The first step in executing this process is to use the Merge Utility to merge the presentation sections of the document with the primary document that will be accepting the new sections. When the Merge Utility is utilized, the dependent Query and Results sections of the secondary document will also be imported into the primary document. The Dashboard Studio Optimize Utility can then be used to move the sections from one Query section to another based on a few rules that are required to be met before the move can be executed. The *Dashboard Studio Optimize Utility* section will discuss the steps and rules for switching a section between queries.

The Dashboard Studio Optimize Utility

The **Dashboard Studio Optimize Utility** contains features to make rapid changes to the composition, ordering, and formatting of the document. The software allows users to make sections read-only, contains the ability to run documents faster by compressing JavaScript, provides the ability to move sections across queries, and fixes corrupt Interactive Reporting documents.

The first step in working with the **Dashboard Studio Optimize Utility** is to access the software from the **Utilities and Administration** folder of the Oracle EPM system folder in the **Start Menu**. The following screenshot displays the shortcut for the product:

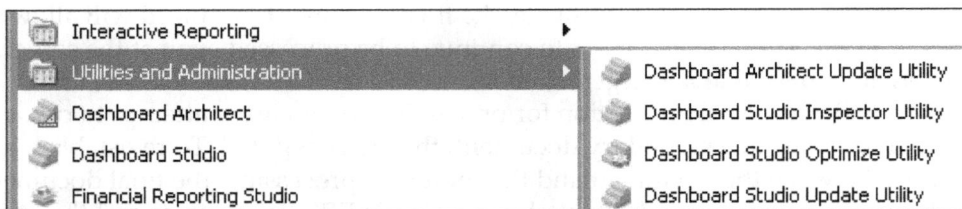

When the software is opened, the **Dashboard Studio Optimize Utility** product will display as shown in the following screenshot and the Interactive Reporting Studio developer utility will also open:

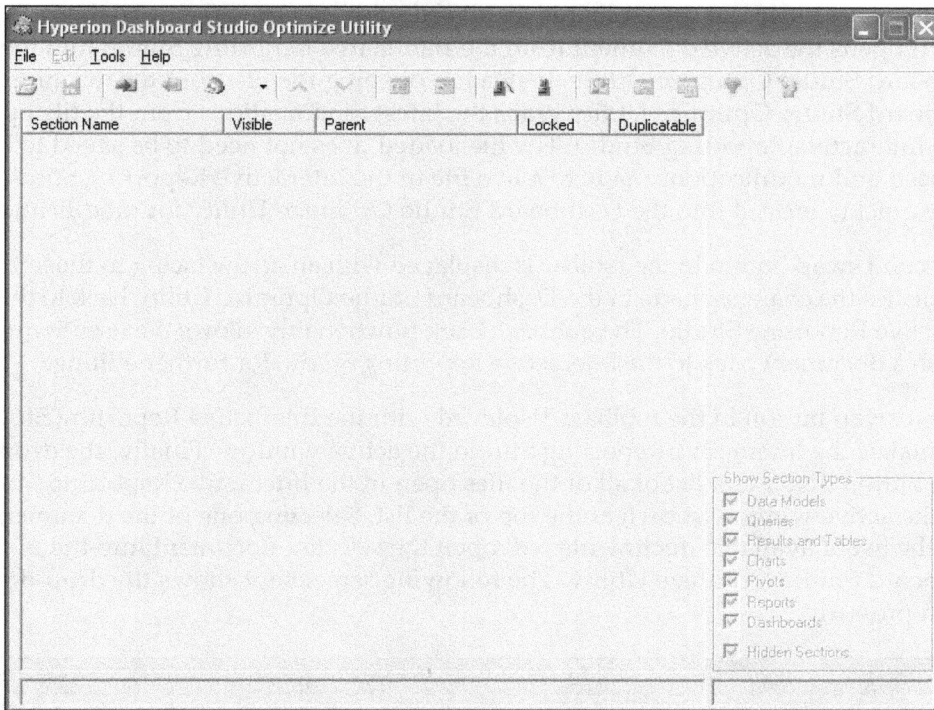

The **Dashboard Studio Optimize Utility** begins with a blank screen ready for the user to open a document into the product. A file is opened in the **Dashboard Studio Optimize Utility** in one of four options: the first method is to use the open shortcut from the **File** menu, the second method is to use the open file button on the toolbar, the third method is by dragging and dropping the file on the local machine into the window, and the final method is to use the Interactive Reporting Studio toolbar button to bring a file open in the Interactive Reporting Studio into the **Dashboard Studio Optimize Utility**.

Interactive Reporting Studio swap shortcuts

The Dashboard Studio Optimize Utility swap buttons are displayed in the Dashboard Studio Optimize Utility toolbar. The following screenshot highlights the three buttons and a drop-down list used to swap documents between the Interactive Reporting Studio and the Dashboard Studio Optimize Utility:

The first swap button in the toolbar is displayed with an arrow facing to the right. It opens the active document from the Interactive Reporting Studio into the Dashboard Studio Optimize Utility. Instead of opening the file from the machine, the Dashboard Studio Optimize Utility grabs the latest modifications from the file open in the Interactive Reporting Studio. The file loaded does not need to be saved to be imported and modifications made to a live file in the Interactive Reporting Studio can be quickly moved into the Dashboard Studio Optimize Utility for modification.

The second swap button in the toolbar is displayed with an arrow facing to the left. It publishes the changes made in the Dashboard Studio Optimize Utility back to the Interactive Reporting Studio. The `publish back` functionality allows the user to quickly publish a document back to the Interactive Reporting Studio for further editing.

The last swap button in the toolbar, displayed with the Interactive Reporting Studio icon, makes the Interactive Reporting Studio the active window. Finally, the drop-down button displays a list of all of the files open in the Interactive Reporting Studio with the active window shown at the top of the list. Selecting one of the documents from the list of available documents will open the selected document into the Dashboard Studio Optimize Utility. The following screenshot shows the drop-down button pressed:

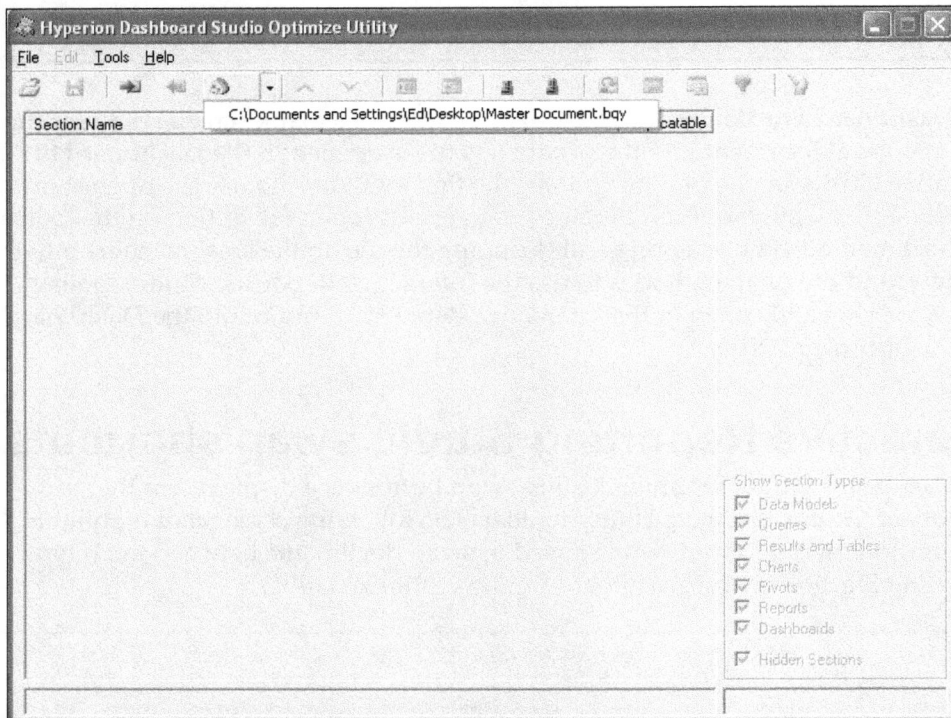

Filtering section types

When an Interactive Reporting document is opened into the Dashboard Studio Optimize Utility, the list of sections is displayed in the main window with a few of the file properties that can be edited using the Optimize Utility. The following screenshot displays a file open in the **Dashboard Studio Optimize Utility**:

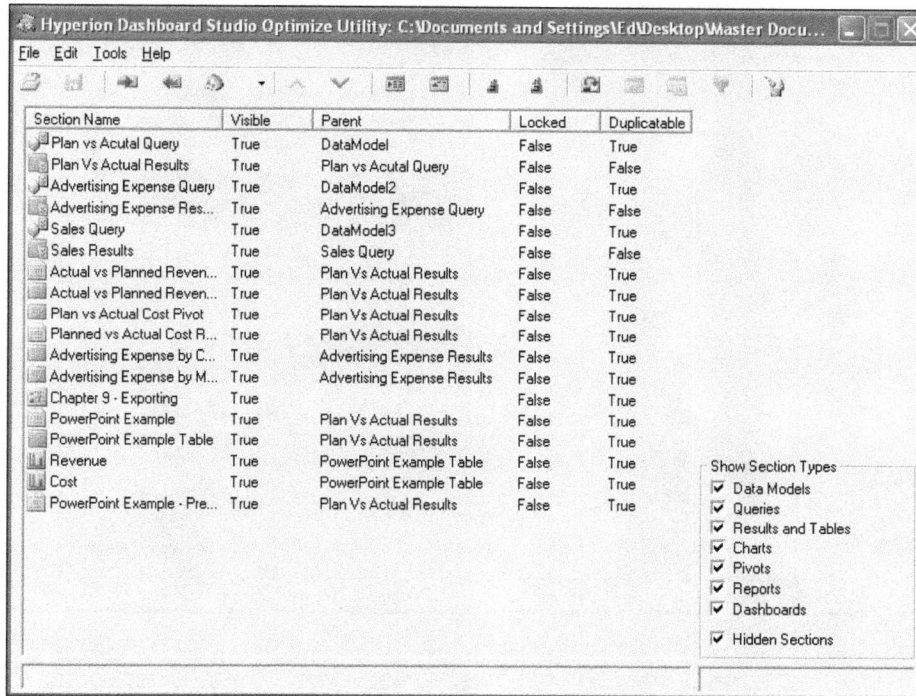

Interactive Reporting documents can contain a large number of sections making the documents hard to edit in the Interactive Reporting Studio. The **Dashboard Studio Optimize Utility** provides the functionality to filter the list of sections displayed in the main window by checking and un-checking section types from the show section type options in the bottom right hand corner of the **Dashboard Studio Optimize Utility** window. The Optimize Utility allows the user to filter to display only a particular type of section or a combination of different sections, including Data Models, Queries, Results, and Tables, Charts, Pivots, Reports, Dashboards, as well as the ability to display or hide the hidden sections of the document regardless of section type.

The following screenshot shows the example from the previous screenshot filtered to display only the **Query** sections of the document:

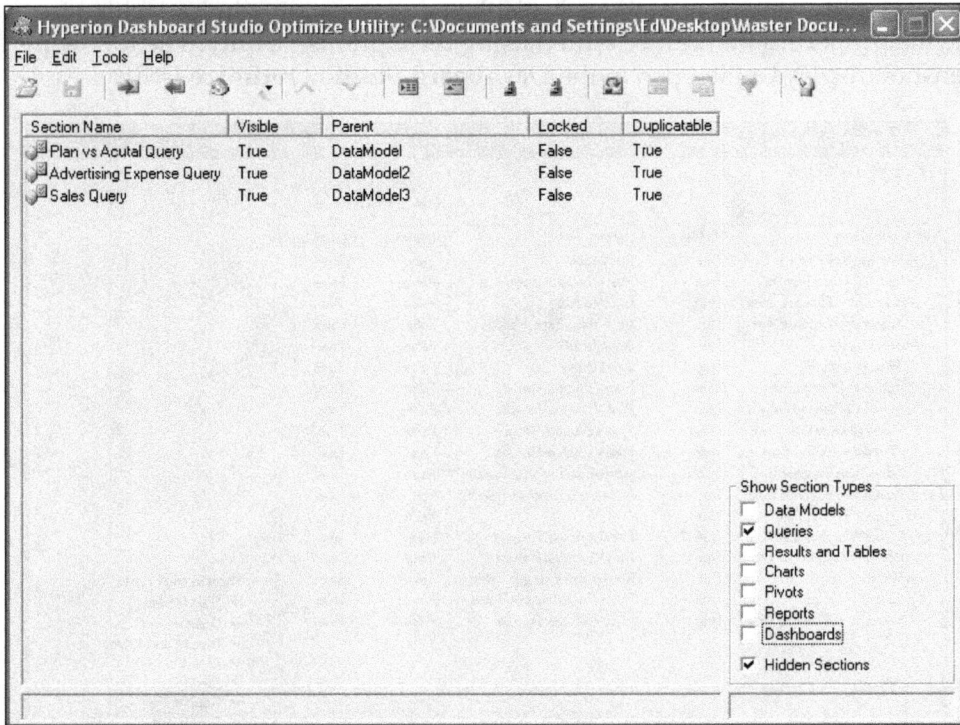

> Only one file can be opened in the **Dashboard Studio Optimize Utility** at a time. Any attempt to open a second file after editing the first file will result in this software prompting to save progress before closing the initial file and opening the new file.

Editing Interactive Reporting documents

The Dashboard Studio Optimize Utility provides the user with the ability to make quick changes across sections of the document that are difficult to complete in the Interactive Reporting Studio. The **Edit** menu, shown in the following screenshot, displays the full list of options that can be executed inside the **Dashboard Studio Optimize Utility**:

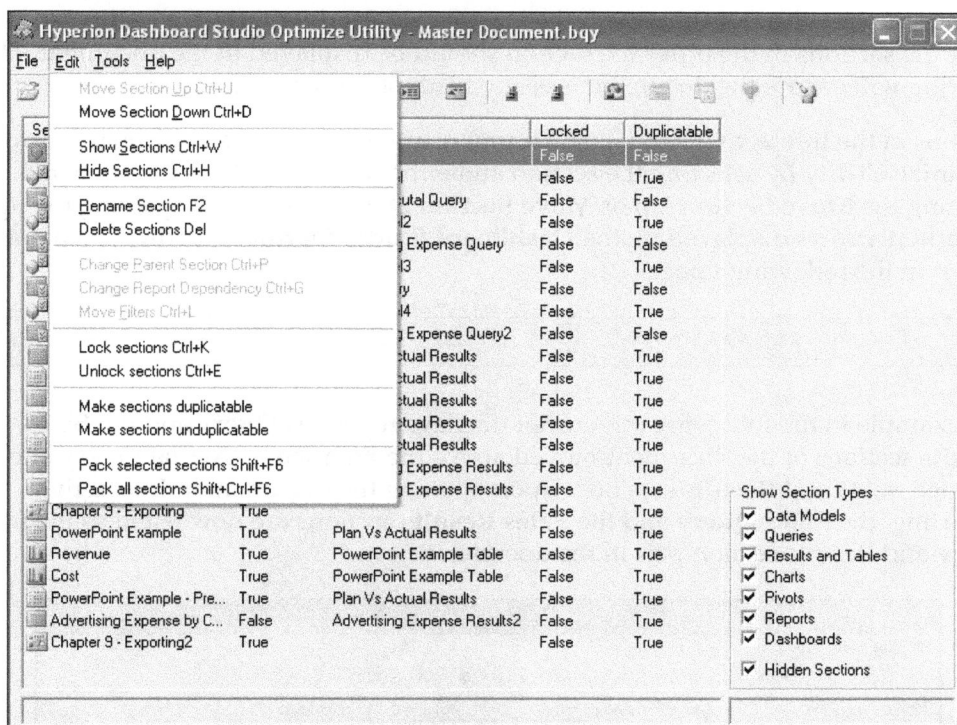

The **Edit** menu options can also be accessed by selecting a section in the main window of the document and right-clicking on it. As the options contained in the **Edit** menu and right-click menu are consistent across the product, the following subsections will discuss editing the sections by using the **Edit** menu or by using the shortcuts displayed on the toolbar.

Moving sections

Moving sections in the Interactive Reporting Studio and Interactive Reporting Web Client product requires the user to duplicate and delete sections to achieve a desired section order. The Dashboard Studio Optimize Utility provides a much easier method for moving sections.

Notice the listing of the sections shown in the **Dashboard Studio Optimize Utility** in the next screenshot. The order of the sections is set by the tool and depends on when the section was introduced into the document. While the section order does not mimic the grouping displayed in the Web Client or Studio product, the ordering of the sections displayed in the **Dashboard Studio Optimize Utility** will impact the ordering of the objects inside the software.

A best practice when working with the **Dashboard Studio Optimize Utility** is to order the sections in the order the section should be displayed in the document. This ordering will ensure the document is easily readable and maintainable.

Sections in the Interactive Reporting document are moved in the **Dashboard Studio Optimize Utility** by selecting the section and either accessing the **Edit** menu and selecting the **Move Section Up** or **Move Section Down** options, or by using the up and down arrows displayed on the **Dashboard Studio Optimize Utility** toolbar as shown in the following image:

The example in the following screenshot displays the **Sales Query** and the **Sales Results** sections of the document moved above the **Planned vs Actual Query** and **Planned vs Actual Results** sections. Upon opening the document in Interactive Reporting, the **Sales Query** and the **Sales Results** sections are now listed as the first Query and Results section pair in the document.

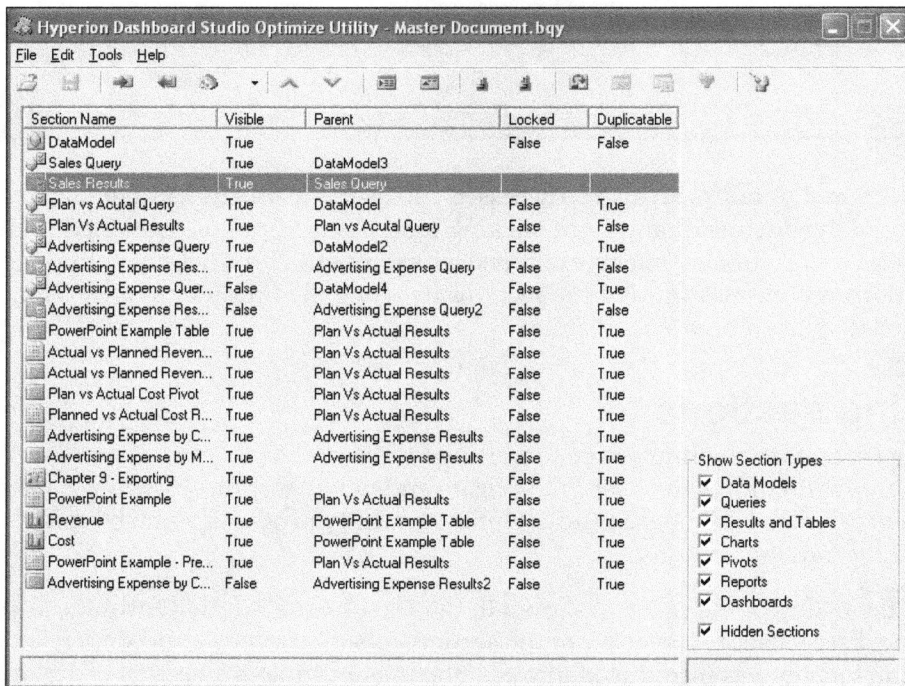

Showing and Cap Hiding

The Interactive Reporting Web Client and Studio product provide the ability to hide and unhide sections of the document. While multiple sections of the document can be shown that were once previously hidden, each section must be hidden individually. The Dashboard Studio Optimize Utility provides the ability to view the visible status of the section in the document and it provides the ability to show or hide multiple sections of the document at one time.

Showing or hiding multiple sections in the document is easily achieved by highlighting multiple sections in the main window and selecting the **Show Sections** or **Hide Sections** menu item, or by using the **Show Sections** or **Hide Sections** button in the toolbar as shown in the following screenshot:

After a section is shown or hidden, the visible column in the main window updates to true or false, where true indicates visible and false indicates hidden.

Renaming and Deleting

The Interactive Reporting Web Client and Studio provide the ability to rename and delete sections from the document on an individual basis. The Dashboard Studio Optimize Utility provides the same functionality, but also allows the user to delete multiple sections from the document at one time.

Renaming or deleting sections in the document is easily achieved by highlighting the section or multiple sections (if deleting) in the main window and selecting the **Rename Section** or **Delete Section** menu item or toolbar button, as shown in the following screenshot:

When a section is deleted, an alert box will appear to confirm deletion if the section is used in dependent sections. Canceling the deletion will prevent the deletion from completing.

Locking and Unlocking

The locking and unlocking features of the Dashboard Studio Optimize Utility are unique in that these features allow the developer to put a section into read-only mode by simply locking the section. The locking and unlocking features are specific to only the Interactive Reporting Web Client, where objects that are locked are not editable by the Web Client user.

Sections in the document are easily locked and unlocked in the Dashboard Studio Optimize Utility by highlighting the section(s) in the main window and selecting the **Lock** sections or **Unlock** sections menu items or by using the **Lock** and **Unlock** buttons in the toolbar, as shown in the following screenshot:

After a section has been locked or unlocked, the locked column in the main window of the Dashboard Studio Optimize Utility will display true if the section is locked or false if the section is unlocked.

Duplicatable and Unduplicatable

Similar to locking and unlocking, a section can be put in a duplicatable and unduplicatable state preventing Web Client users of the product from duplicating a section. While this property can be set in the Interactive Reporting Studio through the **Edit** menu, the Dashboard Studio Optimize Utility allows the user to make multiple sections duplicatable or unduplicatable at one time.

Sections in the document are put in a duplicatable or unduplicatable state by highlighting the section(s) in the main window and selecting the **Make Sections Duplicatable** or **Make Sections Unduplicatable** menu items. After a section is set to a duplicatable or unduplicatable state, the **Duplicatable** column in the main window of the Dashboard Studio Optimize Utility will display true if the section is duplicatable or false if the section is unduplicatable.

Packing section code

Packing the code of a section is used to optimize the speed of the JavaScript processing in the document. Some documents, including documents built by the Dashboard Studio product, contain significant amounts of code that increase the file size and slow down the execution of the document. The Pack Section Code feature provides an automated method to optimize the code execution in the document.

The packaging of code in the documents can be done on a section-by-section basis or across an entire document by highlighting the desired sections and selecting the **Pack Selected Sections Edit** menu item or by merely selecting the **Pack All Sections Edit** menu item. Upon selecting either option, the Pack JavaScript window appears and prompts the user to remove specific sections of code native to the Dashboard Studio in addition to the other packaging features provided by the software as shown in the following screenshot:

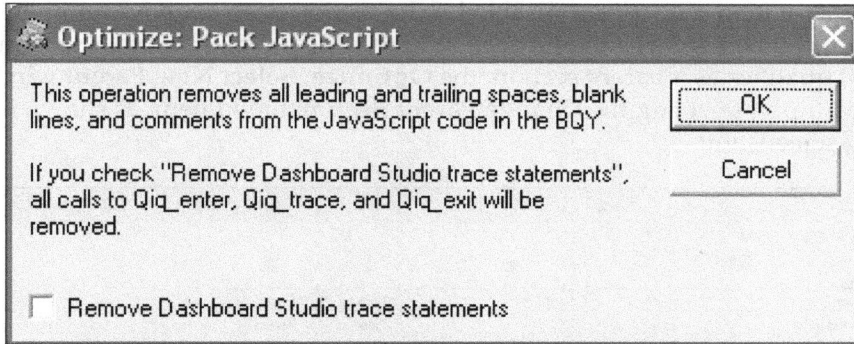

After selecting the **OK** button on the Pack JavaScript window displayed in the previous screenshot, the software will condense the JavaScript code inside the document.

Moving objects and sections across Results

One of the most unique and beneficial features of the Dashboard Studio Optimize Utility is the ability to move sections from one set of results to another as well as similar functionality with filters and objects in Report sections. The functionality allows users to share features created for one specific task across many tasks, which drastically reduces development efforts.

Moving sections across Results or Table sections

The Dashboard Studio Optimize Utility is the only product that provides the ability to move a section of the document from one set of results to a completely separate set of results. The software requires the section receiving the moved object to contain the same column names as leveraged in the current object. In the case of moving a Pivot section between two Results sections, the receiving Results section must contain the same column names used in the Pivot section. In addition to Pivots, Tables and Charts may also be moved under any Results and Table section that contains the same column names.

Initiating the changing of the parent section begins by highlighting the section in the main window and selecting the **Change Parent Section Edit** menu item or by selecting the **Change Parent Section** button in the toolbar as shown in the following screenshot:

The **Edit** menu item will appear disabled if the section does not have another section that can be used as a parent section in the document. If another section in the document qualifies as a parent section, the **Optimize: Select New Parent** window will appear upon selecting the **Change Parent Section** menu item, as shown in the following screenshot:

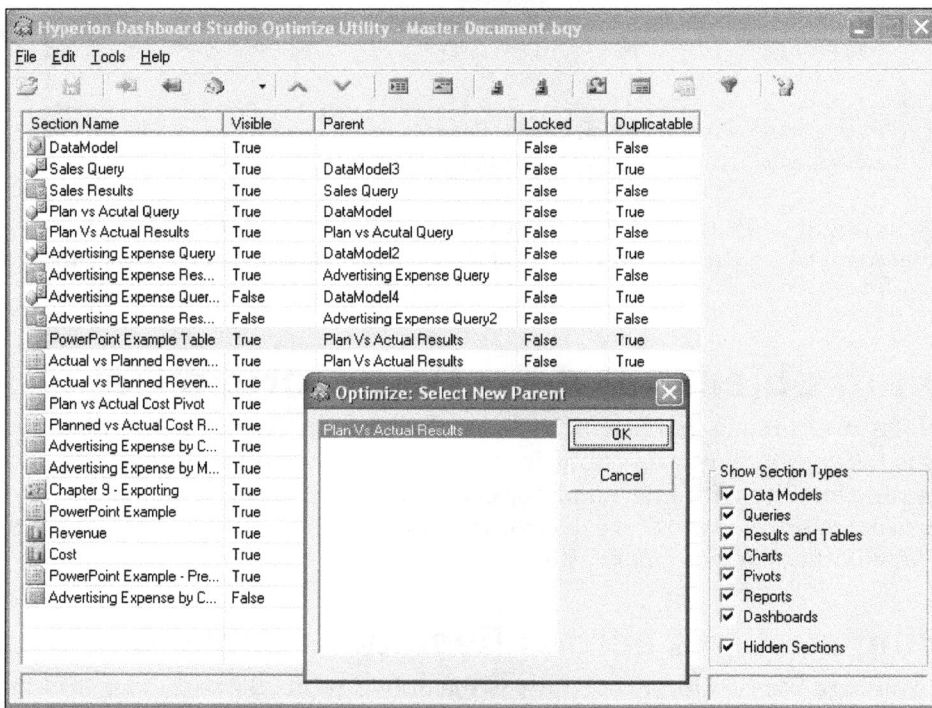

After the parent section of the document is changed, the **Parent** column in the main window of the Dashboard Studio Optimize Utility will display the name of the new parent section. The new parent section can be switched back to the original parent section as desired by following the same instructions for changing the parent section.

Modifying Report Dependencies

Another beneficial feature of the Dashboard Studio Optimize Utility is its ability to take a Report section and change the referenced objects contained within the report across Query, Results, and Table sections. As significant effort is expended in creating Report section templates, the **Change Report Dependency** feature allows the software user to take a report and easily swap out the existing presentation sections in the document to a different section. Once the Report section is modified, the report retains the existing report features and Report Groups, but now displays the new objects in the report.

The **Change Report Dependency** feature is specific to Report sections. The feature is executed by highlighting a **Report** section in the main window of the **Dashboard Studio Optimize Utility** and selecting the **Change Report Dependency Edit** menu item or the **Change Report Dependency** shortcut on the toolbar, as shown in the following screenshot:

When the **Change Report Dependency** menu item is executed, the **Optimize: Change Report Dependency** window appears providing the user with the ability to change the report references in the document as shown in the following screenshot:

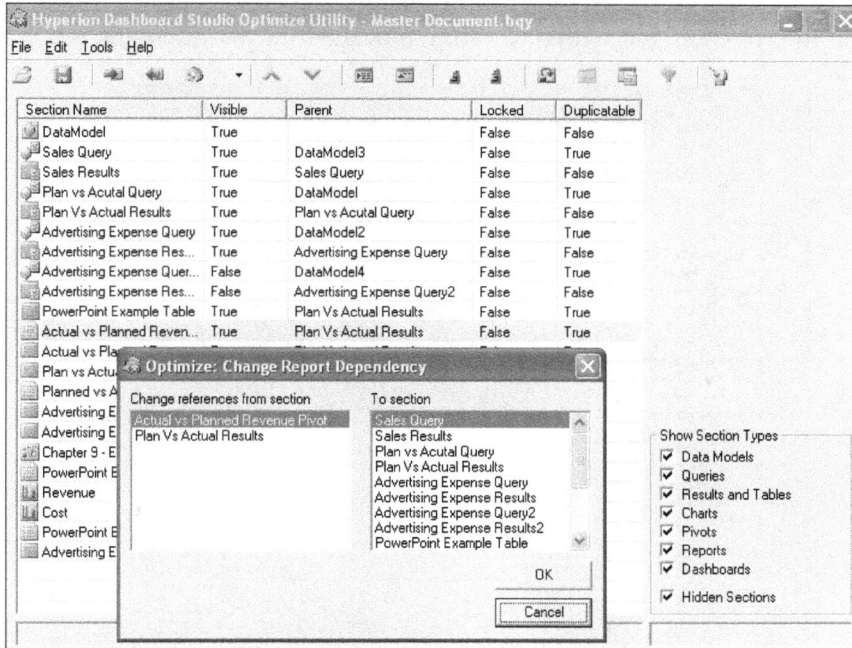

Upon opening the saved document, the modified Report section will display the newly referenced sections in the same place as the section that was replaced in the report.

Moving Filters

The Dashboard Studio Optimize Utility allows users to take filters created on one section and move those filters to another section of the document. The **Move Filters** option is very beneficial as sections of the document may be created with custom filter selections and recreating the filters across sections may require significant effort. Interactive Reporting contains rules for moving filters across the document, where the receiving section must have the same definition for the column as the section providing the column.

Filters are moved to another section of the document by executing the **Move Filters Edit** menu option or by selecting the **Move Filters** button on the toolbar as shown in the following example:

The **Move Filters Edit** menu item will appear disabled if the filters in the section cannot be received by any other document section. When the **Move Filters** menu item is executed, the **Optimize: Move Filters** window appears, providing the user with the ability to change the filters as shown in the following screenshot:

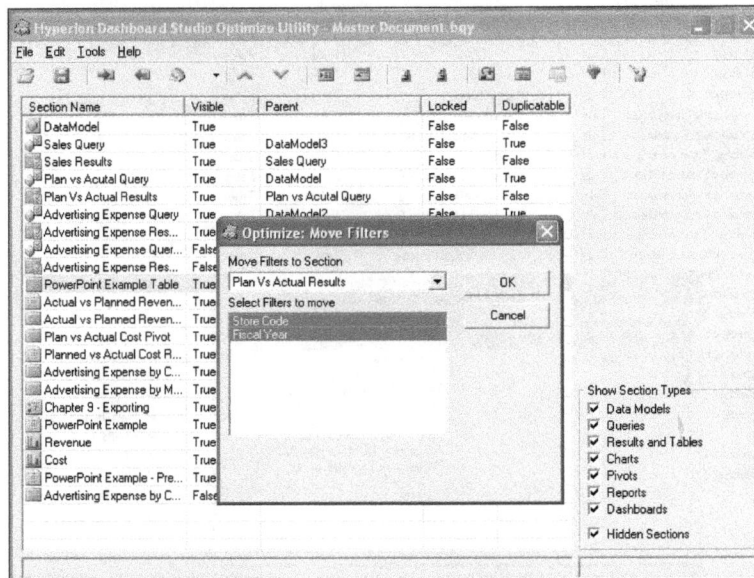

The **Optimize: Move Filters** window allows the user to select the receiving section from the drop-down box and then to select the filters to move into the receiving section. Upon pressing **OK,** the filters moved are displayed in the receiving section.

Fixing corrupt files

Interactive Reporting documents can become corrupted as changes are made to the document over time. When a corrupt document is opened in the Interactive Reporting Studio or Web Client Utility, the report will freeze upon opening or it will display an error window stating Unknown Error. When the document will not open appropriately in Interactive Reporting, the Dashboard Studio Optimize Utility may be used to open the document and in some cases will allow the document to be resaved. The resaving of the document may fix the file corruption that was experienced when opening the document. The file fixing feature is an invaluable resource for users with corrupt files. Users experiencing these issues with a file should send the files to users with the Dashboard Studio Optimize Utility to attempt to fix corrupt files. Additionally, users should save multiple versions of a document to ensure the ability to revert back to an earlier version if the files are corrupt.

Summary

The goal of this chapter was to provide the user and developer insight into tools and technologies that are available for use outside the standard Interactive Reporting Studio and Web Client products. The chapter focused on two specific products: the Dashboard Studio and Dashboard Studio Optimize Utility. The chapter began with an introduction to the Dashboard Studio and Dashboard Studio Merge Utility product. All of the available features of the Dashboard Studio Merge Utility were discussed in-depth, including merging two documents together to merging multiple documents into a single document. After the merge features were presented, the chapter presented a complete guide to the Dashboard Studio Optimize Utility. Quickly editing the document sections and section properties were discussed in addition to details on modifying parent sections, section filters, and report referenced objects. The chapter concluded with the steps to corrupt Interactive Reporting documents using the Dashboard Studio Optimize utility.

Index

Bring To Front option 90

C

CCR
  about 205, 206
  code table, configuring 207
  JavaScript code, preparing 206
  query, configuring 207
  table structure 206, 207
CCR, querying
  about 208
  Code DataModel, building 209
  code query, building 210
  query section, creating 208
  query section, renaming 208
  results section, renaming 208
ceil function 178
center option, object alignment option 91
Central Code Repository. *See* CCR
chart display space
  maximising 50
chart query
  creating 46, 52, 53
chart section computed items 20
check box dashboard control 88
Chr function 179
code
  leveraging, through document 13
code pane 31
code table, CCR
  configuring 207
collections 28
ColMax function 179
ColMin function 179
columns
  referencing 168
command button dashboard control 88
comparison operators, decision logic 36
Compress Document setting 126
computed items
  about 166
  adding 167
  deleting 173
  functions 182
  variables 182
concatenation 33

concat function 180
conditional functions 175
conditional statements, decision logic 37, 38
continue statement 40
controls, dashboard section objects
  about 87
  check box dashboard control 88
  command button dashboard control 88
  drop box dashboard control 88
  embedded browser control 88
  hyperlink control 88
  list box dashboard control 88
  radio button dashboard control 88
  slider control 88
  text box control 88
CountDistinct function 179
Count function 179
CountNonNull function 179
CountNull function 179
cPlanvAct embedded chart section 98
cume function 179
custom dashboard navigation
  implementing 92
  internal navigation, scripting 92-94
custom dashboard navigation, implementing
  external navigation 93, 94
  internal navigation, scripting 92, 93
custom images, adding 74
Custom Values property 154

D

dashboard
  about 24
  BMV USA Executive Dashboard, example
    44
  controls, adding 74
  creating 72
  custom images, adding 74
  data driven dashboard objects, creating 45,
    46
  graphics, adding 74
  hyperlinks, adding 75
  interactivity 76, 77
  objects, adding 73
  planning 43, 44

[PACKT] enterprise

PUBLISHING

professional expertise distilled

Thank you for buying
Oracle Hyperion Interactive Reporting 11 Expert Guide

About Packt Publishing

Packt, pronounced 'packed', published its first book "Mastering phpMyAdmin for Effective MySQL Management" in April 2004 and subsequently continued to specialize in publishing highly focused books on specific technologies and solutions.

Our books and publications share the experiences of your fellow IT professionals in adapting and customizing today's systems, applications, and frameworks. Our solution based books give you the knowledge and power to customize the software and technologies you're using to get the job done. Packt books are more specific and less general than the IT books you have seen in the past. Our unique business model allows us to bring you more focused information, giving you more of what you need to know, and less of what you don't.

Packt is a modern, yet unique publishing company, which focuses on producing quality, cutting-edge books for communities of developers, administrators, and newbies alike. For more information, please visit our website: www.packtpub.com.

About Packt Enterprise

In 2010, Packt launched two new brands, Packt Enterprise and Packt Open Source, in order to continue its focus on specialization. This book is part of the Packt Enterprise brand, home to books published on enterprise software – software created by major vendors, including (but not limited to) IBM, Microsoft and Oracle, often for use in other corporations. Its titles will offer information relevant to a range of users of this software, including administrators, developers, architects, and end users.

Writing for Packt

We welcome all inquiries from people who are interested in authoring. Book proposals should be sent to author@packtpub.com. If your book idea is still at an early stage and you would like to discuss it first before writing a formal book proposal, contact us; one of our commissioning editors will get in touch with you.

We're not just looking for published authors; if you have strong technical skills but no writing experience, our experienced editors can help you develop a writing career, or simply get some additional reward for your expertise.

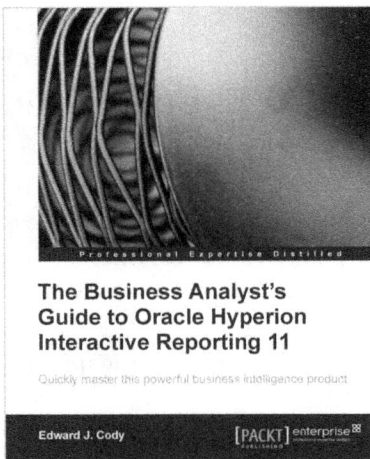

The Business Analyst's Guide to Oracle Hyperion Interactive Reporting 11

ISBN: 978-1-84968-036-3   Paperback: 232 pages

Quickly master this powerful business intelligence product

1. Get to grips with the most important, frequently used, and advanced features of Oracle Hyperion Interactive Reporting 11

2. A step-by-step Oracle Hyperion training guide packed with screenshots and clear explanations

3. Explore the features of Hyperion dashboards, reports, pivots, and charts

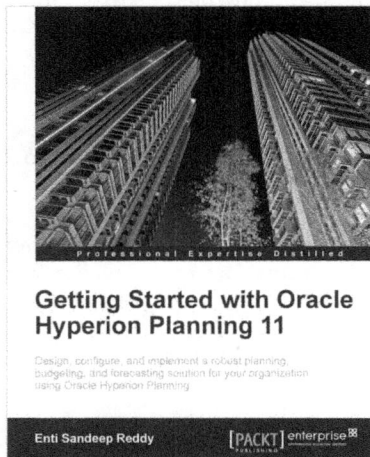

The Business Analyst's Guide to Oracle Hyperion Interactive Reporting 11

Quickly master this powerful business intelligence product

Edward J. Cody   [PACKT] enterprise 88

Getting Started with Oracle Hyperion Planning 11

ISBN: 978-1-84968-138-4   Paperback: 620 pages

Design, configure, and implement a robust planning, budgeting, and forecasting solution in your organization using Oracle Hyperion Planning

1. Successfully implement Hyperion Planning — one of the leading planning and budgeting solutions — to manage and coordinate all your business needs

2. Step-by-step instructions taking you from the very basics of installing Hyperion Planning to implementing it in an enterprise environment

3. Test and optimize Hyperion Planning to perfection with essential tips and tricks

Getting Started with Oracle Hyperion Planning 11

Design, configure, and implement a robust planning, budgeting, and forecasting solution for your organization using Oracle Hyperion Planning

Enti Sandeep Reddy   [PACKT] enterprise 88

Please check **www.PacktPub.com** for information on our titles

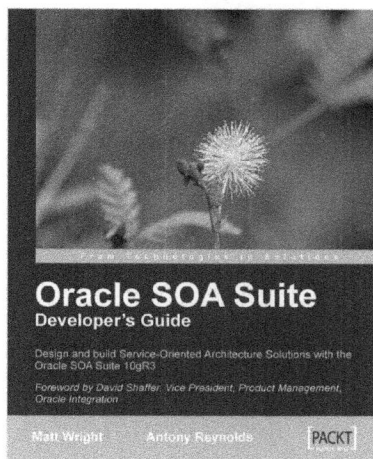

Oracle SOA Suite Developer's Guide

ISBN: 978-1-847193-55-1   Paperback: 652 pages

Design and build Service-Oriented Architecture Solutions with the Oracle SOA Suite 10gR3

1. A hands-on guide to using and applying the Oracle SOA Suite in the delivery of real-world SOA applications

2. Detailed coverage of the Oracle Service Bus, BPEL Process Manager, Web Service Manager, Rules, Human Workflow, and Business Activity Monitoring

3. Master the best way to combine / use each of these different components in the implementation of a SOA solution

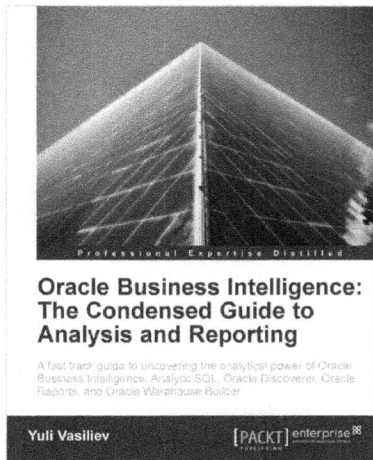

Oracle Business Intelligence: The Condensed Guide to Analysis and Reporting

ISBN: 978-1-84968-118-6   Paperback: 184 pages

A fast track Oracle book and eBook guide to uncovering the analytical power of Oracle Business Intelligence: Analytic SQL, Oracle Discoverer, Oracle Reports, and Oracle Warehouse Builder

1. Install, configure, and deploy the components included in Oracle Business Intelligence Suite (SE)

2. Gain a comprehensive overview of components and features of the Oracle Business Intelligence package

3. Leverage the computational power of Oracle Database

Please check **www.PacktPub.com** for information on our titles